A Unique
Life at Sea

A Unique Life at Sea

Captain Peter Skog

authorHOUSE®

AuthorHouse™ UK
1663 Liberty Drive
Bloomington, IN 47403 USA
www.authorhouse.co.uk
Phone: 0800 047 8203 (Domestic TFN)
         +44 1908 723714 (International)

Published by AuthorHouse 08/30/2019

ISBN: 978-1-7283-9281-3 (sc)
ISBN: 978-1-7283-9280-6 (e)

Print information available on the last page.

Any people depicted in stock imagery provided by Getty Images are models,
and such images are being used for illustrative purposes only.
Certain stock imagery © Getty Images.

This book is printed on acid-free paper.

Because of the dynamic nature of the Internet, any web addresses or links contained in this book may have changed
since publication and may no longer be valid. The views expressed in this work are solely those of the author and do
not necessarily reflect the views of the publisher, and the publisher hereby disclaims any responsibility for them.

Contents

Preface

It was a hot, fine day in the middle of November 2003 in the upper part of the mighty Amazon River, in Iquitos, Peru, where I ended up living for fifteen years, when I started to write about my unique life at sea. I realized my life at sea had been special in every aspect since I started at sea in 1963 as a barely sixteen-years-young teenager who longed to see the real world before I died. I faced some weird events that would shape me for the rest of my future life at sea.

Though I was not a writer, the idea of writing this book emerged in a moment of great sadness in February 2002 in Antarctica. I was commanding the 2,398-ton MS *Explorer*, the world's first expedition cruise ship, the Ship in the Wilderness. My destination was Prince Gustav Sound in the Weddell Sea, east of the Antarctic Peninsula in the Antarctic wilderness. One of my passengers, standing behind my back, suddenly said, "This is really going to make the boys back at the golf club jealous."

Writing about my experiences feels kind of strange. From the start, I knew I was incapable of producing a strict autobiography of all the stunning adventures I have had and the discoveries we made during my years on board the *Lindblad Explorer* in the early 1970s as well as on the *Explorer*. I was now making my second attempt to reach the Larsen Ice Shelf via Prince Gustav Sound, and my chance had arrived to write history. According to the satellite reports, global warming had melted a passage through the ice ahead of us. Even though I believed I'd had one of the longest careers in ice navigation in Antarctic waters on expedition cruise ships, I felt deflated when I had to turn around for safety reasons because pack ice had blocked my way. It was a drama, but I refused to be frustrated that I couldn't make it that year. I had to cheer myself up, and I knew I would try again as soon as the ice conditions became acceptable in the forthcoming seasons.

When I started at sea in 1963, I didn't know that later on I would be fortunate enough to travel many times as a third officer, second officer, and chief officer on the *Lindblad Explorer* and later as a master on the *Explorer*.

On the *Lindblad Explorer*, I was part of the team to open up Antarctica for cruise ship tourism in the early 1970s, and consequently, I experienced a unique time of adventures for better and for worse with world-famous people on board. Together we opened up a new way of tourism in all the remote corners of the world. Those on board were like a big, enthusiastic family discovering new remote places on this earth. I saw the wildlife of the inaccessible corners of the world and the fantastically beautiful scenery of Antarctica, with millions of penguins crowding the slopes of the Antarctic continent. We drove with our rubber Zodiacs through the rivers in West Irian, where we met the Asmat warriors, the headhunters of Biwar Laut.

The Enchanted Islands, the Galápagos, were my favorite place. In the beautiful turquoise water, I went scuba diving in the Devil's Crown, surrounded by scalloped hammerhead sharks. My diving adventures in those islands, which almost took my life, made me pause between my dives.

We stayed adrift outside Bounty Bay in the Pitcairn Islands in November 1977, and the same day, in the late afternoon, I dove down to Fletcher Christian's *Bounty* to caress her ribs. I also visited the South Pacific and its many remote islands and turquoise-colored coral reefs.

My routes with the *Explorer* have been an ever-changing filigree of tracks covering the globe, linking, for the most part, dots in the ocean far from established shipping lanes across all the oceans. Some of these dots were strategic staging posts where international flights could repatriate our passengers and bring in new ones.

The *Lindblad Explorer* (later the *Explorer*) was a wonder in a seaway, and she trod the oceans of the world from 1969 to 2007. Her treasures lengthened, and her logbooks piled higher and higher, until she eventually sank on November 23, 2007, in Antarctica, in the Bransfield Strait. She was without a doubt the most traveled vessel, with the most exciting and varied visual record of natural wonders anywhere on the high seas. I was lucky to be part of the team that experienced bad days and good days, achievements and disappointments, and even moments of danger when we opened the Antarctic Peninsula and the world's remote places for expedition cruising and tourism in the early 1970s. The *Explorer* not only dropped her anchor at hundreds of islands where no tourists had previously set foot but also paved the way for future expedition cruising ships worldwide.

My life became an oceanic amble between the poles. I was on a never-ending journey of discoveries and adventures, which sometimes brought me into trouble from the day I started at sea fifty-one years ago. The incredible adventures we had in Antarctica and worldwide in the 1970s, when we were the only cruise ship exploring the remote and hidden areas of the world, enriched my life tremendously.

I wouldn't have started to write about these events without the mountains of encouragement provided by my old shipmates from the *Lindblad Explorer*, and this book grew out of our time together. My love of the sea and spirit of seeking new fields to explore were part of my life on board the *Lindblad Explorer*. As the *Explorer*, she continued to sail the oceans of the world under the ownership of Abercrombie and Kent in Chicago. She was a ship with style and highly respected by all other cruise ships in

Antarctica and on the globe. The little red ship has a place in shipping history that far exceeds her size. I was her master for eight years, until 2003, when she was laid up in Genoa for sale.

This is the story of my unique life at sea.

Chapter 1

The Sinking of the *Lindblad Explorer*

IN THE YEAR 2007, THE MS *Explorer* (previously the *Lindblad Explorer*), the world's most famous expedition cruise ship ever, was thirty-eight years old and a ship full of style. She wore her elegance and her age with dignity, though she had acquired defects over the years when battling the harsh icy conditions in Antarctica from November to March each year since she was delivered on December 10, 1969. She was not a magnificent vessel, and one could hardly have called her beautiful. From the start, she carried a slight list to starboard, an imperfection we all grew to find charming. The little duck stole the hearts of thousands and rejoining her after being away on vacation was a homecoming. Her hull was purposefully built for the Antarctic; she was a nimble expedition cruise ship with an ice-reinforced hull. She was not an icebreaker, but she was an ice-working vessel with a double hull system.

All the ships that met her in Antarctica greeted her by lowering their nationality flags, showing their deepest respect for the ship that had invented expedition cruising, and giving long blows on their ships' horns as they passed her. It was a magic moment when we saw her sailing toward us sitting like a duck in the water and the PA system on board announced, "The Grand Old Lady is coming toward us." We paid her our respect, and many passengers went to the boat deck to greet her. She was the Grand Old Lady in that part of the world, and she had been, navigation-wise, faultless since 1979 in that unpredictable environment.

However, the night of Friday, November 23, 2007, at approximately 0200 hours, her fate was sealed when she entered the Bransfield Strait, coming from the east. She passed the conical Bridgeman Island, and then, south of King George Island, she suddenly struck ice on her starboard side. Those were her home waters, and she had sailed there numerous times since the early 1970s. She almost found the way herself without the aid of a duty officer on the bridge, until something went wrong on that dark Antarctica night.

The vessel had previously completed a scheduled dry dock in Las Palmas on October 21, 2007, and she had been issued a newly required PSSC (passengers ship safety certificate) by DNV (Det Norske Veritas). But on that night, in the position 62°24'17 S, 57°11'46 W, disaster struck after midnight, at approximately 2:20 GMT, when she was holed by ice somewhere on her starboard side. Those worldwide who had personal connections to the *Explorer* asked themselves what actually had happened to their *Explorer*. The world was stunned, and nobody could understand that the *Explorer* was suddenly in distress, because she was the safest ship of them all down there.

The answer is self-explanatory: the Swedish captain was inexperienced in those treacherous Antarctic waters because it was his first cruise to Antarctica, and therefore, he was unable to predict and understand the hidden dangers. The ill-fated trip to Antarctica as a first-time captain is partly understandable. Unfortunately, he had been employed through a friendly relationship because he had been the master of a small expedition cruise ship in Svalbard for some twenty years, a smaller coastal vessel with space for approximately twenty-four passengers, and as chief officer on bigger expedition cruise ships in Greenland's waters. Therefore, it was assumed he was suitable to be the master on the *Explorer* in Antarctica. Almost every captain commanding a ship in Antarctica previously was a chief officer on board in that environment, which ensured he was familiar with Antarctica.

Antarctica was not the Swedish captain's kind of domain when commanding a ship in that disloyal environment. When commanding a new vessel, a master is extremely careful about his doings, and furthermore, due to the age of the vessel, he should have made a random check of the void spaces, ice frames, and so on to form his own opinion about the vessel's condition prior to his first Antarctic voyage. This was a mandatory procedure and a must-check made by the permanent senior bridge command in the past prior to each upcoming Antarctica season.

Every master and duty officer on a ship entering the Bransfield Strait is supposed to be aware that the strait is full of crystal-clear, diamond-hard ice that is sometimes not visible in the dark nights or with the ship's powerful searchlights, and they must pay special attention when icebergs are visible on the radar screen. Whether small or big in size, all of them produce lethal, diamond-hard growlers that can cause a ship severe problem. Growlers drift with the wind and can sometimes barely be seen day or night on the surface. Nevertheless, the icebergs produce drift ice that drifts with the wind on the lee side from the icebergs; hence, every bridge officer needs to know that he might face a string of ice and consequently slowdown in due time. A ship sailing slowly in the dark Antarctic night always must keep both top searchlights on and crossing each other ahead of the bow.

The master and the new chief officer said the hull penetration was the size of a fist and a limited leak. How could they have known the leak was the size of a fist and limited? To figure that out, the damage-control team had to tear down the outer cabin walls and the insulation to be able to locate the leak. Seemingly, they did all this but never located the point of damage—or did they? —and hence, they were unable to make a temporary repair to keep the vessel afloat as they waded in water.

As a longtime chief officer on board ever since 1974 and part of the *Lindblad Explorer* team who opened up Antarctica for tourism and, later on, as a master for seven years in Antarctica, having some 125 ice voyages to my credit to the continent, I look at this fatal accident with sadness and a head full of questions. It is my opinion the *Explorer* got into distress because the master was not paying enough attention to the ice conditions ahead of him when he sailed into the Bransfield Strait. If the IAATO (International Association of Antarctica Tour Operators) code of rules had been followed, the captain would have had an ice master on board for the navigation of the ship to safely fulfill the cruise schedule. It is, in this respect, difficult to understand why the company did not consider the possibility of having an ice master on board, knowing the incoming captain was a newcomer to Antarctica. Consequently, the IAATO rules were bypassed. It is difficult to ask in retrospect what happened and why the management company in Sweden did not make any comments about this. The answer is simple: they wanted to save money by avoiding a double master salary, so to speak.

It feels as if the right hand did not know what the left hand was doing. The company, based in Canada, must at some stage have asked the management company in Sweden who the new captain on board was, and one can only imagine what kind of an answer they received. The company might have used bad judgment when they accepted an inexperienced master on their ship and allowed him to do his first cruise to Antarctica with a full load of passengers on board. Therefore, some two weeks after the MS *Explorer* sank, experts questioned the official explanation of why the disaster had happened. The initial explanation of the ship's sinking—that it struck submerged ice, sprang a fist-sized leak, and was then doomed by uncontrollable flooding—is far-fetched. Collisions with submerged ice are rare events, and the speed is the key factor. Apparently, her speed was not too much at the time of the incident; hence, it doesn't really add up. She clearly took in water, though.

I can hardly imagine if the company one day wanted the *Explorer* to sail farther south toward the southern polar circle with an inexperienced master, penetrating the ice in the Gerlache Strait, the Lemaire Channel, Petermann Island, and the Grandidier Channel and heading toward Lavoisier Island and Crystal Sound, as we had many times in the past. Heading toward the polar circle, we felt ourselves uncomfortable in that treacherous, close coastal navigation since it was extremely challenging. Antarctica dictates the rules, and as such, the master must comply with them. A master in those waters needs to be one step ahead of the problems rather than one step behind.

When the expedition-cruising world became aware that the *Explorer* was in deep distress in Antarctica and was fighting for her life, people's first thought was *She was unsinkable, and she paved the way for all other cruise ships coming to Antarctica.* She had been doing fine for thirty-seven Antarctic seasons. It was all a mystery.

Many Antarctica experts have told their opinions regarding what happened, saying the leak must have been in the middle of the ship as she sank, because she remained on a level bow-to-stern trim. I agree.

The master was on the bridge, and prior to striking the ice, they kept a speed of some seven to eight knots, and then they slowed down to a minimum speed when entering the ice flows. But the captain must at some stage have been giving a kick ahead from the steering speed to avoid the ice flows, with a subsequent turn to port, and as the stern turned to starboard, they accidentally hit the ice with sufficient power to cause a hull penetration.

It must be said that the *Explorer* responded immediately when giving a kick ahead, with the engine and the pitch propeller as well as her big rudder turning her on a coin. Before making any turns when ice is present, the responsible duty bridge officer always must look over the ship side to figure out what kind of ice is surrounding the hull. Was he doing that? It is doubtful that was the case on that dark Antarctic night, because indubitably, the ship struck ice on her starboard side.

It is obvious that essential pieces of the story are missing. In addition, the bridge command did not bring the VDR (video data recorder, or the black box) with them, as per the rules, when leaving the ship. The chief officer, who was the second-in-command, was equally new on board, and as such, he probably did not have enough knowledge about the ship or how he was supposed to assist and back up the master in case of an emergency situation. Therefore, it is easy to understand he could not give the necessary advice the master needed under those circumstances.

After she struck the ice and it was noted the ship got a starboard list, the commonsense reaction would have been to pump out at least one starboard ballast tank immediately in an attempt to heel the vessel over to the port side and consequently minimize the water ingress on the starboard side. As the ice impact was most likely just below the water line, the closer the fist-sized leak was to the surface, the water ingress should have been minimized to a controllable situation, which the pumps probably could have handled. The vessel had some 190 cubic meters of MGO (medium gas oil) on board, which was sufficient to keep her stability with one empty starboard ballast tank or even two. For this purpose, there was the excellent stability program on the bridge containing the damage stability as well.

In the past, prior to each upcoming Antarctic season, the deck and engine crew held weekly damage-control drills on board. The drills had a priority for obvious reasons, and they were fun to make. Each DC drill was followed by various photos as documentation of what had been done, with a subsequent short report, and the result was filed in a map on the bridge over the aft chart table, and a copy was sent to the management company in Monaco, who had management of the *Explorer* for ten years. The *Explorer* was equipped with a red portable damage-control box containing lots of sophisticated purpose-built damage-control equipment for Antarctica. As far as I can recall, the first engineer—later the chief engineer—who was on board at the time of her sinking was partly involved in constructing the various DC tools during my time as a master on board.

Well, one thing is for sure: practice makes perfect, and I doubt he informed the new master of the damage-control drills held in the past. The *Explorer*, in the past, had been well prepared for any damage-control situation, due to weekly drills.

However, I believe the master on board was, regrettably, not aware of the inadequacies of the chief engineer, who in the past, as first engineer, had been supervised by the chief engineer. When confronted, his standard response was "What can I do?"

However, nobody likes to read the truth or to hear it, and someone came up with the brilliant idea to promote him to chief engineer. As such, he should have had the knowledge regarding how to minimize the water ingress and most likely save the ship, but instead, I believe he was unable to take control of such a serious emergency situation and lost overview of the entire situation. My conclusion is that he was never on top of the problems; therefore, it is likely some vital emergency technical system on board was left behind, which clearly worsened the situation that tragic night. It is my opinion that he was not knowledgeable enough to take care of an emergency situation on board, as one would have expected from him by virtue of his profession as we knew him. We knew him as an engineer who did just what he was supposed to do in his daily work and nothing more. Sadly, that's a fact.

During the numerous accident investigations held in Punta Arenas, Chile; in London with some British lawyers; and with the Liberian authorities, nobody questioned the actions and skills of the chief engineer. This tells me that the accident investigation team was far from having sufficient Antarctica experience; hence, their report was confusing and incorrect.

Below is the *Explorer*'s past checklist in case of a damage-control situation, which was also to be found in a laminated folder above the aft chart table on the bridge. Did they ever look at this checklist?

Damage Control Checklist for MS *Explorer* in Case of Hull Penetration in Ice Navigation

	Damage Control	Required by Deck	Required by Engine	Action
1	Position of damage	Investigate. Alert damage-control party.		CO to locate the damage area with DC team and report to the bridge. Establish radio contact with bridge. Bring equipment.
2	Stop engines.	Bridge		

3	Advise engine room which section is damaged.	Bridge		Advise engine room to be Stand bye with pumps. Confirm if/by high-level alarm.
4	DC party to be sent to point of damage.	Bridge		Commence with temporary repairs. *Bring all DC pumps. Determine the quantity of water ingress.*
5	Close WTD.	Bridge		Check that doors are still closed.
6	Isolate affected area and evacuate.	Bridge	Engine	Chief officer
7	Additional damages	Bridge	Engine	Check secondary point of damages and shock of damages.
8	Determine risk factor.	Bridge		Determine risk factor for vessel pass crew.
9	Trimming possibilities		Engine	Determine if vessel can be trimmed or listed to minimize water ingress.
10	Alert bridge radio officer.	Bridge		Bridge officer to be Stand bye and Alert other vessels in vicinity.
11	Damage stability	Bridge		Chief officer to make a damage stability calculation.
12	Alert passengers and crew.	Bridge		Inform passengers if needed. Sound general alarm.
13	Weather forecast	Bridge		ETO; weather forecast to be determined.

In addition, apparently, some WTD (watertight doors) on the 300 deck were left open, though the captain stated they were all closed, and it remains an unanswered question how he knew this—probably by just looking at the WTD panel indication lamps on the bridge panel.

It is not a secret that during the weekly abandon-ship and fire drills, when these doors were closed from the bridge panel, though the bridge panel indicated they all were closed, the crew down below reported frequently that some still were open, and hence, they were manually closed down below. The master should have told the deck crew to verify the doors were closed via the radio, but this was perhaps never the case. After the impact, the water rose on the 300-deck starboard side from cabin to cabin via the toilet system.

A previous chief engineer who knew the ship well said, "If the crew on board would have pressed down pillows from the cabins in the toilet bowls, this would probably have saved the ship from going down." But nobody, not even the chief engineer, was thinking about this. Why did the investigation team never raise the question about this—or did they? The answer is simple: nobody brought the question to light.

There is an additional aspect that can perhaps shed some light on the huge amount of water on the 300 deck. Did they all forget in the confusion the two vital letdown flaps—each having a diameter of some forty centimeters—situated in the aft cabins 314 and 315 on 300 deck? Each side automatically was supposed to be opened up, according to the PSSC (passenger ship safety certificate) rules, in case of water ingress to allow the water to pour down into the lower bilges and consequently cause a high-level alarm in the engine room. Thus, the pumps would have started automatically. At least during a PSSC inspection, they must have been checked in Las Palmas.

It's important not to forget the ship always had a slight stern trim. In other words, prior to every Antarctic season in the past, the compartments were cleaned of dirt, and the bilge alarms and sensors were tested. This was a standard policy in attempt to make the vessel ready for an upcoming Antarctic season lasting from November to March.

While the water was pouring slowly into the 300 deck level from somewhere behind the cabin walls, passengers described how they had to wade in freezing water up to their knees; hence, it is my belief that the flaps were most likely sealed at the time of the accident, and therefore, the water could not flow down freely into the below compartments and the bilge pumps, which had a capacity of some fifty cubic meters per hour. Secure sources of information mentioned the crew were standing up to their chests while trying to locate the point of damage, and the situation became at some stage under control, when a sudden blackout occurred, and they fumbled around in darkness and, in the end, abandoned the 300 deck. Subsequently, as the water found its way to the engine room, the emergency pump stopped working as well.

I doubt the new captain was aware that the two letdown water flaps existed, let alone that they had to be checked frequently. Consequently, the water found its way through the toilet system from cabin to cabin, and the valves didn't close to the gray water tanks; therefore, the water found its way to the AC room below and to the engine room.

If the toilet system had been shut down, the vessel would probably have stayed afloat, and the water would never have reached the engine room. The vessel had a controllable pitch propeller, and when the water found its way into the engine room, the Kamewa system in the box lost the pressure, and the propeller blades turned automatically to zero pitch because such was the system designed, but in this case, the blades apparently went in reverse, so the ship went astern as well.

The master's comment that the watertight bulkheads on the 300 deck were leaking is far-fetched and not correct. In the past, there occasionally was some minor flooding in various 300-level compartments, and the water never found its way into the adjacent compartment.

The question is this: Why was the vessel issued a PSSC from the DNV during the inspection in Las Palmas, though the master, after the incident, said the watertight bulkheads were leaking? These bulkheads were proven to be healthy, intact, and free from corrosion in 2003. However, during the yearly renewal of the PSSC, it is unusual for the class inspectors to demand a check of the watertight bulkheads on any passenger ship unless they suspect something or are requested to make a check.

On every dark night in Antarctica, the adopted policy was to put the ship in a box, which meant the master drew a square on the sea chart approximately one nautical mile by one nautical mile, depending on the ice conditions, and he then wrote the following in the captain's night order watch book:

> Gentlemen, tonight we stay adrift in the box, as marked in the chart number, so keep the searchlights on, looking for drift ice, and double watch on the bridge. Arriving at the box, we stop one engine unless otherwise is needed. Keep a thorough check on the ship position until daylight, when you start the second engine, and then proceed slowly with a safeguarding speed toward [destination]. Call the captain at 0600 hours or otherwise if needed.

This was any master's standing night order for the duty officers on the bridge for every approaching night in Antarctica during the ship's life span as the *Lindblad Explorer* and the *Explorer* when she was set to drift into a box marked on the chart, or if ice conditions permitted, we sailed with three to five knots—called a safeguarding speed—on the dark Antarctic nights that were presumably ice free. If the ship hit any ice with some three to four knots, then the impact was minimal due to the speed factor. The icebergs and the bergy bits were clearly seen in both radars; hence, they were avoided.

In 1996, I wrote *Ice Navigation and Ice Seamanship*, a manual that was presented to every new bridge officer on board. Several ship companies also received copies. Below is the introduction page.

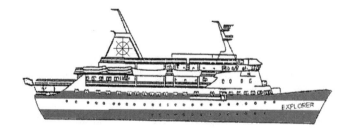

Ice Navigation and Ice Seamanship!

Introduction

This ice manual is written and dedicated to all new bridge officers on ships, that will navigate in Antarctic waters during the Antarctic summer season. The manual will give you ideas about what to do and how to navigate in Antarctic ice. The contents of this practical manual may be seen as basic guidelines, and hopefully it will help any bridge officer, standing on the bridge facing the Antarctic ice for the first time, while his mind is full of questions. If you want to know more about pack ice, then go to the Antarctic pilot books. Each chapter in this manual is based on events a navigator will experience in Antarctica, and the experiences has demonstrated clearly that Antarctica is treacherous and unpredictable when it comes to ice navigation.

An officer on the bridge, can find himself taken by complete surprise when ice is present, therefore be alert, vigilant, suspicious, and never take things for granted when navigating in the Antarctic ice. You will never become an expert since Antarctica is dictating the rules. The author has 100 ice voyages to his credit in this unpredictable environment, and still every day is different and full of new surprises, which gives new experiences. Let there be no mistakes, and as can be seen from the above, when operating in Antarctic ice the safety aspect cannot be emphasized too strongly. If a definition of a good ice navigator were to be attempted, the following could be suggested: A good ice navigator is one who knows how to combine safety of operation in ice and can possibly predict the dangers laying ahead by having ice sense, the feel, and the instinct for ice.

None of these qualities can be acquired in a single day, but for inexperienced ice navigators it would be wise to listen to the advices given to him by an ice pilot if one is employed onboard the vessel.

This practical manual should in no way be held responsible for any wrong actions, which might cause damage to the ship.

Captain

Well, the *Explorer* hit the ice that fatal night in the dark Bransfield Strait. However, people who were shore-based and linked to the vessel, when asked what happened, all chose the simplest justifiable answer: "She struck submerged ice and succumbed to uncontrollable flooding." Yes, the ice was apparently suddenly there, and everybody of ice in Antarctica is submerged, with 90 percent under the surface and 10 percent above.

There is an unwritten rule in Antarctica: if you are in any doubt whatsoever, you stop the ship and try to figure out what's going on. The *Explorer* could have continued to sail in Antarctica and worldwide for many more years to come, provided she was treated with respect and had a knowledgeable bridge command.

The incident was a textbook example of something the Antarctica world had been trying to prevent from happening by making sure the ships had skillful masters on board who knew the Antarctic waters sufficiently. Still, it happened, as nobody followed up on whether the master was authorized to sail in Antarctica or not. In the past, masters were thoroughly analyzed by their companies regarding whether they were competent to be the captain of a cruise ship or not, and they had to have permission from the SWEDISH POLAR RESEARCH INSTITUTE to be approved to work and stay in Antarctica and issued a permit certificate. I doubt the master and the new chief officer were even aware of these permits, let alone the management company in Sweden. In summary, the small management company in Sweden was running its own game and did not show sufficient respect for the knowledge and experience needed to command a cruise ship in Antarctica.

However, we all deeply thank the master that he was able to abandon everybody safely from the *Explorer* to another ship before she went down to her eternal rest in the Bransfield Strait. She was built for Antarctica, and she opened up Antarctica for the cruise ship industry and paved the way for every ship coming behind her. I spent fourteen years on board the *Explorer*, and she enriched my life from the early 1970s on. Her spirit and her memory will live forever.

Chapter 2

How It All Began

THE YEAR WAS 1963, AND I knew nothing about life because I was barely sixteen years old. I was facing the uncertainty of the future. I was born in Helsinki, Finland, and my parents moved to Malmö, Sweden, when I was eleven years of age. I grew up as a young teenager in Malmö without a father because he abandoned us. I had no plans to go to sea at that age, but I always dreamed of seeing the world in one way or another. How could I make my dreams come true?

I had a passion for airplanes, and I built lots of model planes. Before my dad left me when I was twelve, he taught me how to build model airplanes to scale from balsa wood, and I continued to build model planes alone in my boyhood room as much as I could and then test flew them on the huge field close to the beach. If I was not satisfied with a plane, I poured gasoline onto the wings and used a self-timer that ignited the gasoline, and the plane went down like some of the unsuccessful US and RAF flying fortresses over Germany in the Second World War.

I was strong-minded to become a pilot, and I spent my free time as much as possible at the Bulltofta Airport in Malmö, where I went almost every day with my newly received secondhand bicycle. There was an old wrecked Liberator bomber from the Second World War at the far end of the airfield. The pilot, like other thousands of Allied pilots and crew who ended up in Sweden, had apparently returned from a bombing mission over Germany and, as the plane had been badly hit, had to aim for the southern coast of Sweden. Luckily, he barely was able to fly his Liberator toward the coastline of Sweden and make a skillful crash landing at Bulltofta Airport in Malmö. In this plane and wreck, I spent much of my free time from the school. I sat in the damaged cockpit, and in my fantasies, I flew the plane all over the world.

In my teenage bedroom, a world map hung above my bed. I longed to see the world. The last thing I saw before I closed my eyes was the paradise of the entire world out there somewhere.

Paradise is subjective. Ask half a dozen people for their notion of paradise, and you will get six different answers—or maybe twelve. Places to be, states of mind, the successful conclusion to a series of events, the absence of particular annoyances—all of these and more qualify as paradise to different people at different times in their lives. One place, however, long loomed in my imagination as the ultimate paradise: The South Pacific Ocean and Antarctica. Images of that part of the world filled my mind.

The first thing I saw when I woke up was the world map above my head on the wall. I was still studying in high school and had two more years to go until I graduated. Even though I was in school, in my dreams, I was flying the wrecked Liberator bomber over the South Pacific Ocean somewhere, because for some reason, I always dreamed about those islands. I didn't know that some thirteen years later, I would visit that paradise, the South Pacific, though not with a plane. Instead, I would cruise among the wonderful islands of the South Pacific Ocean, making landfall on numerous islands and reefs; walk with some famous people on the warm, sandy coral beaches; and, to my big surprise, be offered a job piloting ships from Yap Island in the Caroline Islands, South Pacific, to Apia in the Western Samoa, and I would come to Antarctica numerous times.

Summer vacation was coming closer. I was off from school from June 6 to August 15. One day I got the brilliant idea to go down to the sailors' office in the harbor area in order to investigate if I could get a job on a ship for a month or so during my vacation. I considered myself mature enough to do this. I came into a huge room crowded with hard and tough seamen of all categories, and most of them were under the influence of alcohol. A little bit scared, I asked one of them where to go and how to get on a ship. I was directed to a window and immediately told to go back home and ask for my mother's permission if I wanted to go to sea. So, I did.

My mother was not surprised when I asked her if she kindly could sign my papers because I was underage and told her I wanted to spend the summer on a ship, going somewhere. She wrote an attestation that she granted me permission to sail out on a ship but with one condition: "I will sign your papers only if you promise me you will never go to the Soviet Union." I faithfully promised this to her. The reason for her demand was that Finland had fought two wars with the Russians.

The following day, I went back full of confidence to the same window as the day before and handed over my mother's attestation to a cranky, arrogant man. I was given in exchange a small blue card and told that all the ships requiring crew in different categories would be roll-called over a loudspeaker at 10:00 a.m. and 2:00 p.m. every day. If one of the called-out ships was something for me, then I was instructed to run up and hand over my blue card to the window.

I left and came back at 1330 hours, full of expectations. I sat in the huge room with lots of seamen from all categories, and I felt kind of lost. At 1400 hours, the call-out of the ships started, and suddenly, a ship by the name of MT *Okturus* (MT stands for "motor tanker") came up over the loudspeaker. The ship was asking for three deck boys for one month of work. That was perfect for me, and I rushed with my little blue card toward the window with two other boys my age, and all of us looked at each other, a little bit scared.

The cranky man behind the counter desk asked me again, "Did you bring the attestation from your mother?"

I said, "Yes, sir, I have it here!"

He looked at me with a suspicious mind and said, "Boy, you are hired as a deck boy."

I couldn't believe it. I'd been hired as a deckhand on a ship that went to the Mediterranean Sea. Within a second, I remembered my mother's words: "I will sign your papers only if you promise me you will never go to the Soviet Union." This I'd faithfully promised her. Unfortunately, I was soon heading for the Soviet Union. I felt guilty as I walked back to her office in all my happiness while looking at my blue card in my hand, which was stamped "MT *Okturus* Deck Boy." I thought about what to tell her, because she'd had confidence in me, and that was why she'd signed my papers. Oh boy!

I didn't know it then, but that was the beginning of an incredible, exciting future life and a special career at sea, a privilege shared by few people.

Still unaware of my coming future and unaware that I would one day visit all the remote places of the world I'd dreamed about, I walked up the stairs to my mother's office on the fifth floor, where she worked at a textile company, eager to enter her office. I said loudly when I met her, with my face like a sunbeam, "Hi, Mom!"

Her first words to me were "Does the ship go to Russia?"

I looked down at the floor and said, "Yes, it goes to Odessa in the Black Sea. I'm sorry, but that's now a fact."

I felt guilty, and from that day on, I did not have a clue what the future would give me, but I became a sailor.

The ship was a tanker of seventeen thousand DWT (deadweight tonnage), which is the maximum weight a ship can load, sailing back and forth from Malmö Harbor to Odessa in the Black Sea through the Mediterranean Sea.

The ship was built in 1955 by Kockums Shipyard in Malmö, and she was 162 meters long. She unfortunately, in 1970, caught fire in the engine room, and in 1971, she was towed to Kaohsiung in Taiwan and broken up.

Chapter 3

Traveling Out for the First Time

SEVEN DAYS LATER, I WALKED up the gangway to the MT *Okturus*, carrying my seaman's bag on my shoulder since I was supposed to look cool. It was a fine day, June 21, 1963. My preparations before joining the vessel had filled me with enthusiasm. The seaman's bag had been a gift from my uncle, who was a former radio operator. As a seaman, I was supposed to have one. The bag was stuffed with all the important clothes I thought I would need for the next four weeks.

My mother had given me a Dixie cap—the flat, visor less US Navy hat—which I wore on my head at a cheery angle while walking up the gangway because I thought I was supposed to look like a cool seaman. Maybe I was cool. Who knows? I was just a teenager.

Coming on board, I was assigned a small cabin that I was supposed to share with another deck boy, a guy I had earlier met at the seamen's employment office. He and I became friends right away. Once I started to unpack my luggage, I found in the bottom of my bag a Bible, given to me by my mother. I guess she was concerned about my first journey abroad, especially because my destination was Odessa in the Soviet Union on a small tanker.

The same afternoon, as we sailed out from Kockums Shipyard in Malmö, I stood on the deck, watching the town slowly disappear behind us. I didn't know what I would face, but I knew I was now alone, and I had to take care of myself to the best of my ability.

Since I was fresh and green in that business and had no experience with ships or a seaman's duties, I did what I was told to do. I was assigned to sweep and clean the decks, chip away rust, and paint. After a week, I was told to do the bridge watch from four o'clock to eight o'clock. The first morning at 0330 hours, I was brutally awakened for my first watch by an older AB (able-bodied seaman), who kicked my cabin door and shouted, "Wake up!" and told me I had to go to the bridge to do the bridge watch. There was always a double watch on the bridge: one doing the constant lookout and the other doing the hand steering.

I entered the bridge for the first time, which was a big surprise. I was surprised to see all the instruments and navigational equipment of various kinds. I got a brief lesson in the darkness with a torch held by the outgoing AB, who told me about the bridge equipment and how things worked. I knew I had to quickly learn my duties as I was told as well as keep a sharp lookout for something—ships, buoys, or whatever was found to be floating in the sea.

I stood firmly on the bridge wing, watching Land's End, England's most southwestern point, pass by. I still remember how impressed I was at seeing the color of the water change rapidly to blue in comparison to the gray water in the North Sea area.

It was the month of June, the best time to sail and to make passages in the North Atlantic and the Bay of Biscay. The weather in June is often settled, and the winds are favorable at that time of the year, so I had a lucky start to my seaman's career. Furthermore, the rest of the crew treated me well. From the beginning, I was fortunate to have good friends I could trust and work together with. I was humble and gentle, and I kept one hand for myself and the other hand for the ship. If one's situation turned out to be the opposite, he for sure didn't continue at sea.

In 1963, life was not easy on-board ships in any category. Of course, twenty to thirty years earlier had been a completely different era in the merchant marine fleets worldwide, and my life at sea was a more modern shipping era and mentality mixed with the old and harsh style. With one wrong word from somebody, a situation could end up with a fight and a nose bleeding!

So, there I stood, watching on the bridge for the first time with an elderly chief officer who was in charge of the four-to-eight watch. I carefully watched his duties in the darkness from the bridge wing door because I was not allowed to enter the bridge as a watch-going deckhand. I found all his duties interesting. He was moving around and doing things continuously.

After a while, when we were well clear from any land in the vicinity, we headed toward the Bay of Biscay. I was then instructed to learn how to steer the tanker. It was a big moment in my life. As nervous as I was, I stepped up onto the helmsman platform, grabbed the huge wooden helm, and felt how the ship responded to my actions. What a nice feeling it was to be in control of a huge ship.

Each watch on any ship in those days had a watch-going officer and two deckhands, which meant one able-bodied seaman (AB) and one ordinary seaman (OS). The deck boys were, however, not allowed to do bridge watches unless the captain approved it. But I was now a deck boy on the four-to-eight watch, the second man on watch, standing one hour on the bridge wing, keeping a sharp lookout for something out there. I was not allowed to enter the bridge unless I first asked for permission from the duty officer.

The Bay of Biscay was almost behind us, and in the early morning at 0500 hours, when it was still dark, I saw the lights of the Cape Finisterre Lighthouse, the most northwestern point of Spain. I reported by shouting into the bridge to the chief officer, according to the bridge rules, whatever I saw out there. I suddenly shouted, "Ship on the starboard side!" but I got no response, though there were some five or six ships ahead of us, and I had no understanding about how to interpret the navigation lights of the ships and what they meant. (By looking at the lights, one can figure out what course the ship has for the time being.) I had only a small clue about the starboard rule.

The bridge was pitch black due to the night vision, and I shouted one more time into the dark bridge, "Ship on the starboard side, sir!" but still received no response. I then slowly entered the bridge cautiously and found the chief officer sleeping and snoring on the bridge sofa. I did not know what to do. I shook him, trying to wake him up, and gave him a polite smack in the face, but still, he slept. I was not a violent person, and I am still surprised that it didn't bother me to strike the man in the face. It seemed right.

He suddenly opened his eyes, gave me a short-lived look, and then again fell into a deep sleep. I became kind of nervous over his reaction, but he just said nonchalantly, "I must have dozed off. What is happening?"

Amazingly, he then immediately fell into a deep sleep again. I felt that my newly started seaman's career was at stake because of this sleeping officer. I had indeed gotten a pretty rough start.

Once in a while, I looked out from the front bridge windows to figure out if the lights ahead of me were approaching. Yes, they were all indeed approaching—and fast! With my knowledge I have today, I realize I should have called the captain and informed him about the sleeping chief officer, but I was too afraid to bother the captain.

One of the ships was, in my opinion, approaching too fast and coming too close, all while the chief mate was in his best sleep. At that moment, as young as I was, I felt insecure while the VHF radio shouted on channel 16 continuously, "The ship on my port side one mile away! This is the ship on your starboard side! Alter your course to starboard!" I knew well at that stage the difference between starboard and port side, and furthermore, the officer on the approaching ship helped me without his knowledge to determine what was going on, as his ship was the only ship approaching clearly too fast. His voice sounded stressed, and no one was answering his calls since I didn't know how to do it yet. I knew we were indeed on a collision course.

The view in front of my bridge windows was soon filled with white lights from the approaching vessel, and I was sure we were about to collide with the lights. The tanker was on an autopilot mode, and I had been taught earlier how to switch over to the hand-steering mode in case of an emergency. This was apparently a case of emergency.

I frantically tried to remember what I had been told about how to turn off the impressive autopilot unit and system full of brass pipes and valves. I turned both the valves I could recognize, and then I cranked the helm over almost hard to starboard and said a silent prayer. The lights from the other ship passed close on our port side. My heart raced as we passed each other and then steamed away from each other. I was scared to death, and I knew I had avoided a collision that probably would have been inevitable if I had not done anything.

Now, as I stood at the helm on hand-steering mode and as the distance grew bigger between our ships, the chief officer suddenly woke up again and saw me standing at the helm. I figured out that he was under the influence of alcohol and probably a huge hangover, and he didn't have a clue what was going on, but apparently, he was now awake. He suddenly said every abusive word he knew to me, threw me away from the steering platform, and deported me to the bridge wing immediately, where I was supposed to be. I felt deflated because I knew I had done something good, but the drunken man had no clue I had just saved his ass.

However, after a while, he realized kind of what had happened and calmed down. He asked me to update him on what actually had happened, and then he finally apologized for sleeping and gave me credit for what I had done. Fair enough from my side, because I knew I had avoided a collision by using my own initiative. My response to the chief officer was quiet, because I had made a lucky guess—a guess that had stood between the completion of my first successful month at sea and grave misfortune.

Images of twisted steel and bodies in the water flashed through my head. He had slept through the whole incident and was surely going to face the consequences from the master. I knew I had to be on my toes the entire trip due to that incident, and I knew the consequences he probably would face. I learned quickly the mentality at sea and the system and bridge procedures, and already, as a barely sixteen-years-young boy, I started to like life on board.

We sailed into the Mediterranean Sea, passing Gibraltar. The azure water made me happy as I stood on the bridge wing as a lookout while the afternoon dwindled, and I watched the sun as it sank into the wake behind the tanker. The blazing orange ball contacted the ocean's surface and disappeared into the cool depths. The last pink faded from the horizon, taking several degrees of air temperature with it. Tugging a sweatshirt over my head, I stood firmly facing the night ahead of me. I thought over the incident while my arms rested on the bridge wing's wind protectors. In the pitch-black night, I felt enchanted upon seeing the fluorescent water torrent in the bow as we sailed under a clear blue sky with twinkling stars above and a glossy calm. I was happy to be down there in that subtropical area, even if only for three weeks on my way to Odessa.

As part of my four-to-eight watch, I was chipping rust; sweeping the decks; and cleaning up after the ABs, the big guys. My white matelot was always on my head, as it was supposed to be. I guess I looked cool under the Mediterranean sun.

After many peaceful days, something happened.

I had my usual dinner in the crew mess during my watch relief for half an hour, according to the bridge watch-relief system. As I was sitting and talking with the old ABs, I was suddenly knocked down from my chair by a clenched hand from one of the opposite guys at my table. I found myself lying dizzy on the floor, and as I climbed back to my seat, I asked, "Why did you do this?"

His only response was "At this table, we don't talk like that!" I was never told what kind of wrong word I had said, but evidently, whatever it was, it was not suitable. Nobody ever told me why. I had learned my lesson, which was to keep my mouth shut once in a while.

That was the first brutal contact I faced at sea and the only one during my forthcoming years at sea. I didn't even start to argue against the existing rules of the table or the mess room due to the sensitivity of the sailors. It was educational. The seaman's strange and harsh reality was there, and for a while, my peaceful days in the azure water were disturbed due to the aching blue eye I got.

Nevertheless, life continued, and we passed the Dardanelles and the narrow Bosporus passage into the Black Sea, heading for Odessa. Our arrival in Odessa, my first foreign port, was exciting for me. My salary was only thirty-five dollars a month, so I didn't have much money to buy things or enjoy myself when going ashore with the big boys. They told me, "Don't worry about your money when going ashore. Go down to the slop chest, and buy blue jeans and nylon stockings." In those days, all the ships had a well-equipped slop chest where one could buy everything from nylon stockings to shirts, chocolate, and aftershave, which was the famous Florida Water.

I bought five pairs of blue jeans, two pairs of nylon stockings, and four nylon shirts. I was told to put on all of the blue jeans and wrap the stockings around my waist. I did all of this and found myself walking ashore like the Michelin Man.

The hidden meaning behind this was that we would sell all the hidden clothes once we went ashore. We would for sure be met by the locals when passing the railway tracks and the wagons, and this business could only take place when it was dark, due to the alert police. Now it was pitch black outside; hence, we were supposed to trade clothes and make some money.

I could hardly walk, but it was not a problem; while we crossed the railway tracks, after no more than ten minutes, ten to fifteen people came out from nowhere in the darkness, asking for clothes to buy. It seemed they knew our bodies were stuffed with clothes. I made more money in less than half an hour by selling all my jeans and the nylon stockings than I had made in a monthly salary on board.

When I finally had sold all my clothes and continued to walk over the rails, a man came and asked if he could buy my nylon shirt. The price he offered for my shirt was too high for me to resist. Neither of us understood each other, but he insisted on buying my shirt. I accepted his offer, and we traded shirts. He got mine, and I got his, which smelled of perspiration to its maximum, but I got my Soviet rubles.

Finally, we said goodbye to each other with a hug, and he told me to disappear quickly into the darkness, where the police couldn't find us. I was loaded with money when I left, and I tried to catch up with my friends, who were far ahead of me. Unfortunately, I lost them in the darkness of Odessa's black harbor area, and I found myself alone in the worst area of the harbor. I had been given an address to a restaurant somewhere but in Russian, and I had no clue which direction I was supposed to go, so I followed something that looked like a main street, in my opinion.

My mother's words rang in my ears while I walked alone on the street, looking for my friends, lost in Ukraine. On top of that, I smelled as if I had been sleeping under a bridge in Odessa for three weeks with that godforsaken, smelly shirt. Nevertheless, I found my friends after a while by asking seemingly half of Odessa's population how to find the restaurant. Finally, we met and had dinner together, my first one abroad in a country different from what I was used to—and they all complained heavily because I smelled!

Four days later, we left Odessa and passed the Bosporus passage in Turkey, heading back into the Mediterranean Sea. The Mediterranean Sea was beautifully calm, and I enjoyed every day of my time on board. The remaining sea days were peaceful, and so was my life on board.

We arrived in Malmö on July 22; at the same berth we had left one month ago. I felt more like a man when I walked down the gangway with my white matelot on my head. I had learned a lot during my first sea voyage, and moreover, I had taken my first step toward seeing the world on the map hanging above my bed in my boyhood room. Last but not least, in my inner self, I had a feeling that my future life should be at sea. It was not easy to figure out what to do as a sixteen-years-young teenager.

Two years later, I finished high school, and finally, the day came when I graduated, and I was on my own. I was free to do what I wanted to do with my life. I had concentrated my ambitions on graduating with high marks because I knew I would need them when I sent in my application to the nautical academy in Malmö some five years later. On my graduation day, my mathematics teacher asked me about my plans for the future, and I responded that I'd like to become a sea captain. He looked at me with suspicious eyes and said, "If you really would like to become a sea captain, then you have to first improve your mathematical skills!" This I knew well since I wasn't the best student in that subject.

What to do next? The Finnish army was calling and hanging over me like a black cloud. I found it better to escape from the army as fast as possible by taking a tramp cargo vessel sailing worldwide. Besides, I needed more experience with life at sea.

Chapter 4

My First Funeral at Sea

I ESCAPED TO THE SEA to avoid the Finnish army, and on July 15, 1965, I said farewell to my mother for the first time for nearly a year. My matelot wasn't on my head that time when I boarded the white 6,228 DWT reefer ship *Coral Sea*, which measured 133.4 by 17 meters and had a speed of eighteen knots, as an OS (ordinary seaman) in Bremerhaven, Germany.

I mustered on board as a deck boy, but the next day, I was promoted to an OS, as the ship was one deckhand short. As an OS, I was supposed to know more about seamanship compared to the new guys and had a bigger responsibility. Since the ship was a fast banana tramp vessel, the crew was hired on the spot in the various ports worldwide, and mostly, the crew came from the Cape Verde Islands, Spain, Finland, England, Denmark, and South America. There was a total of seventeen different nationalities on board.

My mother was concerned when I left her. But I knew that she knew I was going to be careful about whatever I experienced out there on my own—and my God, I would for sure go through many things!

We were bound for Puerto Cortés in Honduras to take on board a half load of bananas, and from there, we would go to the Spanish Sahara in West Africa to load tuna fish for Genoa in Italy. I was doing the four-to-eight watch with the usual bridge procedures and mainly as a lookout watch. I was happy to finally commence with a longer sea time to see the world. As a matter of fact, I sailed on the *Coral Sea* for eleven months in one go, circumnavigating the globe a couple times.

There was a motorman on board by the name of Erik, who had his nineteen-year-old son, Anders, on board. Anders worked as an engine apprentice. In the mid-Atlantic, the bridge suddenly got a message from down below that Erik had become sick and suffered from severe stomach pain. I was told to go down to follow up on what was going on in order to deliver a report to the chief mate, who was on the bridge. Confused and a little bit scared of what I would face in the cabin of Erik, I opened the door and found him in severe pain and lying in the bed. His face was pale, and he was asking for morphine to facilitate the pain. His son was sitting at his bedside with a face that showed he was worried about his father's condition. There was no doctor on board, but there was a well-equipped hospital, as all ships had. We gave him the morphine, and his pain became less for a short while. Later that day, the weather began to deteriorate. Clouds moved into the sky, and it grew suspiciously dark from the north. A storm seemed imminent.

Since we were out in the middle of the Atlantic Ocean and facing a storm, the captain sent out a radio message that we urgently needed medical assistance from nearby ships. There were, however, no other ships within range to assist us and the sick Erik.

At some point, the weather conditions deteriorated and became rough, and the wind increased slowly to force 12 on the Beaufort scale (the scale is from 1 to 12) as Erik's condition became worse. The waves were huge, and the giant crests atomized into foam by the striking wind. The ship had to be switched over from autopilot to hand-steering mode since the waves grew bigger and bigger. When I was not at the helm, despite the horrendous sea conditions, I was instructed to go down to check Erik's condition. His son was there, as usual, holding his father's hand.

The *Coral Sea* was by then pitching heavily in the rough sea, and all of us started to become worried about Erik. The intense darkness of the night and my first storm didn't make me feel too good, and I knew that Erik was probably lying on his deathbed while the vertical walls of water loomed in on either side of us, which was a terrifying sight. Making the blackness more horrible were flashes of lightning that seemed to envelop the *Coral Sea*.

Erik got his usual morphine because there was nothing else we could do for him. The nearest land—some of the outer Caribbean Islands—was seven days away. Anders said to me in a whisper, "I have a feeling that my father will pass away. What can I do?"

I said, "Try to be strong," though I knew my words had no meaning. "I know it's not easy, but all of us are backing you up, and you are not alone." What else could I say as an eighteen-year-old boy? I knew it sounded ridiculous, when we all knew he would most likely pass away.

Three days after he was taken ill, Erik passed away while holding his son's hand. All of us kept our thoughts to ourselves and had tears in our eyes. I eventually went down to Erik's cabin and found his son hugging his father convulsively and, with his eyes full of tears, saying, "Daddy, please don't go! Don't leave me alone!"

Crying, I slowly put my hand on his shoulder, saying, "He is gone. There is nothing more we can do." What we all had feared had happened there in the middle of nowhere in the middle of the North Atlantic Ocean, and we were completely helpless in the severe storm.

We now had a corpse on board and no freezing chamber for Erik until we arrived at the next port, Puerto Cortés, Honduras, which was still some nine days away. Hence, the captain had a long discussion with Anders about what to do with his dead father. Erik's wife back home and Anders agreed to bury him at sea.

As the *Coral Sea* pitched and rolled heavily with the high seas and the wind whizzing in the rig, Erik was wrapped in a bedsheet in his cabin, and the bridge watch was assigned to go down to check that he didn't roll out from the bed. We were just waiting for the storm to calm down to bury him under peaceful conditions.

After a while, it became my turn to go down to check that the body was still in the bed. I found, to my horror, that Erik's body was lying on the floor. The cabin already had an unpleasant atmosphere, and it didn't become better as I struggled to put him back in the bed.

By morning the next day, the wind had become more moderate and good enough that the crew dared to poke their heads above the gunwales. We began preparing to bury Erik's remains at sea. We were told to sew a canvas bag with a pocket in the bottom. I asked why there should be a pocket in the bottom, and the chief mate showed me a table that referred to the amount of weight that was supposed to be used as ballast in the pocket with regard to the body weight.

At noon, the ocean had calmed down sufficiently, and the sun was shining from a clear blue sky. The time for the funeral was set for 1400 hours the same day. The carpenter had been manufacturing a stretcher of teak wood that was varnished with six handles made of cordage.

At 1330, the *Coral Sea* stopped her engines and was set adrift. The captain had ordered us to meet in our best clothes at 1400 hours on the aft deck, which we all did. Anders was with me when his father was carried out on the beautifully made varnished stretcher by six members of the engine crew. The stretcher was placed to rest on the gunwale, and Anders and I placed ourselves at the head of the varnished stretcher with all officers behind us as the rest of the crew lined up. The captain came with a flowerpot from his cabin. Under a sparkling sun, he made a speech, and then he spread out on the canvas soil taken from his flowerpot while reading from the Bible: "From ashes to ashes, dust to dust." Anders buried his face in his father's chest, hugging his body for the last farewell, crying rivers of tears. I cried as well, standing behind him. I couldn't believe this could happen to me, as young as I was.

When the captain was finished with his ceremony, he looked at Anders, who said, "Goodbye, Daddy," and he then gave the permission to let his father go overboard to be laid to rest in the deep Atlantic Ocean. We all bent our heads as a profound farewell as we heard the body splash into the Atlantic water. At that moment, tears ran down all our cheeks. From then on, Anders was alone on board without his father, and I felt at once that his death was gathering upon all of us.

Shortly after the funeral, the *Coral Sea* resumed her voyage toward Honduras with full speed.

Chapter 5

In Jail in Puerto Cortés, Honduras

IT WAS 1964, I WAS seventeen years of age, and we were heading for Honduras. The sun became intense as we approached the Caribbean Islands, so we stripped down to short-sleeved shirts and shorts. Four days after we passed the outer Caribbean Islands, we finally docked at the banana pier in Puerto Cortés. The hills beyond looked mysterious and lovely. White-sand beaches were on each side of the pier. I couldn't believe I was in Central America, and for the first time, I saw palm trees swinging to and fro in the gentle breeze.

The *Coral Sea* was the only ship in the port. We were close to the banana elevators that stood as huge, silent monuments with thousands of two-inch cockroaches running underneath them on the filthy pier.

I felt I was in a land far from home when I looked at all the chickens wandering in and out of the numerous bars no more than fifty meters away from us. The entire street—the only street—had some fifty bars, and all of them were just in front of the ship. There was a strange atmosphere that caused me to think it was a little bit of a godforsaken place.

Girls stood outside the bars, dancing alluringly by moving their bodies gently toward us to the tunes of Elvis Presley coming from a jukebox behind them. They smiled and danced, and they represented a seductiveness in human nature. The waterfront they had was only the banana pier. For the first time, I figured out why the seaman's life was so attracting when I heard the other weather-beaten sailors standing around me say, "Wow, this is paradise!"

It was not a place for tourists but a dream place for seamen. There was a much greater concern with sexuality in that village than with the unstable governmental situation. Behind the bar facades, it was wild, as I soon would experience.

The first arrival day was hectic, as all the deck crew had to prepare the holds to receive the banana elevators that were supposed to be lowered down into the hatches. They were like escalators with canvas bags every three meters, rolling uninterrupted from the pier side down into the holds after being loaded on the pier by hundreds of locals standing in queue. Each held a banana stalk on his shoulder, waiting to place the stalk in the canvas bag.

We would be there for four days, taking on board three thousand tons of bananas. As the *Coral Sea* was a reefer ship, it was necessary that the holds were clean to avoid the bananas becoming contaminated. I was sweeping and cleaning the holds for eight hours that first day, waiting to go ashore for the first time in Central America.

The girls were, of course, working for money due to the poor life conditions they had, and many of them were suffering from gonorrhea, syphilis, and other diseases. They knew they were contagious, but they didn't care, nor did we care.

Puerto Cortés had a population in those days of about two thousand people, and most of them lived in misery. When I finally was permitted to go ashore, I asked one of the elderly seamen, Hans, about rules, if any existed there, to be a little bit safe before I set foot in that exotic country. Hans had been sailing on that route for more than forty years. He suggested I should not bother discussing politics with ladies there. He said, "Just be happy, and enjoy yourself as much as you can." He also told me that traditionally, any white or foreign male could seduce a black woman easily, despite her instinct for virtue (i.e., the economic and social advantages of a white lover and the consequent mulatto children were too great for poor black girls to resist).

What he meant was "Use a condom or Nicholson's cream in all cases." The Nicholson's cream was a story by itself when used! It was a prophylactic cream used in the 1960s to protect against sexual diseases. I made sure I was sufficiently equipped with condoms as well as Nicholson's cream to prevent sexual diseases. I kept them in my pocket when I went ashore. Obviously, he knew about the rules in that part of the world, and I deeply appreciated the advice he gave me, but I never understood why he said not to discuss politics with the ladies, since that was not in my interests. Maybe he had a reason for telling me that.

My sexual experience was on a zero level when I happily went ashore with my friends. It took us two minutes to go to the first bar upon leaving the gangway, and it was a kind of consolation to know that the *Coral Sea* lay just behind us. As soon as we entered the first bar, the Latin music level was increased to its maximum.

Hans had obviously forgotten to tell me that I was a blond Viking, which made the girls go crazy for my hair. If they went crazy for my person, I never figured it out, but I certainly became aware of their predilection for the color of my hair.

The girls became wild, and even before I had stepped inside the bar, I felt I was on the verge of being raped on the muddy street by them. Actually, I enjoyed it very much, but I felt scared as they clung to me like hungry Amazons. It was too much! None of my shipmates cared; they all had grabbed ladies around the waistline, and they disappeared into the dark waiting bars. They all were like hungry wolves after being at sea for fifteen days, and God only knew when some of them had last had a lady who gave them love and care.

I was in paradise and surrounded by wonderful girls who did the utmost to seduce me. I felt excitement while talking and dancing with the girls, but it was not without problems I did so. I soon figured out that their hot blood quickly swelled, and they presented jealousy among each other, which could turn out to be dangerous.

Nightfall was two hours away, and I asked one of the girls, Maria, if she could take me to the beach, and she was more than happy to do so. I didn't have any swimming pants with me because I'd had no plans to go for a swim when I left the ship. Off we went, heading for the *playa*. Since the best part of the playa was farther away, she said, "I have a horse; let's take it." We walked to her house, which looked like a tumbled-down shed, and behind the shed we found her horse, which looked like a limping wreck. We both jumped up onto the limping wreck and took off riding bareback toward the beach. I felt I was in heaven, experiencing my first real adventure in a tropical country, and furthermore, I was sitting behind Maria, who was a beautiful girl.

The sunset was near, and she rode quickly; she didn't really care about my having problems in hanging on to her behind her back. Finally, we were on the beach, and I thought she would stop the animal slowly on the water's edge, but she didn't. Instead, she forced the horse full speed into the water with me clinging on to her back, until both of us fell over the horse's neck and landed with a big splash in the warm water as the sun set. The horse stopped and reared itself on its hind legs. I thought the horse would fall onto me, but somehow, it didn't happen. Maria was a wild girl! The water was as clear as crystal, and I could still see shoals of fish some three meters under the surface when we floated together on the water. It was the first time I had seen that kind of a cobalt-blue water, and I loved it.

The sea was tranquil and took on the colors of the sky while the sun slowly went down in the ocean. There were a dozen young men around us in the water, and they waved and smiled but watched us carefully since I was swimming with my jeans on, and Maria did the same. We played around like kids, splashing water onto each other. The limping wreck was still standing on the beach, waiting faithfully for our return. I had no intention of returning yet, but Maria said, "*Vamos*," despite the fun we had in the water. With water dripping off our clothes, we jumped back up onto the horse and rode away toward her shed.

By then, the sun had sunk below the horizon, and it became quickly dark. We parked the horse in her backyard, and Maria took my hand and showed me the way into her shed. I felt she wanted to give me love, but her shed was filthy, with big cockroaches on the walls and in the bed; it didn't look inviting to me. I knew, however, all my seamen friends on board expected me to give them my full story about what Maria had brought me into, so I thought, *Why not? Let's do it!*

That evening, in that godforsaken shed, I lost my virginity, and suddenly, it occurred to me I had used no condom. My first thought was *Where is the Nicolson's cream?* The cream would later be prohibited, as it caused cancer.

The entire cream package was wet but still usable. The cream had to be applied less than thirty minutes after intercourse, so in the light of a kerosene streetlamp outside her shed, I tried to read the instructions, which said, "Squirt first the entire blue tube inside the urethra, and afterward, smear half the white tube around your penis, and wrap the cotton bag around."

While I was trying to comply with the description on the tube—which, in my opinion, was a complicated one—Maria leaned over my shoulder, asking what I was doing. I didn't answer, as I was heavily concentrating on trying to protect myself from disease. I had been told that the sexual diseases you could face were severe, and I wanted none of them. So, I carefully continued to follow the description, even though Maria thought I was a strange teenager occupied with some strange things around my manhood.

When the cotton bag was finally wrapped around my penis and secured with a nice knot, we both took off to the bar where we had met. There I met my friends, who, by that time of the evening, were more than slightly intoxicated. I met a bunch of wild sailors who were dancing, smoking, drinking, and completely out of order. One shouted to me, "Peter, come here, and tell us about your story with Maria!" and indeed, they got the whole story. After a while, I somehow lost Maria, and since I couldn't find her, I started to talk with another girl, which turned out to be a big mistake.

While I sat on a bar chair, sipping a Cuba Libre, Maria suddenly returned, furious and upset, and started to accuse me, which consequently drew everybody's attention. Her temper peaked, and she went ballistic. She smashed a bottle on my head and knocked me out, and I went down onto my knees.

When I came back to my senses again, I had no clue how long I had been unconscious and lying on the floor. I saw from down below the entire bar in a big fight. I managed to ask one of my friends, "What happened?"

He shouted to me over the music from the jukebox while still involved in fighting with the locals and the girls, "Peter, if you have fun with one girl, never start to talk with another girl! Maria became jealous because you made a mistake!" It was a wild fight with the locals and the girls.

The next thing I saw was the police rushing into the bar and trying to figure out who had started the fighting and why. I was deeply grateful that my friends had been trying to defend me, but the locals outnumbered us, and when the police asked which troublemaker had started things, suddenly, everybody, including the girls and Maria, pointed at me.

With blood still running down from my head, I was taken away to the only police jail in that godforsaken, wild place in the harbor of Puerto Cortés. It turned out the jail was also in front of the *Coral Sea*, no more than a hundred meters away, which was a kind of consolation. But what a jail! The jail was made of wooden planks, with a total inner space of five square meters. The height of the planks was some 1.7 meters, and the jail faced the *Coral Sea*. There was a tiny bunk, which was made of lumber as well, and the roof consisted of corrugated plates, which partly covered the bunk during the rain, which I could imagine.

In the pitch-black evening—I had no idea what the time was—I was taken away in order to spend the night on that bunk partly under the stars, and God only knew for how many more days or hours I would be there. I had no clue. In my opinion, I was an innocent seaman, and it was an embarrassing situation—which had taken place just in front of the *Coral Sea*. What a situation it was! When I got my senses back after being knocked out, I tried to analyze the entire situation, why I was there, and why that had happened to me.

The answer was simple: I was obsessed with the tropical environment and the excitement it offered a young teenager who suddenly had come out into the wide world. I had learned some elementary rules, be careful, take nothing for granted, do not trust anybody, and do not flirt with other Latinas if you are already involved with one. Maria was a nice lady, but obviously I had made a mistake with her.

I saw the deck lights from *Coral Sea* illuminating the banana pier. I felt the wonderful environment had become hostile to me, even though I'd had a perfect and glorious day earlier. I fell asleep on the lumber bunk with my own thoughts, trying to review the events. I knew I had chosen my lifestyle for better or for worse, and the worse was that now I was suddenly in jail in Honduras.

The following morning, I woke up with an incredible headache and heard the sound of raindrops falling onto the corrugated plates above my head. I had a strange feeling in my penis, and it occurred to me that I still had the cotton bag wrapped around it. It was supposed to be removed after twelve hours, but I had forgotten it in all the commotion. While lying still on the lumber bunk, the first thing I suddenly saw was the head of the police chief looking down at me over the wooden planks, along with the boatswain. The police chief shook his head and disappeared. Bosun asked me if I was okay. My first question was "When can I get out of this jail?"

He said, "I don't know, but the captain has been informed, and he is trying to get you out—and believe me, he is not too happy."

I said, "Well, thanks, Bosun, but what about the chief mate, who is supposed to put me to work this morning? I'm not on board."

"Don't worry, Peter. He knows about last night's fighting, and they will release you when they consider the time right. This is Honduras. We'll bring you some breakfast because I doubt you will get anything here, and by the way, I will send an AB down to you to plaster the wounds you have on your head."

I felt I was at least not abandoned, and I could at least see the ship from my jail and what was going on there. Somebody cared about me. I also saw the police chief sitting on a chair two meters away, half asleep, and I guessed he was guarding me so I wouldn't escape.

I got my breakfast, and the AB came with the plaster. Throughout the day, I spent my time watching the locals carrying banana stalks to the elevator. Once in a while, the deck crew waved to me while involved in the maintenance of the ship. Suddenly, the wild lady Maria popped up. She smiled and said, "*Como estas, Peter? Estas bien?*" (How are you, Peter? Are you okay?).

What a stupid question from her! I didn't want to talk with her, and I mumbled that she should go away.

My prison became unbearably hot due to the corrugated metal plates above heating up as the sun shone strongly from a clear blue sky and sweat poured down my face. The temperature was soon 25 degrees Celsius, and I was not psychically prepared for that. I thought, *this is the real purgatory!* I was in great need of water, so I shouted toward the *Coral Sea*, "Please give me water!" Obviously, my shouting woke up the police chief from his beauty sleep in his chair close to me. He came to me, asking what I wanted. I said, "I'd like to have water but only from the ship."

He shook his head again and said something I understood as "Keep your mouth shut; otherwise, you will never be released."

All of a sudden, I started to like him, and furthermore, I saw the captain walking toward my prison. He went straightaway to the police chief and tried to negotiate with him to get me out. I followed their conversation carefully, and out of the blue, the police chief opened up the padlock, and I was a free man.

The captain said to me, "Peter, you have learned your lesson now. Do not ever repeat it." This I faithfully promised while we walked together away from the jail. I thought about what I had just experienced and what kind of adventure I would face next.

The deck crew smiled at me when I came back on board. As I walked up the gangway, I held back my smile because I felt confused and embarrassed. The entire situation had been embarrassing for me.

The next day alongside the berth, I didn't go ashore at all. I had had my fun, and I was happy to be on board. Two days later, as we departed from Puerto Cortés with a strange tugboat that was insufficient with regard to the engine power, I was standing on the forecastle, working with the mooring ropes, when I suddenly saw Maria standing on the banana pier below the ship's bow, waving slowly goodbye to me. I never saw her again, and I could do nothing but wave goodbye to her as well.

Chapter 6

Counterfeit Dollars and Arrest in Genoa, Italy

AFTER FOUR DAYS IN PUERTO Cortés, we departed for the Spanish Sahara in West Africa to load tuna fish. Some twelve days later, we arrived at a group of Japanese fishing trawlers just outside the coast of the Spanish Sahara, and we loaded the frozen tuna straight from the trawlers with huge Yokohama fenders in between.

The hot air from the Sahara Desert covered the ship with a fine layer of sand, and it was a fast operation that took no more than twenty-four hours. The deck crew stood at the derrick controls, maneuvering the slings in the open ocean day and night and checking the preventer guys and the slewing guy manila pendants, which frequently broke. They did this while both ships rolled heavily in the swell.

When the load of tuna finally was on board, we sailed to Genoa. Coming into Genoa we went alongside and close to the famous Via Antonio Gramsci, a street that was a dream place for all sailors. The *Coral Sea* spent approximately five days alongside it. Via Antonio Gramsci had everything, including high crime. Unaware of this, AB Goran went ashore to sell his radio because he needed money for the next evening when we planned to go ashore together. I stayed on board because of my duties. After so many sea days, all of us were keen to see something else, but some of us couldn't due to the watches we had.

The following day, I was awakened by Goran and saw his pale and shocked face when he said, "Peter, do you know what happened to me?"

I said, "No, I don't know."

He said, "I went ashore last night, and since I had no money, I sold my radio in Via Antonio Gramsci for eighty dollars, and I couldn't see that the money I received was counterfeit dollars. What can I do now?" He handed the money over to me.

I took a close look at the dollars, and with my innocent attitude toward the world, I said, "They look perfectly well to me. We can use them!"

It had been fifteen days since we had left Puerto Cortés, so we had a longing to go ashore. Furthermore, our salaries just kept us alive, and none of us had money for the time being. We felt we deserved to have some fun that coming evening. So, what to do now? There we were in Genoa, with no money except for Goran's eighty counterfeit dollars.

Via Antonio Gramsci was a lawless place, with everything from hookers to people robbing each other. We decided to go out and spend the money in Via Gramsci's narrow alleys, even though we both knew it was far from the right thing to do. We didn't come by the decision easily since it was a risk, but we had to cheer each other up.

At 1900 hours, we went ashore, full of expectations and smelling of the aftershave Florida Water, which some thirsty seamen even drank. We aimed for one of the first inviting bars to test the money, so to speak. To our surprise, it worked! Still, we were suspicious, but we felt a little bit more relaxed since the bartender didn't complain about our money. In my inner self, I didn't like this at all, but since I had earlier promised to help Goran, we continued to explore the wild Via Antonio Gramsci, using our dollars where possible. Coincidentally, we came to a Jewish synagogue, and when we had a glance inside the doors, a stocky man in his sixties, wearing a cowl and a tie, invited us to come inside. He looked at us with bright eyes and an expression of good humor. He was probably the rabbi, and we quickly accepted his offer to show us around, though I didn't know why we did so. People came quietly and left equally quietly and vanished into the darkness. Most were elderly women in black clothes who lit candles here and there and knelt as they made their prayers. I wondered why we were there, as we were supposed to enjoy ourselves, so we said goodbye and expressed our gratitude to the rabbi. As we were kindhearted, we dropped a counterfeit dollar into a silver urn, and then we disappeared quickly.

Shortly after that, we came to the famous Tropicana Bar, where we had a memorable evening sitting on a small bench. We sat in almost complete darkness, except the dance floor was illuminated with spotlights, so we watched the performance of a group of dancers. Our mood was on top. The girls were all between eighteen and twenty-five, all vibrant with youth, beauty, and expectations and committed to only one aim: seducing us. We ordered a beer each. We had fun and laughed, and in our seamen's happiness, we forgot we were buying beer with counterfeit money.

Suddenly, in the distance, we heard sirens, and the sound of them became louder, as if they were approaching our area. I told Goran, "Something must have happened in the area."

It was quiet for a while, when all of a sudden, the doors were kicked open with a loud sound that caused everybody in the bar to turn his or her head toward the police who stormed into the bar. There was confusion, and everybody became concerned about what would happen next. The girls on the stage stopped dancing and stood like paralyzed statues. The music stopped, and it was as if lightning had struck from the sky.

In the same moment, the bartender pulled out a strong torch and pointed it straight at us! Disaster had struck for us, and in less than a minute, we were both handcuffed and brought out by two policemen escorting us. Our last words to each other before they separated us were "What are they going to do with us?" We both agreed to say that we knew nothing about the money being counterfeit.

Passing the entrance door to Tropicana Bar, I got the shock of my life: hundreds of people had created a walkway for us as we walked out while the crowd took a good look at us. My first thought when looking at the huge crowd outside was that they probably thought somebody had been murdered and expected to see a corpse carried out on a stretcher or something.

The situation we were in was embarrassing and made us scared. It also was dangerous, but the harm was done, and we had ourselves to blame. With howling sirens, all six police cars took off, with Goran and me in the middle car. I assumed we were heading toward the police station in Genoa. While sitting in the backseat of the carabinieri car, I tried to review the entire situation, but my mind became distracted due to the sound of the howling police sirens from all six cars. Still, I considered myself to be fairly innocent; I'd just been helping a friend who had been unlucky. What *unlucky* meant in that situation I didn't know.

When we entered the central police station in Genoa, they made sure I couldn't talk with Goran and parted us. My pockets were stripped, including my Finnish passport I happened to carry with me. I was taken into an empty room, escorted by three policemen, and immediately brutally forced down onto the floor on my back and kept there by two policemen while the third one took my shoes and socks off. Then he pulled off his belt without saying a word and started to hit my feet. I thought I would faint. I couldn't believe this had happened to me. I couldn't move, and I screamed and begged the police officer to stop because the pain was too much. He stopped for a while and said something in Italian, which I understood as "Where did you get the money from?"

I managed to get a response out from my throat. With my face full of tears and my feet bleeding, I shouted in English, "I fucking don't know! Don't treat me like this! You are idiots, and I do not deserve this!" Or maybe I deserved it. The police officer immediately hit my feet again in anger (maybe because he understood my English) while the other two took an even steadier grip on my body. It was torture, and I was now a victim and treated like a criminal.

I tightened my muscles while my eyes focused on the police officer who prepared to hit me again, and he hit me for a hell of a long time. I did not know what was right or wrong anymore, and the room filled again with the sound of my painful screams. I begged them to stop because I was willing to tell them what we had done.

To my relief, he stopped, and I guess he was satisfied; his duty was to get the truth out of me and nothing else. I also believe he must have liked the view of my bleeding feet. I told him the truth Goran and I had agreed to: I hadn't known the money was counterfeit. I was uncertain how much Goran had suffered, if he had gotten the same treatment I had, and if he had been able to keep our promise we'd agreed to.

It seemed the police were happy enough with my answer and took my word for it. The officer told me to stand up, but that turned out to be easier said than done. With aching pain and bleeding feet, I tried to stand upright, but I couldn't. I had to sit down again, and in a low voice, I asked them if they possibly could give me some bandages for my swollen feet. I became concerned about whether I'd be able to walk again in the near future.

I got the bandages, and in silence, I wrapped up my feet to the best of my ability while sitting on the floor. When that was done, I pulled my shoes nicely together with a slow motion of my hands while raising my left arm with the hopes that some of the police officers could help me up. In a spasmodic attempt to stand on my wrapped feet, I managed somehow to keep my balance. With shaking legs, I was taken to an office in order to meet the police commissioner, who wanted to interrogate me.

The middle-aged commissioner just looked at me without saying a single word. I was quiet because I had nothing to say due to the nightmare I had just experienced.

Thoughts went through my head, when he suddenly said in perfect English, "We believe you that you didn't know the money was false, but in this town of Genoa, there is an overflow of counterfeit US dollars. We don't know where these counterfeit dollars are coming from, but when we catch somebody with this money, we are very tough, and we have to be so. Your friend Goran has been going through the same treatment as you, and he confirmed as well that he didn't know the money was counterfeit."

Upon hearing that, I sent a grateful thought to Goran that he had kept his mouth shut as well. The commissioner continued by saying, "You are free to go. But neither of you will be allowed to return to Italy for the next six months, and your passports will be stamped as *non grata*."

The commissioner took all my family details, and he made it clear to me that he knew I was a young seaman whom unfortunately had been a victim in my innocence of counterfeit dollars. He held my passport, and he stamped it with a powerful bang with a blue stamp that said, "Non grata."

I met Goran a few minutes later, and we looked at each other and both said thanks because we were able to keep our mouths shut. I wouldn't even dare to think about what the penalty would have been if they'd found us guilty. The commissioner came after us and informed us that we had to step inside a police car and go to all places where we had spent the money. The police were keen to trace the money. So off we went to all places where we had been, and luckily, we were able to find the majority of the money. All's well that ends well.

Since none of us had real money for a taxi back to the *Coral Sea* berth, we asked the commissioner if they could provide a car to bring us back, which they did. This time, we sat in the backseat of an Italian police car without any sirens, and the officers talked with us in a friendly way. In those days, seamen were treated as the third category of human beings in the world. Genoa was not an exception.

While sitting in the police car, it occurred to me that I once had read in a Swedish law book from 1861 that the category of criminals included trolley navies, bohemians, gypsies, and seamen. So obviously, I was categorized as one of them!

Two o'clock in the morning, we arrived at the gangway. We nicely said farewell to the Italian police officers who had been kind enough to drive us back to the ship.

We stepped out from the car with our feet wrapped in bandages and with acing pain.

We had been going through a weird story, and as young we were, bearing in mind that we could hardly walk, we said to each other, "You walk first," up the steep gangway.

It was difficult to walk the gangway steps because our legs could not carry us. The gangway watch looked at our feet wrapped in bandages. He asked what had happened to us, but we decided not to mention anything at all about it to anybody since it was an embarrassing story, and we never discussed the matter again.

As dramatic as that incident had been for me, I promised myself I'd be more careful about my life in that early stage of my sea career and avoid further problems in the future. The event deeply affected me, and I was angry at myself for not anticipating the danger by running the risk for possibly bigger problems.

I continued to sail for the next eight months on that tramp vessel worldwide, and I became more mature in my work as an OS and more able to deal with different problems as they occurred. I came to realize that I loved seeing the world and loved that little community of thirty-seven crew members. The *Coral Sea* was not only a lucky vessel but also a happy vessel, a desirable ship that all of us liked. She trod the world and took me to the Far East, where we sailed for almost six months to Japan, China, Okinawa, Korea, Manila, and Mauritius, and after that, we sailed to London, where I signed off the ship almost a year later.

In order to get the widest possible experience from different cargo ships, especially ships with derricks, I applied for the nautical academy in Malmö, Sweden, but before that, I took a turn as an OS on the MS *Sabang*, which sailed for the Swedish East Asia Company.

The *Sabang* was a general cargo ship of 8,535 DWT built in 1955. It measured 147 by 19.1 meters and had a max speed of seventeen knots, a beautiful white hull, and eighteen cargo derricks. She was very much the old type of ship. From her derrick system, I learned the main part of seamanship and derrick cargo handling, which turned out to be invaluable for my future career at sea. I sailed on the *Sabang* for some six months along the coasts of India, Pakistan, and many of the Gulf countries.

Chapter 7

First Time as an Officer

FINALLY, ON FEBRUARY 10, 1968, the Finnish army caught me at the Finnish embassy in London when I was renewing my passport. I was firmly told to show up outside the main gate of the Swedish-speaking Infantry Nyland Brigade in Dragsvik, Finland, on February 15 at 1500 hours.

Finland only issued passports for one year at the time until one had completed the military service. If I by accident was not there, then I would be blacklisted at every Finnish embassy in the entire world. I had only four days to report outside the main gate. Thus, I found myself doing the tough military service for eleven months in the army for better or for worse.

I left the army on January 9, 1969, as a lower grade of a sergeant, and now, with a five-year passport in my hand, I was free to go.

After the military service, I applied for the nautical academy in Malmö, Sweden, where I did three years of intensive studying on the school bench. Three years later, finally, the day came when I graduated: June 6, 1972. It was the happiest moment in my life when I was told to step forward in the lecture theater, and the principal of the school handed me the endorsement of certificate that declared me a master mariner unlimited in worldwide traffic on any tonnage. My mother was sitting among the other parents, and she was as proud as I was. I was twenty-four years of age.

As a brand-new master mariner, I wanted to try my wings as soon as possible. Because of self-explanatory reasons, I stayed within the Swedish East Asia Company, which was a subdivision of the Broström Company, which had some four hundred ships of all categories at the time.

Two weeks after my graduation, I was sitting on an airplane on my way to Balboa in Panama, where I would board the twelve-thousand-DWT MS *Hakone*, bound for Gothenburg.

The *Hakone* was due to transit the Panama Canal, and I would board her while she was slowly sailing toward the Gatun locks with one of the provision boats from the local ship supplier. After spending the night in a cheap and filthy hotel in Balboa, we drove to Colón some two hours (114 kilometers) away on the Pacific side of the canal. Upon coming to Colón, I was told to board the provision boat.

Since Colón was a major place for reprovisioning ships coming from the Far East and vice versa, I found out there was no space for me on board that small provision barge fully loaded with supplies. I looked at the ship chandler and his papers with an inquiring look, and he shrugged, giving me a look and saying, "If you'd like to board this ship, you'd better find a place on top of the provisions somewhere," so I climbed up on top of the lettuce and God knew what with my suitcase, where I sat uncomfortably, watching the *Hakone* slowly approach the locks.

Her arrival time was punctual, when I noted some impending dark clouds coming toward us and felt cold wind, indicating heavy rain was imminent. Then it started to rain suddenly, as if the sky had opened. I was soon soaking wet, drenched in water, and my pants were colored green by the wet lettuce.

While I leaned my wet head in my hands, my mind was full of questions: *Will I be able to make it as a new ship officer on board the* Hakone? *How should I be treated?* My mind was full of thoughts as I watched my first ship arrive where I would be the third officer on board for at least eight months. Amid my thoughts, the barge suddenly came alongside the gangway that had been lowered down, and I climbed up. I was met by the outgoing third officer, who was packed and already standing at the gangway, drunk like a rat, ready to leave the vessel for his vacation. There was no handover whatsoever. Nothing was said from his side as he went down to the supply boat.

A cabin was assigned to me, and I was told to familiarize myself with the second officer, whom I accidentally met on the stairway. That was it; nothing more was said, which made me concerned because in my mind, I had pictured a different reception for a first-time officer on board a ship. My reception was more or less like "Okay, you are here. Accept the deals as they are"—which I did.

As per the rules, I went to the captain in order to introduce myself as the new third officer on board. I knocked carefully on his cabin door, but of course, he was not there, and I realized the vessel was navigating in confined waters, the Panama Canal; therefore, he most likely was on the bridge.

Coming to the bridge, I looked at the bridge equipment with different eyes than I had as an OS. I met the captain, and I approached him determinedly, saying, "Good morning, sir. I am the new third officer, and my name is Peter Skog."

He turned out to be a magnificent and well-shaped man in his mid sixties with the eyes of an eagle. I immediately had respect for him, though he looked at me with an arrogant look. His only comment was "So you are the new third officer. Welcome on board, and don't touch any buttons without my permission." I immediately felt he had an antipathy against new green officers, and my thoughts seemed verified when he added, "Now, you just watch from behind, and tomorrow we start at 0800 hours." Fair enough!

The first mate told me that he was a remarkable man, he went by the name Tarzan, and no one knew the ship better than he did, since he had been on board for five years. He was like a dynamo.

For the first time, I was in the Panama Canal, which was an impressive canal to watch. We passed the Gatun locks and the Miguel and Miraflores locks one after the other, and some eight hours later, we entered the Atlantic Ocean.

The next day, at 0800 hours, I was on the bridge, standing in front of the big chart table, eagerly waiting for Tarzan while analyzing the courses laid out in the sea charts throughout the Caribbean Islands. Tarzan suddenly came. He was doing the eight-to-twelve watch since I was not yet trustworthy, and with all rights, because I had to sail for six months as an unexperienced officer before I could become an experienced officer. He told me at once, "You are not allowed to touch any buttons or similar things until I given my permission to do so. I will do this watch until further notice, and you shall learn from me about the bridge procedure here. Consequently, you shall first of all familiarize yourself with all the buttons today one by one, and tomorrow I will ask you the deep meaning behind each one of them before I let you even touch anything here on this bridge. Is that clear?"

I said, "Yes, sir, it's clear!"

So, we started to go through the buttons one by one, when he suddenly said, "By the way, you shall also from now on forget everything you have learned in the academy. This is your school, and here you will for the first time learn things as they are."

I looked at him, perplexed, asking myself what he meant. A long time later on, I appreciated what he meant.

Three days later, I was instructed by Tarzan to do the eight-to-twelve watch alone without him around. I had until then just been watching his bridge work with a big portion of patience. I was happy to have my own bridge watch, though he frequently checked me up, of course. He instructed me clearly, "If you face any problems or are in doubt about things during your watch, you call me right away. It doesn't matter if it's in the nighttime." Most captains didn't feel safe in their cabins when they had a brand-new officer up there.

I went through all the nautical tables and slowly repeated the astronomy I had learned. I took several astronomical sights from the sun, stars, and moon, and I calculated the sun's meridian passage. I walked on the bridge back and forth from starboard to port side, lost in my own thoughts, proud at seeing the whole ship in front of me, given that the *Hakone* was a cargo ship with the entire superstructure aft. To my delight, dolphins were jumping in the bow in the turquoise water. I loved to watch them. During the four hours my watch lasted, I felt a great deal of satisfaction, even though I knew I had to complete six months as an experienced officer before I was duly responsible for my own actions, according to the Swedish law of the sea. However, I was blissfully unaware of what the near future would bring me.

I repeated my entire navigational knowledge from the academy, which I transferred to practical handling by doing astronomical calculations and sights. As a matter of fact, I had high marks in astronomy from the nautical academy. I loved doing the astronomical navigation, and I loved to see that my calculations were sufficiently accurate.

I converted, during the next fourteen days, my entire navigational schoolbook and skills from the academy into practical action on the chart table. I was enthusiastic, and I took sights from every star and planet and the sun with the sextant as much as possible. During that ocean crossing from the Panama Canal to Europe, I spent my bridge watches in peace, as there weren't any ships around yet. I had not yet been confronted with ship traffic, which was a fundamental part of the work as a bridge officer. I was eager to get some traffic so I could learn how to deal with it.

The English Channel came toward us, along with the dense traffic in the channel. It was a standing procedure that the master was on the bridge when navigating in heavy traffic. I was told to be in charge, and once in a while, he corrected my actions by saying, for example, "Go more to starboard, and when you must alter the course, do it clearly so the meeting traffic can see your action."

With eighteen knots, we passed the Dover Strait in the morning with the white cliffs of Dover on our port side, and we frequently had to determine our position through the land-based Decca system as we entered the North Sea on our way to Gothenburg.

We approached another heavy-traffic area on the Danish west coast from Hirsthals to Skagen. Since we were northbound, that place could be tricky, with a steady stream of ships coming mainly from the north. Approaching Skagen, Denmark's most northern tip, I made my first navigational mistake. My brain had been programmed by the nautical academy with the starboard rule, or the head-on situation, rule fourteen in the international sailing rules, which said, "When two power-driven vessels are meeting on a reciprocal or nearly reciprocal course so as to involve risk of collision, each shall alter her course to starboard so that each shall pass on port side of the other. When a vessel is in any doubt as to whether such a situation exists, she shall assume that it does exist and act accordingly."

So, I acted accordingly, as per the rules, and I complied with them faithfully. I altered the course to starboard for each one of the incoming vessels.

It turned out to be a severe mistake from my side, a blunder I never forgot in my future bridge work. I had been altering the course to starboard for all of the other ships so much that I forgot to check my own ship's position on the chart due to the frequent alteration of my courses. Also, I had forgotten to compensate my course by going back to the original course. My average course in the chart was twenty degrees.

Suddenly, Tarzan came up onto the bridge, and without saying a word to me, he instructed the helmsman, "Port fifteen degrees on the helm." I was petrified upon hearing his words as he took over the command, but within seconds, I realized my huge mistake. The Danish west coast became quickly shallow, no matter where you were along the coast.

Tarzan sailed out to deeper water for half an hour (i.e., nine nautical miles since the ship's speed was eighteen knots on a 280-degree course). Oh boy, that was an alteration of the course by some hundred degrees. When he felt we were safe, he readopted the previous course on the chart, which was twenty degrees true course, and told me to determine the ship's position. I could only speculate what might have happened if he hadn't intervened.

I felt like a fool, but the damage was done. I felt that the captain should have butchered me after that incident, but he didn't. He took me aside to the sea charts, pointed at the shallow areas on our starboard side, and said with a low voice, "Do not forget to compensate the course changes you have been doing for other ships when navigating close to shorelines, and always check the distance from shore with the radar." However, the radars in those days suffered from overheating and broken fuses, and it was a blessing when they worked in dense-traffic areas.

Tarzan said, "We are still afloat, but I felt there was a possibility that this could happen, and therefore, I came up. You continue as before, and I guess you have learned a lesson." So, he had been standing in his front window, watching my actions.

I felt it was a defeat for me, but in my inner self, I felt he was backing me up, even though I was unexperienced. I eventually remembered the principal's words to all of us brand-new master mariners upon our graduation from the academy: "Gentlemen, when you are coming out as new bridge officers and standing on a bridge for the first time, please keep in mind that you only have six months' time when you are allowed to ask any kind of question; after that, you are on your own and duly responsible for your own actions." In other words, "You will end up in court if things go wrong." I realized I was lucky.

On July 5, 1972, the *Hakone* arrived at her home port, Gothenburg, in Sweden for discharging her cargo from the Far East. She had a turnaround period in Scandinavian ports of approximately fourteen days until she again was outbound for Japan and the Far East after loading partially new cargo in various European ports. She sailed out from Rotterdam in Holland, her final port in Europe, on her round-the-world voyage, which took five months. Tarzan signed off the ship for his scheduled vacation, and I said goodbye to him at the gangway and expressed my thankfulness toward him since he had taught me many valuable things.

I completed the round-the-world voyage without any further problems, and five months later, we arrived again at Gothenburg on December 22. I had two months to go until I became an experienced deck officer.

Chapter 8

My First Grounding

On Christmas Eve 1972, at 1600 hours, we sailed out from the Gothenburg harbor in a freezing ten-degree-below-zero-Celsius temperature, again bound for the Far East. It was my second time making that round trip.

Passing the *Göteborgs grund*, we increased the speed to approximately the full seventeen knots as we proceeded toward the confined area with a buoyed fairlead through the enchanted, beautiful archipelago full of bare rocks on each side, with screaming birds and scenery that took one's breath away. Christmas Eve was emotional for everybody, and at that time of the year, it was almost dark, and the atmosphere was enchanted as the hull broke the thin ice that sounded like crushed crystal glass. Indeed, it was winter, and that day was so cold the water began to freeze.

The archipelago demanded the utmost attention because it was rich with rocks, and pilotage was compulsory. The mood was good on the bridge, and the pilot was involved in a discussion with the captain. As we approached the new Scandia container terminal, passing shortly the company flagship, MS *Nihon*, which was alongside that berth, the captain instructed me to greet her since it was policy to greet the company ships always. I went up onto the monkey island, the top bridge, and lowered the Swedish flag. I was pleased to see that they recognized our gallantry by lowering their flag too.

With full speed, seventeen knots, we made the turn around Gäveskär to starboard in the fairway marked with several buoys, since the pilot had ordered the helmsman to go to starboard ten on the rudder. While we were turning, the pilot was deeply involved in a conversation with the captain, and he forgot to instruct the helmsman to go back to amidships rudder. I was standing, as usual, next to the helmsman in order to follow up the commands, and for some seconds, I waited with excitement for the pilot to compensate the turn since the vessel was still under a heavy starboard turn. There was not much space in that narrow fairway, and there were underwater rocks everywhere.

Since the pilot did not react, nor did the captain, I shouted, "Mr. Pilot, change the course, for heaven's sake!"

The pilot then realized the seriousness and quickly shouted, "Hard port rudder!" but it was too late.

The *Hakone* reacted slowly, and the captain shouted, "Stop the engines!"

The pilot shouted, "No, don't do that! We need the steering speed!"

It seemed to take forever until the vessel reacted on the hard port rudder. Ahead of us, we could see submerged rocks rapidly approaching with the breaking water flushing all over. I thought, *This is our unavoidable destruction*, and I prepared myself for the coming grounding by grabbing the rail in front of me. The loud sound of steel crushing against granite shortly filled our ears. When the ship finally reacted on the port rudder, it was far too late.

A few seconds later, with a tremendous bang, we went right up onto the submerged rocks with seventeen knots of speed. We heard the keel plates crush against the granite bottom as shock waves went through the entire ship, and we felt the hull struggling to keep us together. The impact was immense, and the force of the grounding caused all of us to fall forward and grab the handrail below the bridge windows to be able to stand on our legs as the vessel forced its way over the rocks with a continuous crashing sound that never seemed to end. Some 156 meters of underwater keel struggled to pass over as the high speed enabled her to jump over the rocks with a tremendous effect on the hull. We asked ourselves if she would stay afloat when she finally came to rest on the other side of the rock. She undoubtedly had a severely perforated underwater keel that could sink her once she finally stopped.

We had lost the steering and the engine power as well, so we could only watch in which direction she was heading. She hit a second underwater rock just on the port side of the fairway, which came to act as a buffer and caused her to bounce back, and then she finally came to rest.

Everything was now silent, and all of us looked at each other with astonishment. I was stunned but got quickly back to my senses and power of action. I knew I had to make notes about the time of accident and so on, so I wrote down all the relevant times while the captain, who was pale and sitting on the emergency parachute rocket box, screamed, "Why did this happen to me?" Then he blamed the pilot for negligence, and they accused each other for everything. They shouted at each other, using abusive words.

The high-level alarm from all the bilges and the engine room sounded, indicating that the vessel was rapidly taking in water.

A complete sounding of the ship was made quickly in order to see how watertight she still was, and the report was presented to the captain: she was taking in water fast. The chief engineer called us up from the engine room and said, "The engine room is filled with water. We are pumping as much as we can, but it seems the water ingress is bigger. We are abandoning the engine room since we are unable to keep the water level down, and the water level is rising quickly."

The boatswain came up onto the bridge to report in his drunkenness to the captain regarding the condition of the forepart of the ship. The captain gnashed his teeth over his condition and said, "You drunken pig. What do you have to report?"

Carefully articulating and trying to sound convincing, he said, "Well, sir, my entire storeroom down below in the bow is filled with water." Not a word was spoken for several minutes, and the silence was profound. However, we had our doubts about whether that was the case or not.

I was instructed to carry out an inspection of the forepart of the ship. After Bosun's report to the captain, I was halfway down the stairs in the bow of the ship no more than ten minutes later.

I had luckily brought with me a torch since the entire ship was partially black due to no power on board. Even though the emergency generator was running, it didn't give any power to the lights in that part of the ship. I climbed down the stairs, fumbling in the darkness, and passed through some manholes until I came down to the far bottom. In the light of my torch, I saw the water gurgling, and I was unable to figure out where it came from, but it was there. The intoxicated boatswain had obviously been right, but his storeroom was not filled with water.

I thought, *We are actually sinking slowly,* and I had been an officer for just five and a half months. The engine room had been abandoned. We radioed the harbor control, asking for assistance, but the answer was that no one was available, as it was Christmas Eve. We stood crosswise in the fairway but afloat with a huge stern trim. Apparently, she was floating on the tank top. No one was available to give us appropriate assistance (i.e., a tugboat to assist). I couldn't believe that was possible, but obviously, it was possible.

Coming back to the bridge, I found the captain in a state of shock, and he couldn't talk normally. I gave him my report of the bow part, but his response was kind of absent. He was sitting on the emergency rocket box, repeatedly saying, "Why did this happen to me?" We had been asking for tugboat assistance, but the big, powerful tugboats were all alongside and unmanned. The harbor control managed finally to send out a small tug after some three hours, which was supposed to take a headline from our bow for towing us back into the harbor. We were not surprised when we understood the entire crew, including the tugboat crew, were more than slightly intoxicated since it was Christmas.

The *Hakone* lay crosswise in the fairway but afloat, drifting in the wind until we presumably hit something else. The tugboat crew and our own crew worked slowly on the forecastle to connect a headline to the tugboat. They were not in the best condition, but at least something was done.

After an eternity, the headline was finally connected, and the small tug started to tow us slowly back into the harbor. Shortly, we again passed the company flagship, *Nihon,* and the OS on watch said, "Sir, shall I go up on the top deck and greet them with the flag?"

The captain said in wrath and embarrassment, "No, we do not greet them with the flag!"

The *Hakone* was barely afloat when she was put alongside in one of the inner harbor basins in Gothenburg to wait for a dry dock to become ready for her. It was not an easy task since it was Christmas Eve.

The fire brigade came with additional pumps to lower the water level in the engine room and kept them there until the dry dock was ready. Two days later, we were towed into dock.

When the dock was dry, I went immediately to see the extent of the damage, and what I saw was a disaster: she was completely ripped up across the entire bottom. Not one single steel plate was intact. She had been staying afloat only on a weak and dented tank top.

The maritime declaration started the next day in the courthouse in Gothenburg. Since I was not an experienced officer yet by fourteen days, I only had to leave my statement of the situation, which I deeply appreciated. If I had been an experienced officer and deemed part of the reason for the accident, then the juridical decision would have been different. In the worst-case scenario, one can lose the endorsement of certificate for a certain time or receive jail time, depending on the seriousness of the situation. During our grounding in those confined waters, we'd had a pilot on board, along with the master on the bridge, who had the last responsibility. It was unlikely that the officer on duty would be blamed much, since he did not have the knowledge of the area.

Leaving the courthouse, I had mixed feelings. I felt sad that I unfortunately had been part of a bridge team that had run a big ship up onto the rocks.

I learned a lesson for my future: never take things for granted, and never believe you know everything, even if you have been sailing in the area a thousand times. Ever since that incident, I have always tried to be one step ahead of problems rather than one step behind, and I always remind myself of what I have to do and to be observant. That became my policy after the grounding incident on my next round-the-world trip. I circumnavigated the world two times on the MS *Hakone*.

Chapter 9

The *Lindblad Explorer* Shipping History

THE *LINDBLAD EXPLORER*'S HISTORY IS filled with visits to remote places, adventures, science and art, diplomatic missions, and heroic rescue and salvage operations. During her trips, she carried thousands of cruise passengers, scientists, artists, and crew members—and a special bear from the Amazon called Kinky.

The late Lars-Eric Lindblad was the first operator to commission his own cruise ship. His dream had always been to design a purpose-built ship. In 1968, contracts were signed for a special ship to be designed by the noted Danish marine architect Knud E. Hansen. Captain Edwin MacDonald, who had retired from service on the US Navy icebreakers and had a great deal of experience in the Antarctic, was a consultant.

The ship was built for $2.5 million by Nystad Varv in Finland, where there was plenty of experience in ships operating in extreme ice conditions. Finland has been building superstrength icebreakers since the 1900s, and the *Lindblad Explorer* will be regarded as a thing of beauty and joy forever.

She was named the *Lindblad Explorer* by Sonja, Lars-Eric's first wife, in July 1969. The owners of the new vessel were K/S A/S Explorer and Company, managed by Lars Usterud-Svendsen of Oslo, and she flew the Norwegian flag. With a length of seventy-three meters and a draft of just more than four meters, she was able to sail into places other passenger vessels could not go. The hull was a type of double-hull system and reinforced and had the highest ice classification. She was painted orangish red, a color often used on Arctic and Antarctic vessels since it makes them conspicuous and easier to find. The top observation deck was designed to give unsurpassed views on all sides. There was also a small crow's nest for passenger use. At the time she was launched, she had the most up-to-date navigational equipment available.

Technically, the *Lindblad Explorer* was not an icebreaker vessel. She was an ice-working vessel and was designated by Lloyds as ice class 1A. She had a reinforced hull, an ice knife on the rudder, and a protected variable pitch propeller. For added operating ease, she was fitted with a bow-thruster unit. In order to increase her sailing range, she had evaporators to produce fresh water from seawater, and she had the fuel capacity to cruise for seven thousand nautical miles. The hospital was designed by two US physicians: Roy Sexton and John Stubenboard.

The most important part of the accommodation was the penguin room, now called the lecture hall, which was designed for films, lectures, and demonstrations and was one of the most used spaces on the ship on many of the cruises. The original penguin room contained a bar that was used for parties and carnivals for passengers and crew. The back of the room leading to the pool had huge glass doors from starboard to port side.

Another innovation was the introduction of inflatable rubber landing crafts powered by outboard motors. These Zodiacs were fast, safe, and easy to use. They provided the opportunity to land passengers in places where there were no formal docking arrangements, and they drove across reefs and sand banks and along narrow channels in the Amazon basin and opened up many exciting places to tourists, from the polar regions to small tropical islands.

She looked like a splendid private yacht, and she was a unique ship. She carried a unique crew, who seldom found their ship alongside in port. More likely, she was at anchor in a small bay, protected from winds, which made landings in otherwise inhospitable regions possible.

The initial cruises were fully booked just by word-of-mouth advertising, and voyage number one was to have the late Keith Shackleton as expedition leader. He was distantly related to Sir Ernest Shackleton, the famous Antarctic explorer.

Finally, the brand-new *Lindblad Explorer* was delivered on December 10, 1969, in Nystad, and the shakedown cruise began, calling first at Southampton before starting the long trek southward to Buenos Aires. She sailed from Southampton to Madeira, the

Canary Islands, and the Cape Verde Islands and then across the Atlantic to Rio de Janeiro and Buenos Aires.

As she set out from the Finnish shipyard, she began a unique life at sea filled with firsts, including the following:

- 1970: First passenger ship in Antarctica
- 1972: First passenger ship to sail to 77°53′ S on the Antarctic Peninsula
- 1973: First passenger ship to do partial circumnavigation of Antarctica from New Zealand to Argentina
- 1974: First ship to explore the Amazon River to Peru
- 1979: First ship permitted to cruise the rivers of China
- 1980: First passenger landfall on Antarctica's Bouvet Island
- 1981: First passenger landfall on Antarctica's Paulet Island
- 1982: First passenger ship to circumnavigate Franz Josef Land above 82° N
- 1983: First passenger landfall on Antarctica's Snow Hill Island
- 1984: First passenger ship to traverse the Northwest Passage
- 1988: First passenger ship to visit Provideniya, Siberia
- 1996: First passenger ship to transit Herbert Sound, Antarctica
- 1997: First ship to circumnavigate James Ross Island
- 1998: First passenger ship to penetrate eighty nautical miles beyond Iquitos, Peru, upriver to the confluence of the Maranon and Ucayali rivers

However, misadventures were to be the order of the day. Generator problems beset the ship near Kiel in Germany, and new generators had to be loaded for installation in Southampton. Then one of the two MAK main engines failed, and the ship was forced to limp to Dakar in West Africa on the remaining engine. In addition, it was found that no primer had been painted on the hull, and there was a serious rust problem, along with peeling paint. However, repairs were quickly made, and the ship continued across the Atlantic.

Everyone was just beginning to relax, when, in the mid-Atlantic, the ship was on fire. The oil in the deep fryer in the galley caught fire and burned so fiercely that the deck above the flames was beginning to melt. The steering cables were destroyed by the fire, and the ship began to go in circles. Control was regained using the manual emergency-steering system from the steering-gear room while orders were passed by walkie-talkies and headphones from the bridge to the helmsman in the steering-gear room. The *Lindblad Explorer* limped directly to Buenos Aires and into the dry dock. The first Antarctica cruise was canceled. The second voyage, in February 1970, went via the Falkland Islands, South Georgia, and Tristan da Cunha to Cape Town. In the Indian Ocean, she carried out twenty-four cruises among Mombasa, the Seychelles, and other islands.

On July 1, 1971, the *Lindblad Explorer* played a part in a dramatic sea rescue. About four hundred miles east of Madagascar, the crew spotted a Taiwanese vessel, *Chin Fu*, hard aground on a coral reef. Huge waves were pounding her, and the crew was still on board, as few of them could swim. Four Zodiacs, under the command of the first officer, pulled close enough for nine crew members from the *Lindblad Explorer* to swim through the waves, board the stricken vessel, and bring the twenty-two crew members to safety. The rescue operation took eighteen hours. Later, the HMS *Beagle* arrived and took the rescued men to port. The late Sir Peter Scott described the rescue as one of the most amazing displays of courage he had witnessed.

In 1971, the ship completed five trips to the Antarctic, including one in which she became the first cruise ship to travel below the polar circle. In 1972, she sailed from Cape Town for Antarctica, South Georgia, and the South Shetlands down the Antarctic Peninsula to almost 70 degrees. She was the first passenger ship to travel that far south along the Antarctic Peninsula.

In February 11, 1972, disaster struck again. The *Lindblad Explorer* went hard aground in Admiralty Bay, King George Island, and started taking in water. All the passengers were rescued, but the first attempts to free the ship failed. Two Chilean and two Argentine naval vessels; the HMS *Endurance*; an American ship; and a Russian ship all hurried toward her. The Chileans made four unsuccessful attempts to refloat her, and one of them eventually took her passengers and most of the crew to Punta Arenas in Chile. Finally, *Arktis*, a powerful salvage tug sent from Cape Town, managed to pull her off. The double hull held, and the ship was towed to Buenos Aires for temporary repairs and refit, and she was back in operation by August 1972.

Meanwhile, her owners had sold her in her still-damaged state to United Cruising Company of Bermuda—an offshoot of the Swedish American Line, which in turn was controlled by the Broström group of Gothenburg—and a new company called *Lindblad Explorer* SA. Paul Palsson, the chief executive of Broström, said that when Lars-Eric Lindblad was asked whether the grounding would affect bookings for future cruises, he replied that it would make the ship more popular than ever. The late Mr. Palsson also commented, "The very experienced Swedish officers and crew did a lot to popularize her cruises. A job on board the *Lindblad Explorer* was much sought after. It was rather odd for a ship registered under the Panamanian flag to have an expensive, mainly Swedish crew."

The scheduled Arctic cruise was able to go ahead only a few weeks late. The ship was now, for all intents and purposes, a new one.

On Christmas Day 1979, she left Paradise Bay in Antarctica, heading for Neumayer Channel and Port Lockroy and hit a rock before the entrance to the channel. Please read further about the grounding of the *Lindblad Explorer* in 1979 on Christmas Eve.

As on previous occasions, a major mishap was followed by a change of ownership: Broström sold the ship to the China Navigation Company, the shipping arm of Swire and Sons. The new arrangement did not last long. In July 1982, China Navigation bowed out, and the ship was sold to the Salen group of Sweden. She then flew the Swedish flag.

The charter to Lindblad Travel Service ceased, and marketing was handled by Salen Lindblad Cruising, a separate firm despite the similarity of name. On occasion, passengers had close but unplanned encounters with wildlife. King Karl's Lane, Spitsbergen, a place noted for its polar bears, was reached in fine weather. Shortly after arrival, a dense fog descended, and several people got lost. Lars-Eric and his group came across a small hut occupied by two scientists. The occupants of the hut quickly let the unexpected visitors in. There were seventeen bears in the area. Along with the scientists, who had rifles, they immediately set off to the ship in the now lifting fog. The ship's horn was sounded to summon the passengers back. After embarkation, it was found that one lady was missing, as a roll call always was made upon the passengers' return.

Keith Shackleton, Lars-Eric, and two Norwegians took off to search and found her sitting unharmed and not distressed on a rock. Engrossed in her own little adventure, the lady had not heard the warning horn. Not far from where she had been, they came across a whole group of bears.

The crew came mainly from the Tonga Islands in the South Pacific, and one of them, the motorman, was related to the king of the islands. When the ship arrived in Tongatapu, there were always arranged visits to the palace. Huge barbecue pits in the ground were arranged at the homes of some crew members for all passengers and crew.

At various times during the ship's travels throughout the world, two chimpanzees, six monkeys, one boa constrictor, and parrots lived in the crew cabins. On the Amazon River, the late Professor Lyall Watson from Bermuda brought on board a coati (coatimundi bear) named Kinky. At the captain's welcome party, the Swede carried Kinky on his shoulder and introduced her to the passengers as a crew member. Passengers were told to get used to seeing Kinky around because she had free access to all parts of the ship. Being a night animal, she prowled during darkness and slept during the daytime. Passengers were warned that Kinky would go into a cabin if the door was open and crawl into the bed to sleep. Usually, Kinky would walk up onto the bridge to find a comfortable place to sleep. The officer on duty used to place Kinky inside the port radar hood for her to sleep, putting a sign on the radar hood: "Occupied. Kinky is sleeping." After sunset, when it became dark, she kicked up the radar hood and jumped out of the radar to have her breakfast, which, in the Amazon River she came from, consisted of big black beetles that covered the boat deck. She took her position at the end of the deck, opened her mouth, and swept the deck clean by running back and forth.

A major feature of the *Lindblad Explorer*'s visits to unusual, remote places was that almost everywhere, many of the local people were invited on board. This was particularly the case at isolated research stations or small communities. Often, we had the opportunity to meet scientists from a multitude of nations, including many from behind the Iron Curtain—remember that Glasnost was not even a dream in the 1970s and early 1980s.

During the early voyages, the *Lindblad Explorer* notched up another first for a passenger ship: the circumnavigation of Milne Land, a large island in Scoresby Sound off Greenland's east coast. Later, cruises went to the Canadian Arctic, Ellesmere Island, and even the magnetic north pole. Among passenger cruise ships, the *Lindblad Explorer* holds the record for the farthest trip north; she circumnavigated Franz Josef Land, more than 82 degrees north.

In 1974, when she came up from Antarctica to Carcass Island in the Falklands, there was, as usual, a barbecue ashore for passengers and crew. On one occasion, the wind suddenly picked up to a severe gale. On order of the captain, who was ashore at the time, the mate on watch had to take up the anchor and ride out the storm outside while passengers and crew spent the night sleeping in a hut together with sheep as pillows.

In 1976, the *Lindblad Explorer* became involved in the first incident of the Falkland Islands conflict. An Argentinian destroyer, the British Antarctic survey ship *John Biscoe*, and the *Lindblad Explorer* all departed Ushuaia in the southern part of Argentina at the same time, heading for Port Stanley. The following day, the destroyer requested that *John Biscoe* stop her engines to be boarded for inspection.

At the time of the incident, we were some fifteen hours away from Pembroke Lighthouse outside Port Stanley. I was the duty officer on watch on the *Lindblad Explorer* bridge and overheard the entire conversation on the VHF radio, and therefore, I called the captain to attend on the bridge because that was something unusual. The captain of the *John Biscoe* refused to stop and was then told by the Argentinian destroyer that they would fire a warning shot across her bow if she didn't follow the instructions. The *Lindblad Explorer* overheard the entire conversation between the two ships, and then the first shot came to our surprise. The *John Biscoe* remained silent on the VHF, and the bridge command on the *Lindblad Explorer* held our breath, waiting anxiously for what would happen next. The destroyer threatened the *John Biscoe* again; however, from nowhere, a huge fogbank appeared and rescued the *John Biscoe*. Shortly afterward, she arrived at Port Stanley. Due to the severe incident, the entire crew on board the *John Biscoe* went ashore to the local bars and refused to embark their ship again unless England sent down warships. Consequently, the Royal Navy sent down an aircraft carrier to the region to mark their presence.

In May 1979, the *Lindblad Explorer* became the first vessel from the Western world to cruise with passengers in the Yangtze River and the coast of China. She spent almost six months cruising along the rivers and the coast.

US president Jimmy Carter sent some senators from the US Senate as tourists with the *Lindblad Explorer* on a China river cruise to try to ease the tense relations between the two countries.

In 1984, the *Lindblad Explorer* made a historic voyage. On August 20, she sailed from St. John's in Newfoundland in an attempt to cross from east to west the Northwest Passage, the hazardous sea route through the polar waters north of Canada. When she arrived at Point Barrow, Alaska, on September 14, she was the first passenger ship to travel the Northwest Passage without icebreaker assistance. Ninety-eight passengers had paid up to $20,000 each for the forty-one-day voyage and cruise, which ended in Yokohama, Japan, a distance of 4,790 nautical miles. Two months later, the ship was at the other end of the globe, sailing in Antarctic waters.

Soon after completing her epic 1984 voyage through the Northwest Passage, she was sold to a joint venture between Society Expeditions in Germany and the Heritage Hotel group. Within a few months, however, she was bought by Vienna International Shipping Corporation and registered in Monrovia, Liberia. The new company was associated with Discoverer Reederei in Bremen, the owners of the rival expedition ship *World Discoverer*.

In September 1985, she emerged from a major four-month refit in Singapore with the name *Society Explorer*, registered in the Bahamas and chartered back to Society Expeditions. Her accommodations now included two suites. In August 1986, the *Society Explorer* made several cruises to Vancouver and the inside passages along the coast of British Columbia.

In January 1989, the ship was involved in another Antarctic incident but this time as a rescuer, not a victim. She and the *Illiria* took on board eighty-one passengers from the Argentinian navy supply and tourist ship *Bahia Paraiso*, which sank in the Bismarck Strait close to the US Antarctic Palmer Station. Today when a cruise ship visits the Palmer Station, choosing to use the eastern entrance, occasionally, outbound from Palmer, the *Bahia Paraiso*'s hull can be seen.

In March 1991, *Society Explorer* was seized by creditors while in a shipyard in Talcahuano in Chile and remained under arrest for several months. In 1992, Society Expeditions filed for chapter 11 protection from their creditors. *Society Explorer* was sold to another firm specializing in exotic and cultural holidays, Abercrombie and Kent in Chicago. Now named *Explorer* and flying the Liberian flag, this important little ship continued to operate much as she had throughout her long career.

Today her achievements do not seem as impressive now that cruise operators can charter powerful icebreakers converted for passenger cruising. However, none of these behemoths can equal the exploits of the Little Red Ship. During her fifteen years with Lindblad Travel Service and Lars-Eric Lindblad, this unique adventure ship carried enthusiasts, artists, and naturalists to the remotest parts of the earth, venturing farther north and farther south than any passenger ship had before. She visited inaccessible landscapes with undisturbed wildlife colonies during her 1.5 million nautical miles and dropped her anchor more than five thousand times.

The passengers came in all shapes, sizes, and dispositions. With a maximum of a hundred passengers, there can be no generalizing: each voyage hosted a group of individualistic individuals. In general, it was a privilege to work for them. From the earliest chartering days, the emphasis was on academic studies, so the scientific staff changed with the theaters of work. Antarctica saw a predominance of naturalists, supplemented by glaciologists and expedition historians. Anthropologists and divers marked the tropical islands and reef areas, while places like the Amazon called for botanical and linguistic skills. Lars-Eric Lindblad was a great believer in seeing that the potential aboard not be wasted, and the logbooks of the vessel were crammed with material that since has proven a valuable source of information in all kinds of unexpected areas, particularly because much of it covers places seldom visited. The log keepers were too numerous to list and enormously varied in their approaches. Some books contain copious drawings; others contain the written word alone.

Nelson Rockefeller sailed with the *Lindblad Explorer* in 1973 to the Asmat and Agats region in West Irian, the old Dutch New Guinea, trying to figure out what had happened to his son Michael Rockefeller, who had been lost in circumstances of sinister mystery.

Each year, the *Lindblad Explorer* was in the Antarctic ice for the summer season, migrating north like the Arctic tern to follow the daylight. Her routes were an ever-changing filigree of tracks covering the globe, linking for the most part dots in the ocean far from established shipping lanes across the Pacific, Indian, and Atlantic.

The *Lindblad Explorer* took soundings in several passages and uncharted bays where no ships had ever navigated before her, and today her soundings are invaluable and have paved the way for future cruise ships. She also played an important part in the general awareness of the need for conservation worldwide.

Chapter 10

The *Lindblad Explorer*

AT THE END OF 1973, I returned to Sweden and to my mother, this time as an experienced officer. One day I got a phone call from my company in Gothenburg, and they asked if I wanted to sign on to the expedition cruise ship *Lindblad Explorer* as a third officer at the most southern tip of Argentina, in Ushuaia, and join the ship there. I had no idea where Ushuaia was, nor did the head office in Gothenburg. They had no clue where Ushuaia was on the map, but according to them, it was somewhere very far south at the bottom of South America.

Indeed, it was far south: it was the world's most southern town. It had some five thousand inhabitants and was not far from Cape Horn, a town hidden on the maps.

The *Lindblad Explorer* was ordered by an American Swede, Lars-Eric Lindblad from New York. Lars-Eric was born in 1927 just north of Stockholm in Sweden. He immigrated to the United States in 1951 and became an American citizen. His dream had always been to design a purpose-built ship for expedition cruising. Lars-Eric had been able to use the Chilean ship *Navarino* up until 1968, when the ship had to be used as a naval transport. The *Navarino* was used three times to travel to the Antarctic, though one of the trips had to be aborted due to a broken rudder, and all the passengers had to be sent back to the United States.

The idea of his own ship sprang from the problems he had had with the *Navarino*, and he came to the conclusion that in order to continue the Antarctica voyages and be able to navigate safely in ice, a new ship would have to be ice-strengthened so she could push the ice pack or slide through it. Hence, Lars-Eric became the first operator to commission his own cruise ship, the *Lindblad Explorer*.

The ship pioneered cruising to Antarctica, the Arctic, Tierra del Fuego, the Falkland Islands, the Seychelles, and the islands east of Bali. In 1968, Lindblad Travel Service's staff had grown to more than seventy worldwide, including many specialists and consultants. In 1984, Lars-Eric led the first voyage on board his own cruise ship through the Northwest

Passage from Newfoundland over the American continent and via the Bering Strait to Yokohama, Japan.

Lars-Eric Lindblad died in 1994 of a sudden heart attack while on vacation in Sweden, at the railway station in Stockholm.

Keith Shackleton was a British naturalist, explorer, and painter who concentrated on landscape views and animals. He also produced limited-edition prints. He was a friend of conservationist and fellow painter Sir Peter Scott, with whom he traveled to Antarctica. He was one of the best-known wildlife artists and president of the Royal Society of Marine Artists, and he was distantly related to Sir Ernest Shackleton, the famous Antarctic explorer. Keith Shackleton was appointed a member of the Order of the British Empire in the 2012 Birthday Honours for service to the conservation of wildlife. He died on April 17, 2015, peacefully.

I was informed by the Broström company in Gothenburg that the *Lindblad Explorer* sailed to every remote corner of the world and was the perfect ship for me. Without hesitation, I accepted the offer. The *Lindblad Explorer* turned out to be a turning point in my life, and with her, I would experience many incredible adventures in the hidden corners of the world.

In January 1974, I was sitting on an airplane, heading for Ushuaia in Tierra del Fuego, the Land of Fire. I was going to the cross the Drake Passage to the bottom of the world, Antarctica. I couldn't believe it. I felt I was on my way to a wonderful world. Finally, my dreams had come true, and I'd made everybody jealous back home. I thought about the world map that hung above my bed and my dreams I'd had.

Walking along the pier in Ushuaia, I saw the ship lying alongside. She was not an imposing vessel, no bigger than a channel ferry. I could hardly call her beautiful or even pretty. With her slight list to starboard, she looked like a duck with one wing low. My first impression was that she had an imperfection I loved from the beginning. While walking on the pier toward her gangway, I didn't know that this ship would provide me with the most consistently enjoyable fifteen years of my life.

She was a vessel I became fond and proud of. The Little Red Ship, as she was called, was 250 feet long and 2,398 gross tons, with a draft of just under fifteen feet, or five meters, to enable her to sail into places where other passenger vessels could not go.

I was introduced to the Swedish captain, who had been on board since the ship was taken over by the Broström Company and had managed her since 1972. He had been the master of the Swedish American Line cruise ship MS *Gripsholm* in the past and had taken over the command of the *Lindblad Explorer* at Kristiansand, Norway, in the summer of 1972. He was her senior captain for the next fifteen years.

The second officer, Goran, was from the southern part of the Swedish archipelago, in Blekinge. Later on, he was promoted to chief officer.

Goran's pleasure was to tie fishing nets in the cabin, which was ready for use in the archipelago of Blekinge. He was a sailorman and a keen fisherman. He knew the sea, and he knew his job, and the others respected him for it. He would later become the captain of the *Lindblad Explorer* in the early 1980s.

As we walked around the ship, Goran introduced me to the officers, who were all Swedish, and to the deck crew, who came mainly from the Tonga Islands and some from the USA. Jack, the first radio operator and a genuine fly fisherman, was a special man. He had the biggest waxed mustache one could imagine, with a big curl on the end. He went by the name Jacken, and he was a skillful radio operator and full of jokes. He was universally liked for his unfailing good humor. He could have a sharp, satirical tongue sometimes, but he could take a joke against himself without losing his good spirits. It was not always easy to get the best of Jack in an exchange of response, though.

He took great pride in his work, and he was good at obtaining HF (high-frequency) radio contact with the world with our three-kilowatt radio transmitter, which was, in those days, extremely powerful. He carried his profession with dignity, but unfortunately, he was under the influence of alcohol every day. He always started his days with one whiskey and a beer, and in his daily work, he always walked around in his socks.

He had a big predilection for fishing and fly-fishing all over the world. Fishing was his life and his everything, and whenever there was time left over, one could find Jack sitting in his radio station, fabricating fishing flies with his special tools for that purpose.

Jack suffered from chronic seasickness, which made his days a lot more difficult. However, he was also the first one to escape the area when the captain was on the hunt looking for a scapegoat among the officers if things for some reason went wrong. He immediately sensed when the captain was on the hunt, and he always disappeared with the speed of a missile. However, for some reason, the captain always had his mind set on Jack first—nobody really understood why. When he found him, the first thing Jack always said was "Captain, it was not me. I know nothing about this. I am not involved in anything." But Jack got his share anyway.

The entire ship figured out right away when Jack was under the influence of alcohol in his radio station, because the last lines in the daily incoming American radio news transmitted over the high frequency usually said, "Due to atmospheric disturbances, there is no more news today," or "The remainder of this bulletin was lost due to radio and other forms of interference." He even wrote, "Tomorrow's news has been canceled due to lack of interest."

By reading this, everybody knew that the radio station was in a happy-go-lucky state and that Jack was under the influence of alcohol. Usually, the news was then short. We all knew Jack soon would be visiting the bar and participating in the social life. He was a true entertainer in public. Eventually, Jack met a passenger lady who became his life partner and wife, and she made him stop drinking. Today he lives in Calgary, Canada, running his own fishing tour operation and business.

Once, on Kodiak Island in Alaska, a bunch of officers went ashore for fly-fishing, with me as a Zodiac driver for the occasion. As I was sitting on the Zodiac pontoon, watching the guys in their waders' fish for salmon with water up to their hips, I suddenly saw a Kodiak bear walking on the beach, heading for us. I shouted as loudly as I could, "A bear is coming toward us!" All the guys ran toward my Zodiac to escape the bear as I pushed it out toward deeper water, except for Jack, whose bag was on the beach some thirty meters away from himself. The bag contained a couple salmon, which the bear probably could smell. In our horror, we suddenly saw Jack run toward his bag and toward the bear. All of us watched anxiously from the Zodiac as the distance between him and the bear decreased to the point that we thought the bear would finally catch up with Jack. He barely managed to get his hand on his fishing bag and then ran in a hurry toward our barely floating Zodiac in the shallow water, shouting, "Start the engine!"

The Zodiac was still partly grounded, and the engine was tilted due to the shallow water. While the engine was idling, Jack came running in a panic into the water up to his knees with the bear only about fifteen meters behind, trying to catch him. The bear was apparently upset and right behind, and still, the outboard was tilted, which caused us to plunge into the water to push the rubber boat into deeper water.

When Jack finally reached the Zodiac, we pulled him on board with his fishing gear in his hands. He was anxious that the angry bear would be able to catch him. Despite the panic, somehow, in our fear, we managed to start the engine as the bear was still running toward us. We were all in a state of shock at what we had just seen.

The second radio operator, Ove, who was from the northern part of Sweden, was a helpful man, but he also enjoyed sneaking away to his cabin for a drink. He was a gentleman and a skillful, reliable radio operator, and most of the time, he could be found in Jack's cabin, where they sat and told stories to each other. He knew the fine art of staying away from trouble, especially when the captain was on the hunt.

Klemens, the other second mate, was a cautious guy, but he never missed a good party. Most of the time, he was found in his cabin, writing letters to his female circle of acquaintances.

Hans, the first engineer, was a professional diver from the Royal Swedish Navy. He knew every bolt in the engine room, and he was a skillful engineer.

His roommate was a big, unique, well-traveled Amazonian parrot, a scarlet macaw by the name of Lulu, which had almost lost all its feathers. Hans's hobby was teaching Lulu to greet everybody repeatedly. Upon coming to his cabin, we were greeted sometimes with some surprising and shocking sentences, such as "You are ugly," "Hello," or "Sit down!"

The late chief engineer, Gote, was a polite man, and he was seldom in the engine room.

If there were any problems, they were solved using the drawings of the engine room in his cabin in front of the engineers. He was a married man in Gothenburg, Sweden, but had his longtime mistress, the late Miss Grace from the USA, on board most of the time.

The other engineers were a bunch of happy-go-lucky sailors who knew how to have fun twenty-four hours a day, but they were all hardworking and felt their responsibilities. The third engineer, Nisse, arrived in New York in 1974 and quickly became a popular person. The second engineer, Leif, was like a pleasant host and minister of amusement in the lounge whenever the prospects looked good. He never missed an opportunity for amusement. Last but not least was the Polish electrician, Anton.

Anton was an aristocratic person in his behavior, but when he was under the influence of alcohol, he kind of lost the plot. His hobby was to collect fossils as well as prehistoric remains. All of us deeply admired Anton's nicely organized fossil collection, which he had in his cabin and sometimes showed to us, especially when he was under the influence of alcohol. He was a peculiar sort of man and very serious in his daily life on board, and he had a special way of keeping track of the ship's wiring problems when they occurred. He always made drawings of different electrical units that nobody could understand except for Anton himself. He understood the ship drawings, but in his opinion, they were not accurate enough; therefore, his own drawings were helpful whenever a problem occurred. All of us knew he could be counted on to do his share and whenever things went wrong in the engine room.

Generally speaking, the officers on board the *Lindblad Explorer* could hardly have been a more mixed collection of individuals, which would be proven in the coming years.

Goran introduced me to the expedition leader, Francisco from Buenos Aires, who was in charge of planning the shore excursions for the passengers, and I was introduced to some famous people. Goran told me, "This is a very special floating world." The staff on board consisted of famous people in the expedition world, such as Keith Shackleton, Edmund Hillary, Ron and Valerie Taylor, and Sir Peter Scott.

Francisco came from an aristocratic family, and his exterior and manner displayed perfect politeness. I was informed by Goran that his wife was the daughter of Argentina's minister of economy from 1959 to 1962. She was elected to Congress in 1985 on her father's ticket as secretary of natural resources and sustainable development, but her relationship with the recently divorced late President Carlos Menem was discussed because she became his mistress. Maria was appointed to the union of the democratic center and became an outspoken advocate of free markets during the presidency of Raúl Alfonsín from December 10, 1983, to July 8, 1989. She married Francisco and had two sons with him. When Menem left office in 1999, financial transactions in her name came under scrutiny, and Maria was ultimately convicted of misappropriation of public funds in 2004, was sentenced to three years in prison, and served twenty-one months.

In the 1960s and 1970s, Francisco became a naturalist, Argentine conservationist, and keen wildlife photographer. Thousands of his photographs have illustrated books and magazines of Argentina, Spain, Great Britain, and the USA. He went to Antarctica in 1964 to collect material for the Argentine Museum of Natural History, sailing with the Argentine Navy. He then visited many of our future destinations with the *Lindblad Explorer*. He spent five days in Paradise Bay and camped for twenty days in Admiralty Bay, King George Island. The four of our team were at the time the sole inhabitants of the island and had no communication with the outer world. All in all, it was a two-month campaign.

Beginning in the 1960s, he set aside his training as an industrial engineer to go to work for a company that specialized in international ecotourism trips, Lindblad Travel Service, on the *Lindblad Explorer*. He guided stakeholders in the wilds of nature on all continents and seas, even on remote islands, making photograph safaris.

In 1967, he received the Wildlife Photographer of the Year award from *Animas Magazine*, forerunner of *BBC Wildlife* magazine, and in 1996, he was recognized as the pioneer of Argentine wildlife photography by the Academy of Visual Arts Foundation and the photo Club Buenos Aires, who awarded him their first Silver Pyramid for his lifelong career in nature photography.

Francisco was a ladies' man and tried to seduce the ladies when the opportunity was given. However, one day, as we were alongside in Ushuaia, an out-of-the-way port where passenger ships normally did not go but where we always repatriated our passengers, Francisco came to me and said, "Peter, I have a girl in my cabin, and Maria Julia is on her way down to see me. When you see her coming on the pier, please delay her. Bring her to the bar and tell her I am occupied."

After a while, I saw Maria approaching the gangway, and I became concerned when she asked for Francisco. I stammered when I saw her and said, "Oh, Maria, welcome on board. Francisco is busy, but please come to the bar and wait for him." I thought Francisco must have been out of his mind, having a girl in his cabin while his wife was waiting for him in the bar; hence, I rushed to the reception desk and called Francisco urgently on the phone in the suite. I said, "Francisco, Maria is in the bar, waiting for you."

He replied, "Peter, please give me five minutes more. I am not finished yet."

I almost fainted when I heard his answer.

Well, when he finally came out of his cabin, he was out of breath and red in his face. He met Maria Julia in the lounge bar, and I thought, *What a brave man. This will never end in a good way*, because he was playing with fire. As a matter of fact, they both played with fire and got divorced.

The mentality on board was "One for all, and all for one." Most of the staff and crew were involved in sexual activities, and everything on board was waterproof; no one betrayed anyone on board.

As I was introduced to the ship's crew, I met two guys with curly, big hair. One said, "Hello. I am Tevita Matavalea, and he is Frank Lovo, and we are from the Tonga Islands. What's your name?"

Taken by surprise at his approach, I said, "I'm Peter."

Tevita asked me right away, "Which sea watch are you going to have?" I responded that I didn't know yet about that.

It turned out that Tevita and I were on the same sea watch for more than two years, and we became good friends and experienced an exciting life together. He was a happy-go-lucky man who grabbed every opportunity to have some fun. Tevita later married a lady from Switzerland by the name of Flavia, and they lived together in her country, where he became a bodybuilder. Later on, I figured out that he was very curious, and to satisfy his curiosity, he climbed outside the vessel's topside on the rails to see what was going on in the officers' cabins. The deck crew and the engine crew came partly from the Tonga Islands.

Goran told me that all of the Tongans had the same character, and they missed their islands very much. They were big guys, but in their inner selves, they were like small kids. I could always trust them no matter what, but I learned after a while that they often were homesick and talked about "My island" with tears in their eyes, saying, "I miss my island so much." But they were excellent Zodiac drivers; it was incredible what they could do with a Zodiac. A Zodiac is a safe rubber dingy certified to carry fifteen persons and stable-powered by a twenty-five-horsepower Yamaha outboard engine in those years.

On the outside boat deck, we met a man walking with samples of small penguin craniums in his hands. Goran said, "Oh, Peter, by the way, may I introduce you to Sir Peter Scott?" I had no idea who Sir Peter Scott was; I knew, however, about Scott's race to the South Pole with Amundsen, and I couldn't believe he was the son of the famous Antarctic explorer Sir Robert Falcon Scott. Peter Scott was the founder of the World Wildlife Trust, and he was a frequent lecturer on the *Lindblad Explorer* and one of the many well-known artists who became her lifelong friend. Scott was born in London in 1909 as the only child of Antarctic explorer Robert Falcon Scott and sculptor Kathleen Bruce. He was knighted in 1973 for his contribution to the conservation of wild animals. In the tropics, he gave the passengers plates with contours of fish, and everyone sat on the bottom of some five to ten meters of depth like in a school class and colored the fish that swam past with underwater pens. He was only two years old when his father died. Robert Scott, in his last letter to his wife, advised her, "Make the boy interested in natural history if you can; it is better than games." He was named after Sir Clement Markham, the mentor of Scott's polar expeditions. He died of a heart attack in 1989.

Edmund Hillary became the first climber to reach the summit of Mount Everest on May 29, 1953, with Sherpa Tenzing Norgay. Hillary reached the South Pole by tractor on January 4, 1958, and climbed Mount Herschel (10,941 feet, or 3,335 meters) in 1967. His was the first expedition to climb it. Hillary wrote many books about his adventures, including *High Adventure* (1955), *The Crossing of Antarctica* (1958, with Fuchs), *No Latitude for Error* (1961), and *Nothing Venture, Nothing Win* (1975).

Tenzing was on board often, and he was a good friend of Lars-Eric Lindblad. It was said that Tenzing only had one dollar a day when he worked for Hillary. Tenzing Norgay went on to become the greatest of climbing Sherpas, even before he set foot on Everest's summit in 1953.

Ron and Valerie Taylor were from Australia. The Taylors were prominent Australian shark experts. The Taylors' first underwater film, *Shark Hunters*, was sold to US television in 1963. Afterward, their expertise was called upon for films such as *Jaws* and *Jaws 2*, *White Death and Blue Water*, and *Orca*. They were regarded as pioneers in underwater cinematography and produced some of the earliest underwater footage of great white sharks. Ron died on September 8, 2012. He taught me how to dive with sharks in many of the world's remote corners.

The picture below of the three of us was taken in 2005 on board the MS *Orion* as we cruised the Great Barrier Reef in Australia.

The late Thor Heyerdahl and Bengt Danielsson from the Kon-Tiki expedition later met up with us as we proceeded north toward the tropics. Goran said, "You will meet them all as we are cruising in the warm climates, and they are all very special in their topics." Bengt Danielsson was a Swedish anthropologist and a crew member who participated in Thor Heyerdahl's Kon-Tiki raft expedition from Callao, Peru, to Raroia in the Tuamotu Islands in 1947. He was the Swedish consul to French Polynesia from 1961 to 1978 in Papeete. When the *Lindblad Explorer* came to Papeete, he always arranged for a barbecue for the crew. He and his wife were particularly outspoken critics of French nuclear tests at Moruroa and Fangataufa atolls. Because of that commitment, he was deprived of his 1978 title as consul. He died in July 1997 following a deterioration in his health.

Thor Heyerdahl was a Norwegian adventurer and ethnographer with a background in zoology, botany, and geography. He became notable for his Kon-Tiki raft expedition in 1947, during which he sailed eight thousand kilometers across the Pacific Ocean in a hand-built raft from Callao, Peru, to Raroia in the Tuamotu Islands. The expedition was designed to demonstrate that ancient people from South America could have made long sea voyages, creating contacts between separate cultures.

Chapter 11

My First Journey to Antarctica

I WAS FULL OF EXCITEMENT when we sailed out from Ushuaia the next day at 1800 hours. The cool, refreshing air of the Beagle Channel intensified my anticipation as I stood on the bridge wing, watching the beautiful scenery pass by. Farther south some 550 nautical miles (i.e., two days' crossing) was my destination: the Antarctic Peninsula and the South Shetland Islands, a group of more than twenty islands.

I learned the bridge procedure, and I was assigned the sea watch between eight and twelve with Tevita. We sailed through the Beagle Channel without a pilot on board, as that was not yet compulsory. Francisco was contemplating where to explore Antarctica—of course, with the existing weather conditions in mind. The Drake Passage is a notorious stretch of open water between South America and Antarctica. I was told it was a bleak, miserable place plagued by fierce winds and turbulent seas—an unforgiving environment that had given many fine sailors a hard match.

As I took over the bridge watch the first time, just after we passed the narrow Paso Mackinlay in the Beagle Channel, Tevita told me while gesturing with his hand, "Peter, Drake Passage very rough. Ship plenty up and down!" I appreciated his sense of humor.

The next morning, when we had the legendary Cape Horn behind us and began to pitch heavily in the high seas, I figured out it was better to keep one hand for yourself and one for the ship.

Three oceans—the Pacific, the Atlantic, and the Southern—converge at Cape Horn; each one is ruled by a different current. The South Pacific gyre approaches from the west, strikes the west coast of Chile, and deflects to the north. The South Atlantic gyre moves down the east coast of Argentina and then veers sharply west. Finally, the Antarctic circumpolar current girdles the globe.

There is no land to impede the wind south of Cape Horn, so in the Antarctic Ocean, waves build from the west, circling the globe forever. Each current is driven by its own prevailing winds. Thus, it's not only the water that collides but also the air above it, which creates unpredictable winds and almost constant rain.

The earth comes alive when the forces of nature collide. Hurricanes and tornadoes arise when hot and cold air masses smash into one another. The steepest, most dangerous waves develop along the boundaries between opposing currents.

There are few places, called triple junctions, where three opposing influences, such as different currents, wind systems, or tectonic plates, collide. There is only one place on earth where three triple junctions meet at the same point: Cape Horn. I soon discovered I was in the stormiest seaway in the oceans, and that was why we were bobbing up and down like a toy duck in a Jacuzzi. Tevita had been right!

To pass the horn meant wind, and by the law of averages, thereabouts wind meant gales, so the reputation of Cape Horn was assured. The Drake Passage started to claim its first victims, and the ship's doctor became busy with plastering fingers that had been squeezed in the heavy public bathroom doors. While I watched from the bridge, a close escort of dolphins played in the bow. As we went farther south into the Drake Passage and away from Cape Horn, the *Lindblad Explorer*'s movement became gentler and more organized in the ten-meter-high sea.

We sailed on dead reckoning and common sense because we didn't have a GPS in those days. The last accurate position was determined by taking a visual bearing from the Cape Horn Lighthouse with the diopter, and then we had to keep our hopes up that we could get a fix from the sun with the sextant somewhere south if the sun at all became visible during the Drake Lake crossing, as it was called. The admiralty current charts showed us the direction of the current, and they were a reliable source when crossing the Drake Passage, but since the current and the wind in general were setting from the southwest and west to east with some 0.5 to 1.0 knots in the Drake Passage, we compensated by increasing the course with some ten degrees until we were able to get a new astronomical fix with the sextant.

We had a lively evening with a hard wind and rough sea as we approached the South Shetlands. The *Lindblad Explorer* pitched in the more organized sea and swell as we came farther away from Cape Horn, occasionally taking some waves and sea spray over the forecastle. There was still no sign of a clear sky; therefore, we were unable to determine our position by using the sextant.

As usual, the first day of convenience was weather dependent. It was the captain's welcome dinner with a cocktail party that evening, and everybody was dressed up in his best clothes. I was invited to join the dinner. We slowed down to a comfortable speed, altering the course to the best we could find to minimize the rolling as long as the event took place, since all of us wanted to have a peaceful dinner, as long as it would take.

After the dinner, I went to bed and fell asleep, excited about the first iceberg sighting, which probably would happen soon.

A day and a half later, all the passengers and I wondered when the first iceberg would be seen, including repeat passenger Mr. Warren Kendall from Fort Lauderdale. He always traveled with his mother, and he was a big, corpulent man. His passport said he was a sportsman! His father, Donald Kendall, was a famous lawyer and became the president of Pepsi-Cola in 1963. He brought Pepsi to Russia.

An iceberg contest was announced: the first person who spotted an iceberg bigger than a bergy bit would be the lucky winner of one bottle of champagne. The captain gave me a brief instruction about how to navigate in ice and how to attack the ice. He told me clearly, "The strongest part on the ship is the bow."

When navigating in any kind of ice (e.g., pack ice, ice floe, growlers, first-year ice, second-year ice), the ice should be taken on either side of the bow. In contrast, the weakest parts of the ship are the shoulders, where penetration of the hull is most likely if the speed is too high. "Therefore, Peter," he said, "if you must have impact, always take the ice on the bow. Keep in mind that the speed is the key factor." I was grateful for the quick lesson, which would be an invaluable help for my future ice navigation in Antarctica.

The wind had subsided to a minimum, and the sea had calmed down. We were approaching the Antarctic convergence, the area where the cold Antarctic water met the slightly warmer water from the north. The temperature there dropped about three to four degrees, which meant we were under the influence of the white continent in the south. Some people say it's possible to see the water color change after passing the convergence, which I can agree to. When passing the convergence, one could always expect fog in one way or another.

I was informed that the fog usually lasted for a day until the conditions were normalized, and it was a common phenomenon. The radar showed no icebergs around, but the captain told me they would pop up once we came closer to the South Shetland Islands. We had information that a huge piece of iceberg (0.5 by 1.0 nautical miles) was drifting north from the South Shetlands. We approached the Antarctic convergence, which could only be found by taking the seawater temperature continuously every half an hour. When the temperature suddenly dropped some two to four degrees Celsius, we were under the influence of Antarctica.

The Antarctic convergence is a curve continuously encircling Antarctica where cold northward-flowing Antarctic waters meet the relatively warmer waters of the sub-Antarctic. Antarctic waters predominantly sink beneath sub-Antarctic waters, while associated zones of mixing and upwelling create a zone high in marine productivity. Passing the convergence meant we had to keep a sharp lookout and double watch, looking for ice of all kinds.

Suddenly, we were given fair, clear weather. The fog disappeared as quickly as it had come, and I looked for danger, such as ice, on the horizon. To my surprise, there was suddenly a huge, distinct white echo on the radar screen some twenty miles dead ahead of us. It was my first iceberg, even though only still visible so far on the radar.

An announcement was made over the PA system that in about two hours' time, we should pass close to a giant iceberg on our port side, and everyone was soon out on the decks, searching for the iceberg as we closed in on it. Antarctica was so close we could smell it, and the color of the water was different.

Albatrosses were flying low around us since the wind had almost died out. They do not like calm conditions, as remaining airborne in the calm winds demands a sustained flapping of the wings, and to an albatross, exertion of that kind is both vulgar and wholly out of kilter with its accustomed lifestyle. But they do not need to wait long, as calm sea conditions are rare down there.

Coming closer to it, we could see the iceberg was well shaped, as if it had been sawed out from the ice shelf, with straight edges. We proceeded close to it and took a good look at it. It is said that the best moments in Antarctic travel are when you see your first iceberg and when you see your last iceberg. Yes, that's true. During all my 125 voyages I made to that remote continent, it was a love-hate relationship. Each time I looked over my shoulder and saw Antarctica vanishing behind me, I said to myself, "I hope I never see this continent again." But every time we passed the Antarctic convergence southbound, I was always happy and looked forward to battling the environments down there, though I knew I had to tiptoe to survive in that harsh environment; otherwise, I would be the loser at the end of the day.

The giant iceberg was there, and I had been told I should call down to the engine room half an hour in advance for them to switch over from the shaft generator to the auxiliary engines since there was a possibility we had to start to maneuver because we wanted to have a close look at the huge, icy natural wonder.

The bridge and the forecastle were crowded with passengers since we had an open-bridge policy, and everybody said, "Oh my God, I can't believe my eyes! What a huge iceberg!" We altered the course slowly to port, and we slowed down to a minimum safeguarding speed. The captain took over the command and parked the vessel on the leeside of the iceberg at a safe distance so everybody could have a close look, and if worse came to worse, we could retreat if we had to (i.e., if suddenly a huge part of the iceberg calved with an enormous swell as a result, the ship could easily have been sucked in toward the iceberg).

It was my first iceberg ever—reflective blue ice with caves and fissures of a deep indigo. Since the sea was sufficiently calm, the captain allowed the passengers to go out onto the forecastle to have a close look at the beautiful, huge piece of ice that wallowed slowly in the swell, a piece of the southern landscape that had broken off and was drifting north to show Antarctica's first face to arriving strangers, as we were.

It was massive, delicate, and softly blue, but up on the bridge, we had to look out for the pieces it launched like torpedoes—chunks of ice called growlers, which lay awash and invisible to the radar yet were big enough to cripple a ship.

The iceberg was flat on top like an aircraft carrier, which gave me the impression it could break up at any minute and cause a heavy swell toward us. One could see it was slightly moving up and down for the gentle swell we had, and occasionally, there were avalanches on one side, which gave us the impression it was fragile and could break up more into bergy bits or growlers and finally become brash ice. With all these anticipations, we decided to back out to a safe distance and resumed our voyage to the south.

We continued to sail for the rest of the day and night south, and we expected to see the South Shetland Islands by early tomorrow morning. The South Shetlands Islands, which lie just north of the Antarctic Peninsula, are the most accessible part of that remote, dramatic region of the earth. These islands of the peninsula are unpredictable. They are exposed to the lash of the Drake Passage but also to the tempering effect of the sea. While the rest of the Antarctic coast is locked away for the winter by the ice pack, I was told the South Shetland Islands are often accessible to ships year-round.

Antarctic territory officially begins at a latitude of 60 degrees south, but a ship approaching Antarctica usually passes its first big chunk of ice somewhere north of Smith Island. Depending on the course and the schedule, some ships reach the shelter of the South Shetlands by turning around to the northeastern tip of King George Island. Others slip between Smith Island and Snow Island in the Boyd Strait, as we did.

Antarctica is the wildest and most beautiful desert on earth. *Desert* means Antarctica is the driest continent on the planet, with almost no rain. No one lives there permanently apart from base personnel, who change regularly, and there are no diseases. In Antarctica, there are different environmental hazards from wind, sea, ice, and intense cold.

But there is life aplenty, and it is for the most part unexploited. There too a permanent deep freeze creates unexpected problems. Garbage, for instance, survives for years, so it must be burned. Climate change is more sudden than anywhere else within my experience, and when the weather seriously misbehaves, sea conditions in the Southern Hemisphere are probably more severe than anywhere else on Earth.

The four and a half million square miles of the Antarctic are uniquely isolated. Much of the rock surface beneath the ice is below sea level, so the sheer volume of frozen water is almost unimaginable.

The *Lindblad Explorer* is a symbolic name, and we were the first passenger ship to enter that hidden part of the world. Indeed, the name of the ship itself provided some pointers.

I began to understand what a privilege it was to stand on that bridge as a watch-going officer as we approached the South Shetlands Islands with the bridge crowded with red parkas due to the open-bridge policy. All wanted to take part in every step we made on the bridge from a navigational point of view as we approached the bottom of the world. At that time, none of us knew much about Antarctica, and we didn't know that Antarctica would be heavily targeted by the tourism industry in the future, to the extent that big cruise liners carrying up to a thousand passengers would visit that remote continent and travel to areas that were navigationally unsafe.

In the early morning hours of my watch, I saw land on the radar on my port side. We would shortly enter the Boyd Strait, and I could see that we were about ten miles more to the east, with Snow Island dead ahead of us, since the current had been affecting us. Ten miles from the course line in those days was not so bad, actually, because we had sailed all the way from Cape Horn only on dead reckoning, and there had never been an opportunity for us to use the sextant for astronomical sites to determine our position. However, to the north of Snow Island were millions of underwater rocks that had to be avoided; hence, we altered the course toward the Boyd Strait. Now we only navigated on the radar, keeping the required distances from the shoreline, watching Antarctica come closer. Livingston Island was now on our port bow, and with stunning suddenness, the crescendo of light seemed to be everywhere, despite the shallow angle of the sun. The mountains were dazzling white with snow and gave a wonderful reflection in the calm sea. The air was clean and clear, and the visibility was phenomenal. The bridge was again full of passengers wearing their red parkas, and everybody said, "This is breathtaking, and I can't believe I am seeing all this!" but I thought, *Great God, this is an awful place.* I thought it was the most unsmiling and beautiful land I had ever seen, and I was drawn to it immediately in ways and for reasons I did not understand. Words failed to describe what an interesting and amazing continent it was.

We met white and blue drift ice and growlers, which caused us to slow down as we sailed into the Boyd Strait. Its purity was perfect and reflected the colors of the ice in the water. Many say that the most spectacular scenery in all the continent—and, in my opinion, in all the world—is there.

Francisco announced that we would go straight to Deception Island to gain time. The island lay some three hours to the southeast from the Boyd Strait, depending on the ice conditions.

The captain had invented a new term called the *echo sounder lookout* since the Simrad paper echo sounder was our best friend in those uncharted waters. In 1974 and earlier, we had no clue that we were paving the way for all the world's future cruise ships coming to Antarctica. They would sail in our wake.

As we slowly navigated in uncharted waters in the Antarctic Peninsula, we made continuous depth entries in the sea chart for our future reference, and we made daily soundings and surveys of every uncharted new bay or inlet we encountered. We daily produced our own charts, mud charts, and landing reports, which were accurate and reliable and proved to be invaluable for us and for the future cruise ship industry as we sailed farther south into Antarctica. We were amazed at what we had achieved.

The bridge officer kept his eyes on the Simrad paper echo sounder continuously as we sailed in the treacherous waters with a slow speed. He kept one hand on the engine control while keeping a close eye on the paper echo sounder. We sailed south and inland into a world none of us had visited before. The bottom was full of pinnacles and surprises that kept our blood boiling. It was all a touch-and-go thing, and it was an adventure on a high level with the world's most distinguished passengers on board, who'd paid a fortune to be part of the history and to discover that remarkable new world no one had ever seen before.

We were like a big family, and in my happiness, I gave friendly claps on the back to royalty and the presidents of companies in the excitement we shared together for the time being. We were all sitting in the same boat in the middle of the nowhere in Antarctica, and we had a blast.

The echo sounder was our most important equipment in those days on the bridge, with its small needle writing a bottom curve that suddenly could steadily rise up until the watch-going mate on the bridge lost his nerve and had to stop the engines and then sail slowly with safeguarding speed, watching while he kept his eyes on the echo sounder. If things became serious, we called the captain, who attended on the bridge, but he was equally in doubt about what lay ahead of us. Every day kept our blood boiling, and numerous times, we found ourselves in deep guano, which caused us to immediately launch an echo-sounding Zodiac with a mate on board and with a VHF radio, and he crisscrossed ahead of our ship bow in attempts to figure out what lay ahead of us while giving the bridge the sounding figures as we produced a fairly reliable chart.

Chapter 12

Deception Island

DECEPTION ISLAND IS AN ALMOST circular volcanic crater lying at the southern end of the South Shetlands chain. It is shaped like a South Seas atoll, a horseshoe, with a lagoon in the middle. The only entry from the outlying ocean to the central lagoon is inconspicuous compared to the size of the islands. The island is a working volcano, and you can sail and swim in it. The water within the caldera can be much warmer than one would expect.

The average breadth of the horseshoe is about three miles, and the island's circumference is about twenty-three miles. The early sealers, looking for a natural harbor, at first thought there was none, until at last they happened on the 0.25-nautical-mile-wide strait known as Neptune's Bellows. To the right of the Bellows lies the empty central lagoon, known as Port Foster. It is calm and sheltered, though the katabatic winds sometimes whip it up.

Deception is an active volcano with hot springs and warm fumaroles, and the island is either black or white. There was an eruption in 1924, when the lagoon literally boiled, and the sulfur and the heat together stripped the paint off every ship inside the place.

In 1820, Nathaniel Palmer, the sealer who sailed his forty-seven-foot sloop *Hero* across the Drake Passage, sheltered in the Deception before casting southeastward across the unknown strait that was later called the Bransfield Strait. He was perhaps the first to see the coast of the great white hidden continent. Many ships have fled to Deception Island to avoid storms, and many have also fled from it, chased by nature's fire.

Deception is a sleeping volcano that sneezed in 1967 and 1969 and a place of shelter and ruins. Sudden, incredible strong winds up to ninety knots can come down from the ash-covered hills.

It's a perfect ring of rock broken only by the narrow entrance of Neptune's Bellows. Hot springs raise steam along the shoreline, especially from Pendulum Cove to the northeast. Farther around the caldera is an Argentinian base that is still occupied as a summer camp and was used as an emergency shelter for the crew of an Argentinian supply ship, *Bahia Paraiso*, which ran aground in early 1989 on Anvers Island, southwest of the only existing

American base, Palmer Station. She still lies there, showing her belly for the arriving cruise ships.

In the middle of the 1980s, the US research vessel *Polar Duke* once spent a windy afternoon working with a trawl to see what grew on the bottom of Deception's caldera. Bits of volcanic rock came up, and when the catch was dumped onto the deck, it was startling. The deck squirmed with thousands of thin-legged starfish slowly moving—a heap of unexpected life. It turned out that the floor of Deception was paved with brittle stars.

In the afternoon, Neptune's Bellows was straight ahead of us at a distance of one mile. The captain lined up the vessel so that we had a due westerly course of 270 degrees. All of us were looking intensely with our binoculars to see if the narrow entrance was open and not blocked with ice.

To our disappointment, an iceberg lay just in the middle of the entrance, which prevented us from sailing through. While approaching slowly, the captain said, "Let's turn the ship around, take out a mooring line with a Zodiac, and then pull the bloody thing away!"

Keith Shackleton offered to go out with two of our Tonga deck crew in a Zodiac to tie the mooring line around the iceberg. The Zodiac was lowered, the *Lindblad Explorer* went slowly astern, and the captain parked the ship with the stern inside the Bellows, pointing toward the caldera close to the iceberg, while the Zodiac crew tried to arrange the mooring line around the iceberg. Luckily, there was no wind for the time being, so the prospect of success was looking good.

Keith radioed that the mooring line was in place, connected with a huge shackle, and we started to tow the iceberg. The aft decks were full of passengers and crew watching the mission we had thrown ourselves into. Since the iceberg was grounded, it took a while until things started to happen.

The stern line was as tight as a rubber band, when the iceberg suddenly lost its point of balance and flipped over with a big bang as the line ricocheted back toward the ship, and the iceberg rolled around its axis, breaking up into pieces. The captain ordered everybody back on board while he again slowly turned the ship and proceeded with safeguarding speed through Neptune's Bellows. The entrance was now filled with bergy bits, growlers, and brush ice but was navigable. On a distance of 0.06 nautical miles of our starboard side, we sailed through the Bellows into the caldera of the snoozing volcano. Everybody was pleased, especially Francisco, who had his plans ready for the crater.

The *Lindblad Explorer* was the first passenger ship inside Deception Island, and she would continue to enter the Bellows undisturbed until 1975, when the next expedition cruise ship, the *World Discoverer*, became her competitor in Antarctica. Until then, we were alone in that untouched, hidden continent, and we explored that undisturbed, remote part of the world by ourselves for many years.

At the time, I didn't know that twenty-four years later, Antarctica would be my field, and I would complete some 125 voyages to that continent and be the captain on board the ship (by then named the *Explorer*), trying to reach the Larsen Ice Shelf in the Weddell Sea. Nor did I know I would look back on those pioneer years as being part of the team who opened up Antarctica for cruise ships and tourism due to my new hobby, which was to make soundings and surveys and produce mud charts of many of the inlets in the Antarctic Peninsula to facilitate future navigation. The homemade mud charts turned out to be invaluable for future cruise ships down there. We also worked closely with the BAS (British Antarctic Survey) vessel *John Biscoe*, which was fully occupied in servicing the British scientific bases. She also collected the results of the soundings we made to enhance the British admiralty Antarctica charts in the peninsula.

We dropped the anchor in Whalers Bay at a depth of forty-five meters, giving out five shackles in the water (each shackle is twenty-eight meters). The bay is very deep, all the way up to two cables (i.e., three hundred meters) from the shoreline, but from that distance from the shoreline, it shallows up rapidly. The anchor holding turned out to be not too good since the bottom consisted of ash and dust from previous volcanic eruptions.

It was my first landing in Antarctica, and I was astonished to know we were inside a volcano's crater with snow-covered hillsides. Everything was white and beautiful. The captain told me to keep a good check of our anchor position, as the vessel could start to drag quickly since there was a bad anchor holding. Once the *Lindblad Explorer* was peacefully riding her anchor, I scanned the hills around me from the bridge wing where I stood. My first impression was that a harsh landscape surrounded us, and we were not on the same frequency in that scene in terms of wisdom of the things that could happen weather-wise and only God knew what else.

I felt lonely while standing safely on the bridge wing and scanning the hills. I had an impression that this thing could have an outburst any minute. But somehow, I was attracted to the unpredictable scenery I was looking at. Port Foster, as it also was called, was not as safe as it looked. Someone had painted faces on five huge old fuel storage tanks that stood listing in volcanic dust and gravel. There was one face on each tank; each was twenty feet tall. They stared out across the bay, permanently astonished at the penguins that came to strut beside them, the fur seals that barked on the beach, and the first passenger ship ever to steam slowly through the clouds of cape pigeons at Neptune's Bellows.

Beside the faces of the tanks were rows of bleached and broken barrels left over from the old whaling station that once had occupied the shore. On the other side of the tanks were buildings and the remains of an old Twin Otter aircraft abandoned by the British when the volcano became aggressive.

The others passengers and I were astonished to be at last in Antarctica. In the future, people asked me why I wanted to go back to Antarctica and to that awful place called Deception Island. I used to say, "In short, it has much to do with the charm of the wilderness and the challenge Antarctica gives you. You try hard to find something new, and if you make it, you feel very proud." The knowledge of where I was and the sense of being alone in that magnificent wilderness were as near as possible to what I would call absolute paradise.

Frank Wild, who was the right-hand man to Sir Ernest Shackleton and joined him on several of his Antarctic expeditions, went again and again to Antarctica in the early years of the twentieth century and became stranded on Elephant Island on April 15, 1916. He said that he returned to Antarctica because he could never escape "the little voices." He said, "What do the little voices whisper? They remind you of all the faces you have seen in Antarctica faces on fuel tanks, faces of friends, and the many contrary, wonderful, and deceiving faces of the island." This I agree with.

I always had a love-hate relationship with that fearsome continent and its islands. Many who travel to the Antarctic find themselves drawn to it again and again. Travel there is a kind of religious experience, and it is as much about the inner journey as about the actual distance covered. It is the one place in the world virtually untouched by civilization, and it is likely to remain so as environmentalists struggle to preserve its pristine nature.

We started to land the passengers in our Zodiacs powered by forty-horsepower outboard motors. The Zodiacs were fast, safe, and easy to use. They provided the opportunity to land passengers in places where there were no formal docking arrangements.

It was indeed a peculiar feeling to be in the caldera of Deception Island.

Great God, this is an awful place. That was where my own little voice took me first. I didn't know I would in the future sail repeatedly through Neptune's Bellows.

From the bridge wing, I saw red parkas walking on the beach close to some bull fur seals. I counted seventeen through my binoculars. They were lazing on the beach, and one bull fur seal remained seated in the Zodiac and proved difficult to remove. Our staff tried to remove the stubborn fur seal with paddles and whatever they had, but they failed. After one hour, the seal slipped into the water.

Francisco had divided the passengers up into groups since some wanted to go hiking up in the mountains and toward Baily Head, which lay to the east and just on the other side of Port Foster. Some walked along the beach and up to the newly created lake where the old runway had been in the past for the Twin Otter that rested against the old hangar.

The wind was nipping cold for the passengers ashore and for me standing on the bridge wing, watching the Zodiac operation done by the Tongans. With the binoculars, I could see a red parka sitting alone on the beach in front of an easel, painting a penguin that obviously knew it was not supposed to move for some time. It was senior naturalist doctor Roger Tory Peterson from the USA, creating one of his famous wonders.

Some four hours later, without a warning, we faced suddenly some strong katabatic winds coming down from the hills. They caused Francisco to collect in a hurry all the red parkas back to the beach. Many people had already left the beach well before the last Zodiac was announced, as it seemed people had a profound respect for that godforsaken place. The wind picked up to some thirty knots, which was a clear indication we'd better get the hell out of there because more could come. In those years, we had hardly any proper weather information or weather charts. Once in a while, we could receive some blurred weather facsimile charts from Chile.

Finally, after an eternity, everybody was back on board, including Roger Tory Peterson, who was the last person to board the last Zodiac from shore. While the wind whizzed in the ship's rig, we pulled up the anchor and made a big turn inside the caldera in order to line up the ship toward the entrance on a due course of 90 degrees east. We sailed out from the dreadful crater through the Bellows, and I heaved a deep sigh of relief to be outside as we sailed into the Bransfield Strait.

In my heart, I never liked Deception Island, and I would never appreciate that dreadful place in the future. It was my first time there, but I would come back again and again since the small voices called me back.

As we entered the Bransfield Strait, we met the BAS *John Biscoe* of Port Stanley in the Falklands. She was named after the sealer John Biscoe. She was small, a little more than 1,500 tons, and in 1979, she had an extensive refit to construct a suite of laboratories for oceanographic research. She also carried out some underwater surveys in the Antarctic waters, including South Georgia.

Recently, trawl mechanisms and nets have been improved for the capture and detailed examination of krill. Wet laboratories are essential in all marine research but particularly so with krill, which becomes contaminated by the atmosphere within four hours of being caught.

The *Lindblad Explorer* was now heading down toward the Gerlache Strait.

In the future, however, we would once in a while meet in South Georgia, Grytviken, to spend New Year's Eve together if our cruise schedule allowed us to do so. The *John Biscoe* always spent that special evening with the British garrison troops there.

Chapter 13

Grytviken and a Crazy New Year's Eve

As we once in a while made the long cruise from Ushuaia to the Antarctic Peninsula, to the South Orkney Islands, and onward to South Georgia, ending up in Port Stanley in the Falklands, which took some twenty-one days, we usually ended up in Grytviken for New Year's Eve, celebrating the special evening in peace and mostly likely with the *John Biscoe* in the bay.

South Georgia is the most attractive island of the Antarctic in the variety of its landscape and animal and bird life. Legend has it that the island was discovered in 1512 by the Florentine explorer Amerigo Vespucci, which seems unlikely. The first person to survey the northern coast and land was Captain James Cook in January 1775. He landed in Possession Bay and then sailed to the large inlet with arms stretching east and west, which he named Cumberland Bay. Tucked below the entrance to Cumberland East Bay are Grytviken, which for sixty years was the capital of the Norwegian whaling industry in the Antarctic, and King Edward Point, where the magistrate responsible for South Georgia has his seat.

Anyone wishing to land on South Georgia must seek clearance for immigration from the magistrate, an authority assigned to the base commander of the BAS.

The whaling industry on South Georgia was founded largely through the vision of one man, Captain Carl Anton Larsen. Larsen first saw South Georgia during his second voyage in 1894, and two years later, he made inquiries to the Royal Geographical Society in London about the possibility of setting up a whaling station on the island. There was clearly money to be made, but in the past, Larsen had failed to find backing in Norway, just as Scotsman W. S. Bruce had failed after his 1892 voyage to interest his country. By Christmas 1904, Larsen had found backers in Argentina and formed his Compañía Argentina de Pesca, and the first whales were processed at his new South Georgia shore station of Grytviken. The place got its name in 1902 during a Swedish Antarctic expedition under geologist and polar explorer Otto Nordenskjold when they found old English pots used to make seal oil and even tombs from English and American sailors. The Antarctic expedition noted, however, that in the literature and the British charts, there were not any records to be found on that place. The Swedish archaeologist and geologist Johan

Gunnar Andersson have been identified as the one who came up with the name, but in his book *Antarctic*, he only notes laconically, "We gave this small ideal safe harbor the name Grytviken."

Grytviken was founded on November 16, 1904, by Carl Anton Larsen, a Norwegian captain, whaler, and explorer. Larsen and sixty compatriots built in one month a whaling station on the site, which was a base for industrial whaling for more than fifty years. The whale population in the waters around the island was rich, and the business was originally very profitable. However, the whales declined over the next sixty years due to overfishing. In December 1966, Grytviken Station was shut down, as the whale population was so low that the station was no longer profitable. Remnants of whaling can be seen on the beaches, and whale bones can be found. Old factories for the extraction of whale oil and abandoned whaleships can also be found nearby.

Quickly, Cumberland Bay was packed with humpback whales, and the abundance of easy prey close to shore made for rapid profits. But as the industry expanded with further stations springing up in the island's other natural ports, the whale catchers were forced to sail farther out into the ocean. Every summer until 1966, tall chimneys belched steam from specialized boilers lined up in the blubber, meat, and bone cookeries and the guano factory. However, the visible heart of the operation feeding the cookers was the flensing plan, a huge wooden deck sloping gently up from the shore.

A total of 175,000 whales were harpooned in the waters around South Georgia according to Reader's Digest Book Antarctica. It was a "Horrible, murderous business, wasn't it. As whales became scarce, the shore-based industry became less profitable, and by 1965, all whaling from the island ceased.

On January 2, 1975, I wrote the following in my diary:

> Now looking at the Grytviken station as we approached this place 9 years after it had closed, I felt unhappy. There was a blur of a few buildings and high radio masts, dwarfed by the crags and mountains rising directly above. Below the peaks the vegetation, grass and moss, was clear emerald green and mostly the sky was bright. A dazzling glacier shone on the *Lindblad Explorer*'s port bow as the sun began to appear through the fine rain.

On each side of the old wooden wharf, dotted along the shoreline were clumps of gentoo penguins, and at the far side, the roaring sound of the elephant seals was heard as they looked at the vessel and the some twenty red parkas who watched the spectacular scenery from the forecastle of the *Lindblad Explorer*. The roar was a long, rolling belch amplified by air pumped into the nose.

In the water, there were two or three small steam whale catchers with their funnels, masts, and superstructure almost horizontal in the water. The best preserved, the *Petrel*, lay in the water off one of the big slipways. She carried the colors of Argentina because she'd belonged to the Compañía Argentina de Pesca, the first whaling company to operate a station on South Georgia, which had traded at Grytviken from 1906 to 1959. In all, seven stations were established on the island:

Grytviken, Leith, Stromness, and Husvik, which operated until the early 1960s, and Godthul, Ocean Harbor, and Prince Olav, which suffered crises and closure in the '20s and '30s. At the height of the whaling industry, about six thousand men, mostly Norwegians, worked at the stations.

Behind the factory buildings stood the manager's house, and beyond to one side was the white wooden Lutheran church, with its pointed steeple. The church was framed by the jagged granite peak beyond with the snow-covered mountains behind. The church was specially built for Larsen. It was built in Norway and transported in sections to the present site in 1913.

We arrived at the fragile quay without putting any pressure on our mooring ropes to spare the pier without causing any damage. I was speechless at the beautiful scenery surrounding us, but we also could see a sprawl of pipes, chains, hawsers, empty warehouses and sheds, and acres of rusty corrugated iron clanging in the wind. It was impossible not to be overwhelmed by the Antarctic scenery. I thought, *South Georgia is an extraordinary place.*

The most prominent grave, with a stone obelisk, is that of Sir Ernest Henry Shackleton, who died in Grytviken on January 5, 1922, as he was preparing to set out on his fourth Antarctic expedition. He was struck by heart disease, and his body was shipped to Montevideo for passage home before his widow suggested it would be more fitting for him to be buried on South Georgia.

So there I was on South Georgia, the Gateway to Antarctica, as the island was called by Shackleton.

One hour later, we saw the RRS *John Biscoe* enter the bay, and shortly after that, we heard the sound of her rattling anchor chain as it echoed among the snow-covered hills. It was a nice summer day in the late afternoon, when the peaceful bay was suddenly interrupted by the sound of the laughing crew from the *John Biscoe*. Obviously, the *John Biscoe*'s crew had been given permission to party and go ashore, as we saw and heard at 2000 hours a Zodiac approaching the wooden wharf with a bunch of happy sailors who were more than slightly intoxicated. They came on board to have a cocktail in our lounge and fraternize with our passengers, who had a great time that lovely evening. Since our New Year's Eve dinner commenced at 1930, our fellow crew members from the *John Biscoe* left in their Zodiac, singing and screaming with the promise that before midnight, they would return to the *Lindblad Explorer* to fire their fireworks, which later proved to be the red distress rockets.

At that time, I made friends with Malcolm "Marty" Shakesby from England, chief officer of the *John Biscoe*, whom I would stay in touch with for the next years as long as we were in Antarctica. He stopped working at sea in November 1987, prior to departure to the Falklands to fill the position of general manager of Sullivan Shipping Agency. He was awarded the MBE (Member of the British Empire) medal on the New Year's honors list by Margaret Thatcher on December 4, 1987, for his role in the rescue operation of the *Herald of Free Enterprise*, which capsized off Zeebrugge in Belgium, and he received the MBE from Her Majesty the Queen at Buckingham Palace on March 8, 1988. Today he is running his own company, Marine Consultancy, in Dorset, in the offshore sector as well as being the director of Poole Harbor Authority. In February 2001, he was elected local conservative counselor.

When we had finished our New Year's Eve dinner, it was decided that the first engineer, Hans; the second engineer, Leif; the electrician, Hugo; the third engineer, Nisse; a passenger who was the owner of Bata Shoes; and I would go ashore to figure out if Grytviken could once again be illuminated—after being shut down in December 1966—by finding and starting the old generators in the engine room hall.

However, none of us were sober as we set out on the mission in our best uniforms, with polished black shoes, walking across the sprawl of pipes, chains, and more to find the engine and the generator. Equipped with torches for checking out each shed and warehouse, we finally found the engine room. After so many years of darkness, if anybody could illuminate the ghost town again, it was Hans, Leif, and Hugo, who were the perfect team for it. They made a thorough examination of the equipment, and after an hour of investigation, Hugo suddenly said, "It's amazing—everything seems to be in a good condition, and I believe we should be able to start the generator!"

I thought the established order of silence perhaps soon would be broken after the height of the whaling industry. Also, I asked myself what the reactions of Francisco and everybody else, including the crew on board the *John Biscoe* and the base commander, would be. The base commander had arrived on November 11, 1969, with a party of ten on board the *John Biscoe* to take over the base. He had accepted a five-year contract as base commander of South Georgia. The arrangement was that he would spend the summer in Grytviken to control the station, but subsequently, a wintering deputy would run the base while he returned home to help organize the requirements for the following season. So began the continuous occupation of the somewhat unusual base. He was required to clear every ship for customs on arrival and departure, levy the harbor dues, and charge for water taken on board. Each summer brought a constant stream of visitors, including a number of Russian fishing vessels with their assistant tankers, many of which came to take on water and give their crews a spell ashore. The *Lindblad Explorer* was the first passenger ship to go alongside the wooden wharf in Grytviken.

But my consolation was that to my knowledge, on that evening, everyone in that beautiful bay was having a good time, and perhaps nobody would pay much attention if they found the ghost town suddenly once again illuminated. It turned out I was wrong! Nevertheless, I fully supported our crazy mission.

Somewhere from far behind in the darkness, I suddenly heard Leif shout, "There is still fuel in the tank! Hans, start the engine!" God knew where the tank was, but obviously, there was fuel enough somewhere. It was pitch black in the hall, but in the light of the torches, they managed to get the auxiliary engine running.

Unexpectedly, the hall filled with the sound of the running engine in the darkness. The noise was incredible, and I thought, *Holy hell, what the heck are we doing?*

In the light of the torches, I saw Hugo leaned over the generator in his best uniform with tucked-up sleeves and his face covered with oil. He shouted to the first engineer, Hans, "Pull down the circuit breaker—now!" It was amazing: Grytviken became once again completely illuminated.

All of a sudden, I saw a heavy snowfall begin to fall slowly outside. We stood in the entrance door, paralyzed and silent, watching the big falling snowflakes, which made a romantic, enchanting impression on us as they fell in the light of some alley lighting that was still partly intact. It was a magnificent sight we experienced as the time came closer to midnight.

Again, I tried to figure out what the BAS base commander was thinking as he saw his Grytviken illuminated. Nevertheless, we all agreed that it was a breathtaking sight as we stood silently at the entrance to the shed, watching the magical sight.

The generator and the auxiliary engine stopped ten minutes later at 2230 on December 31, 1974, and everything went silent, and Grytviken once again went back to its eternal sleep after eight years of silence. At the time of this writing thirty-eight years later, I am convinced the sound of the auxiliary engine has never been heard again after that night.

Cheerfully, we walked back to the inviting *Lindblad Explorer* in a gorgeous snowfall. We were completely covered with snow. There were only sixty minutes left until the New Year, and the captain and Keith Shackleton were scheduled to make a speech to everybody, including the base commander, who was supposed to say a few words. I feared the worst was yet to come. Francisco was furious about what we had done.

However, John Green came to me with his usual smile at the corners of his mouth and said, "Peter, what you and your friends did tonight I will never forget as long as I live. Well done!"

My answer was simply "Thanks, John!"

There was an exceptionally happy atmosphere when I met Hugo in the lounge. He had a big smile on his lips. Goran, the other second officer, said, "You must have been crazy when you did this, but it was great."

Marty from the *John Biscoe* came over and was in a particularly good mood when he said, "Peter, I am a sailor by trade, and I have been in Grytviken many times working for BAS, but none of us on board the *John Biscoe* could believe what we saw tonight! All of us felt something when we saw Grytviken become illuminated. It was like *Arabian Nights* or like the soft tones of *The Sound of Music*. The *Lindblad Explorer* is indeed a wonderful ship!" Bear in mind, the year was 1974.

The captain grabbed the microphone fifteen minutes before the New Year and made a short speech. After his speech, which was kind of emotional, he handed over the microphone to the base commander, and I was waiting for the worst to come. The three of us who had been in the engine room hangar starting up the generator looked at each other like guilty schoolboys when the base commander spoke. He said after the usual introduction and courtesy phrases, "During my years that I have been in Grytviken as a base commander, this is something I would never have believed to be possible. As I have walked around in the haze of these rusty buildings in the Grytviken station in the nighttime, the station has been resting in peacefulness, except for tonight, New Year's Eve 1974, when the entire station became, to my big surprise, illuminated."

He didn't say it in public, but he said afterward that the only thing missing was Mozart's piano concerto when the station was lit. Well, I was moved at what I heard, and so were the others, but there was an undertone: "Do not do it again!" Hans made a funny face and laughed uneasily while I turned red in my face.

By then, we had most of the *John Biscoe*'s officers and crew, including the captain, on board. He'd joined the *John Biscoe* in 1964 as second mate and become her master in 1972. The crew were very much under the influence of alcohol, and they'd brought some of their expired pyrotechnical distress rockets with them to inaugurate the new year, which was only five minutes away.

The bar personnel were fully occupied with refilling all the empty glasses and bringing in the champagne glasses, as per the rules. For a few minutes more before the ding-dong at midnight, the atmosphere in the lounge had an old-world air, and all were preparing themselves for the big kiss and hug ceremony. By a mere chance, I overheard one lady next to me say to her husband, "I don't think it was in the program that Grytviken was supposed to become illuminated tonight."

At the stroke of midnight, to the tones of the ding-dong made by the captain's tapping a cognac glass with a teaspoon over the public-address system, everybody shouted, "Happy New Year!" Serpentines filled the entire lounge, and endless cheek kissing began to the left and right. Francisco, as precautionary as he always was, was watching the blast and, as usual, standing politely a little bit aside, rubbing his hands, expecting probably the worst still to come, as we had a big part of the *John Biscoe*'s crew on board, who by then were more wild than tame.

I cannot recall the names anymore of some of the *John Biscoe*'s crew, but one guy said, "It's time for the big fireworks," and off he went.

Suspicious as I was, I followed him since he seemed to be a happy-go-lucky person in his intoxication. As I came outside, the moon was shining beautifully from a crystal-clear sky, and I saw that some distress rockets already had been fired off from the *John Biscoe*. It was a fascinating night.

When the passengers realized that fireworks were in progress, they became enthusiastic about the new surprise and made their way out to the open deck areas. It was a surprise, and it became a scary one after a while, when I saw the happy-go-lucky guy from the *John Biscoe* step down—or perhaps he fell down—into a Zodiac with one of his friends, who was more than intoxicated from alcohol. I figured out that was where he had his pyrotechnical rockets hidden. They drove a little bit out from the wharf and started to fire the rockets off.

A midnight horror commenced for the next twenty minutes. The distress rockets were fired off repeatedly from the small Zodiac one after another, and once the rockets reached the vertex, they slowly started to fall down from their high altitude exactly above the *Lindblad Explorer*'s sundeck, where we had our fifty-four gasoline tanks in storage for our outboard engines. The happy duo in the Zodiac were singing and having a great time as they continued to shoot the rockets, but they unfortunately failed to see that they were in danger of blowing up our vessel as the rockets started to land on our sundeck, still fully burning. Discipline no longer seemed paramount among the two crew in the happy Zodiac, and it was a matter for the utmost regret.

In my imagination, I could see an enormous explosion that could dome the ship, triggered by the rockets as they eventually landed in the highly exposed and explosive tanks. Tevita, the quartermaster from the Tonga Islands, who happened to be around, shouted in the same second I reacted. Some rockets failed to land on the sundeck, but many did. By then, I was running around with Tevita and two more deck crew on the sundeck in a desperate attempt to kill the falling rockets before they hit the gasoline tanks. The rockets were indeed beautiful to watch for the passengers as we had a terrifying time in trying to kill them. I alerted Tevita to one approaching rocket that seemed to have the perfect trajectory toward the gasoline tanks as some were still burning around us on the decks. The two other deck crew, Siua and Frank, were doing their best to extinguish them. We shouted down to the Zodiac to stop firing off the rockets, but they just happily continued.

Tevita and I stood firmly waiting on each side of the gasoline tanks with lifted arms, ready for action, as the rocket, in its parachute, slowly came closer. It was nerve-racking to wait and watch the one that had the perfect path toward the tanks with their surrounding gas vapors. We both knew the consequences if we failed to grab it. Neither of us had gloves, which made it a lot more complicated.

All our attempts to shout to the two lighthearted guys in the Zodiac to stop firing their rockets received no response. I wondered how many rockets they had left since they already had sent up several.

Two rockets were slowly falling down with the ideal path toward our fifty-four tanks, and they appeared to be some of the last ones since there were no more to be seen in the crystal-clear sky. They had a slightly different path. I gathered that the men must have fired a total of some fifteen rockets, which easily could have become devastating.

Just before one red flare touched down on top of the gasoline tanks, we both made a high jump at the same time in an attempt to reach it. Tevita barely managed to throw it away but in the wrong direction, so it grazed my uniform and made a big burn mark on it. At least the danger was now over, but there was one more surprise to come that night. As we walked down from the sundeck, we felt spiritless due to that last exciting event, and we knew we had escaped lightly. I went down to the half-tilted wooden wharf because I wanted to have a stiff talk with the two happy-go-lucky guys out there in the Zodiac, when I suddenly saw a strange situation going on in their Zodiac: as drunk as they both were, one of them had fallen into the freezing-cold water with no life vest on.

As I watched the incredible situation, feeling helpless, the crew and passengers were already shouting and screaming to each other to do something. The man in the water was clinging on to the Zodiac with only one arm, while the other one made hopeless attempts to pull his friend up as he apparently fell backward in each rescue attempt.

We had to get him back before he finally slipped down into the Grytviken bay forever. Since he was heavily intoxicated, it was assumed he didn't have much power left. He had been in the water for about four minutes, and still, no rescue Zodiac had been sent out from the *Lindblad Explorer*, for unknown reasons.

Suddenly, a Zodiac appeared from the vessel's stern, heading toward the scene of the event. He was quickly pulled on board by strong Tongan arms and taken to the wooden wharf, unconscious and suffering from heavy hypothermia. His heart was still beating but weak.

The Tongan crew had the presence of mind to get a stretcher quickly down as the ship's doctor treated him for hypothermia. His body temperature was dangerously low, and he was enfolded with blankets to regain normal body heat. As his general condition slowly improved sufficiently, he was carefully transferred back to the *John Biscoe* in a Zodiac.

The doctor said, "If he would have been in the water for another minute or two, he would never have survived." Malcolm, the chief mate, told me later on that when he regained consciousness, he had no memory of that night's exciting, sad events.

The captain decided to sail out from Grytviken in the dark night while saluting the *John Biscoe* with a long blast on the ship's horn, and they, as usual, responded with the same. We would most likely spend the next New Year's Eve together in Grytviken again.

Over the years in the Southern Hemisphere in the 1970s, the *John Biscoe* and the *Lindblad Explorer* reached a feeling of affinity that became invaluable for both of us.

Now we were heading for the Falklands and Ushuaia in Argentina, and the day passed in idle enjoyment. On the decks, there was constant sun, a breeze, and the delightful sensation of being surrounded by wandering albatrosses. The *John Biscoe* was also bound for Ushuaia.

Chapter 14

The First Naval Incident between Argentina and Great Britain, with the *Lindblad Explorer* in Between

IT WAS FEBRUARY 1975. I cannot recall the date, but the *Lindblad Explorer* was alongside the berth in Ushuaia to repatriate the passengers and receive a new group who would be sailing with us for the next twenty-one-day cruise via Port Stanley, the Falkland Islands, and South Georgia to the Antarctic Peninsula. The BAS ship *John Biscoe* was alongside the pier ahead of us in Ushuaia, and they departed at approximately 1800 hours. We departed shortly after that.

Alongside us as well was an Argentinian destroyer. The *John Biscoe* cast off her lines; we did as well; and immediately after us, we noted that the Argentinian destroyer departed too. We felt it was strange or perhaps just a coincidence. All three of us sailed in the Beagle Channel toward the open sea. We knew the *John Biscoe* was bound for Port Stanley in the Falkland Islands, as we were.

Leaving the Beagle Channel, we headed northeast toward the Falklands, and thirty-six hours after that, we had an approximate position some two hundred nautical miles from Isla de los Estados, the most easterly island of Patagonia, when I suddenly overheard a message on VHF channel 16 from the Argentinian destroyer: "This is the Argentinian Navy ship [I cannot recall the name of the destroyer now, unfortunately], and we ask the British *John Biscoe* to stop for inspection since you are entering the territorial waters of Islas Malvinas, Argentina, without permission."

I was stunned at what I had just heard over the radio, and I called the captain and told him, "You'd better come to the bridge quickly to hear this conversation on the VHF radio." He immediately attended the bridge. Both of us were shocked at what was going on over the VHF radio.

The *John Biscoe* was clearly visible ahead of us and fairly close, and the destroyer was to our port, approximately a nautical mile away. The *John Biscoe* remained silent until the next VHF message was heard, and this time, it was more hostile: "This is the Argentinian warship. If you, Captain, do not stop your engines, we will fire a warning shot."

There was a profound silence on the radio, and the captain and I looked at each other with concern. The situation was unreal, and we thought, *What is actually going on?* We were taken by surprise.

The weather was overcast, as usual, with an obvious approaching fogbank in the distance ahead of us. We thought if the *John Biscoe* only could reach the fogbank and Volunteer Point and Pembroke Lighthouse some seventy nautical miles ahead of us, she would be safe.

The *John Biscoe* continued to be silent, and half an hour later, we heard a huge bang. The destroyer had fired a shot with sharp ammunition just in front of the *John Biscoe*, fully visible for us, and we observed a large column of water ahead of the *John Biscoe*. We were paralyzed on the *Lindblad Explorer*'s bridge, which was now silent. The captain called the engine room, asking for permission to increase the speed, and we did. Slowly, we were able to speed up, and we placed ourselves at the port side close to the *John Biscoe* to act as a shield protecting her from the Argentinian destroyer's hostility. It was a brave action, as we were now acting as a shield with passengers on board between the destroyer and the *John Biscoe*, and we asked ourselves on the bridge if we would be shot by mistake. All of us were constantly watching the destroyer in our binoculars. The passengers, however, had no clue what was going on.

We and the *John Biscoe* sailed together for a while until the long-awaited fogbank surrounded us. On board were our expedition leader and the cruise director, Francisco from Argentina, and Keith Shackleton from the United Kingdom, a lecturer and famous naturalist. Due to that incident, there became a profound bad temper between the two of them, which was partly understandable.

When the *John Biscoe* arrived at Port Stanley, something strange but fully reasonable happened: the entire crew of the *John Biscoe* went ashore in protest over the incident with the Argentinian destroyer, and they refused to come back on board unless England took some appropriate actions.

After that incident, the *Lindblad Explorer* sailed south to Antarctica twice, when suddenly, a British aircraft carrier marked its presence in the waters outside the Falkland Islands. This was the first incident between the United Kingdom and Argentina and later on led to the Falkland War on April 2, 1982.

Chapter 15

Hope Bay and the Horrible Lifeboat Journey

OUR NEXT ANTARCTIC CRUISE BEGAN on January 19, 1975, in Ushuaia, in southern Argentina, and passengers' introduction program contained the following information: At Hope Bay, the arrival point for the Antarctic continent, is a large military establishment bearing the legend over the landing jetty "Welcome to Antarctica!" Effective occupancy is still the name of the game, and it all began with the import of a pregnant Argentine lady in 1975 in an attempt to claim partial possession of the continent. Since 1940, Argentina and Chile have been in competition for ownership of Antarctica. Many other countries are involved in this competition for the territory, but no one truly owns the land or has actual sovereignty. Almost all dropped their claims after the Antarctic Treaty of 1959, which was signed by forty-five countries, blocked any one nation from trying to take over the winter wonderland. Argentina and Chile remained in competition even after the Antarctic Treaty was signed. Both claim that the Antarctic Peninsula is a continuation of the Andes Mountains. Now a little school stands there for a handful of young ones, hopefully with a vacancy for a geography teacher!

Because the bay was deep, the only possible place to drop the anchor in the bay was a shallow and small patch with approximately seventeen meters of water some six cables (one cable is 182 meters) from the far end of the bay and two cables from the southern ice cliffs.

In my chief mate's cabin on January 24, 1976, I wrote the following in my diary about Hope Bay:

> Yesterday at 1300 hours we sailed into Hope Bay and dropped the anchor
> on the usual 17-meter bottom curve. [The same depth is shown in the curve
> in the chart.]

The passengers' daily program for January 24 read as follows:

Quote:

The *Lindblad Explorer* shall be at anchor at Hope Bay. Here we shall visit the larger Adelie Penguin rookery and the Argentinian Army Station, "Esperanza." This is one of the last stations to use husky dogs and, should the weather be good, we shall have an opportunity to watch dog-sledge demonstrations. Also, you may visit the abandoned British Station under the competent leadership of John Green from England.

Unquote:

John Green was an Antarctic polar explorer born in 1922 who had done partial mapping of the Antarctic Peninsula in the 1950s and early 1960s and spent many years in the Antarctic Peninsula. His knowledge of the Antarctic Peninsula and especially Hope Bay had come from his doing a lot of mapping on the Antarctic Peninsula with British Antarctic explorer Sir Wally Herbert. Therefore, John Green was highly appreciated among the passengers and staff. He was a Zodiac driver and a lecturer when he was sober. We sailed to Hope Bay because of his famous hut, which was just behind the existing Argentinean base Esperanza, where he overwintered.

In his obituary in *Polar Record*, the following is written about him:

He was born in Birmingham on May 28, 1922, and was in World War II, reaching the rank of captain. He joined the Falkland Islands Dependencies Survey in 1949 and was base leader at Base B (Deception Island) in 1950 and at Base F (Argentine Islands) in 1951. Upon his return from Antarctica, he became SECFID (secretary of FIDS) in Port Stanley until 1962. Then he was transferred to London, where he became operations officer until 1967. When he left FIDS/BAS in 1967, he worked for Outward Bound and tour operators. He retired to Cornwall and died in Lisbon on May 29, 1988

The passengers' program was as follows:

Quote:

7:30–9:00 a.m.: Breakfast 8:30. First boat leaves for shore, and half hourly shuttle service will be maintained between the station and the ship.

12:30 p.m.: A lamb barbecue luncheon onshore at the Argentinian station

2:00 p.m.: John Green will lead those wishing to climb Mount Flora to search for fossils.

4:00–4:30 p.m.: Afternoon tea for those on board

6:00 p.m.: The last boat returns to the ship. The Argentine personnel will join us for cocktails and dinner.

7:00–8:30 p.m.: Dinner

9:00 p.m.: Briefing followed by "A Year and a Half of Russians on Ice, or Wintering with Vodka," an illustrated slide lecture about life on a Soviet Antarctic expedition, by Gregg Vanc

Unquote:

We had invited eight people from the Argentinian military station Esperanza for cocktails and dinner. Hope Bay and Esperanza were also the scenes of the first shots fired in anger in Antarctica, when an Argentine shore party fired a machine gun over the heads of a British Antarctic survey team unloading supplies from the *John Biscoe* in 1952. The Argentines later extended a diplomatic apology, saying that there had been a misunderstanding and that the Argentine military commander on the ground had exceeded his authority.

The evening was an absolute enjoyment. The bay was calm, and both Antarctica and Hope Bay were at their colorful best. I wrote in the ship's logbook at 1800 hours: "Barometer 995 MB, wind speed 15 knots, wind direction East and partly cloudy." A worrisome atmosphere settled over the area as I watched the upper layers of the clouds sail along the sky. I had learned to be observant of the slightest changes in cloud movements and to observe the barometer, and I grew suspicious about the conditions in the bay because we had experienced sudden windy conditions on previous visits.

I always kept one bridge door open in order to feel the wind and any changes in wind speed. As the sun slowly dipped beyond the snow-covered mountains, I continued to observe the weather. At 2000 hours, the end of my watch, I wrote in the logbook, "Barometer 985 Mb, wind speed 25 knots, wind direction East—steady." I was now quite concerned about what the weather had in store for us, and since we had guests on board who at some point were to be taken ashore, I went to the lounge to inform Captain Kjell about the rapidly falling barometer.

The captain was the most wonderful man I had ever met. He was humane and a gentleman, a native of Sweden, and he was a true seaman and a little bit religious in his nature. He believed in God, and he was a ladies' man and a charmer. I admired his perfectionism and the passionate speeches he gave to the passengers.

In the lounge, I saw the eight Argentinean station personnel having a great time, dancing, drinking, and enjoying themselves with the passengers, as the wind picked up more and more. I politely whispered to the captain, "The wind is picking up, and the barometer is falling quickly—what shall we do?"

"Let's wait and see what happens," he replied.

Some hours later, I returned to the bridge, watching with the second officer the descending barometer needle, which was now showing 953 MB. When the barometer fell rapidly in Antarctica, one could soon expect strong winds. As was usually the case when lying at anchor, both our powerful searchlights scanned the ice conditions.

From the mouth of the bay, some light pack ice drifted toward us and slowly filled the area. My first thought was that the approaching ice and the increasing wind from the east represented a degree of danger and that we should leave the area. It was bad to lie at anchor in strong wind when surrounded by ice. But I recalled that the Argentinians were still on board, and the sea was becoming rough because of the easterly wind.

The wind then started to gust and become katabatic—a term for the strong Antarctic winds caused by cold, dense air flowing out from the polar plateau of the interior and down the steep vertical drops along the coast at the edge of Antarctica. I realized we had to get our guests ashore as quickly as possible, so again, I went to consult the captain, who agreed.

By midnight, the barometer had dropped to 945 MB, and the wind force was now somewhere around sixty knots. Extremely low barometer readings, such as 940 MB, are normal in Antarctica, though if these kinds of barometer readings occurred in the United States or Europe, roofs would become airborne, and people would not be able to walk the streets. Surrounding Antarctica, there is normally a belt of low pressure, the circumpolar trough, containing multiple low centers. The continent itself is dominated by high pressure, but meaningful analysis of surface pressure data is difficult because of the elevated nature of much of Antarctica.

The captain informed the eight Argentinean guests of the deterioration in the weather and said they would have to remain on board while the *Lindblad Explorer* left for the Antarctic Sound to ride out the storm. The Argentinians refused and insisted they be sent ashore, so despite the circumstances, we agreed. They were told to meet at the gangway hall in less than half an hour for their transfer ashore.

Since all the guests had been thoroughly enjoying themselves, with many under the influence of alcohol, including both our deck officers and those from the base Esperanza, they were still dancing and ignored our instructions to leave the ship. In the midst of that chaos, we debated using Zodiacs or a lifeboat to take them ashore. Given that the weather outside had reached gale force, we decided against the Aodiacs, for it was pitch black, and the bay was now full of ice. So we deployed a lifeboat meant for twenty passengers. The captain asked for an officer to volunteer to take charge of the lifeboat. All the deck officers refused to go out under that kind of weather, as they knew they were not sufficiently clearheaded. The captain turned to me and said, "I have been trying to convince the Argentineans to stay overnight until the weather conditions improve, but they insist on leaving now, so can you go?"

After I glanced down at the two-meter-high waves, my answer was not convincing: "Okay, I will go, but I will choose the crew myself."

I knew I was facing probably the most dangerous situation in my life when I accepted, but I had already picked out the crew in my mind. The deck crew would be from Tonga: Tevita; Siua Palu; and Sione Matavalea, the brother of Tevita. I knew those men would be reliable under the conditions, and they were strong. The engine crew included a Spanish fitter, Lago-Tajes, who knew everything about lifeboat engines; Ketut Mupu, a motorman from Bali; and, from the Tonga Islands, Ketoni Tuita, an outboard mechanic who was related to the queen of the Republic of Tonga Islands.

When the lifeboat crew was chosen, I had a short briefing with them on the boat deck. I told them that they should understand that we were being given a difficult task and that I was counting on their goodwill and fortitude to get the job done. My immediate impression was that they were deep in their minds and silent after my briefing, but I could tell they were determined.

I felt that now I had to put my shoulders to the wheel in order to survive out there with the eight Argentineans and the crew in the pitch-black night. Soon the gale winds were up to sixty to seventy knots amid numerous pieces of drift ice in the bay. We all dressed in thermal jumpsuits, and I had a walkie-talkie radio. I briefed everybody on the quick-release system in the lifeboat, since I knew that once we had contact with the breaking waves, we'd have to unhook the boat fore and aft simultaneously and immediately. If it for some reason didn't work out as planned, the risk was imminent that the boat would end up hanging in one davit block only, and disaster would strike. Hence, I delegated for safety reasons two Tongan crew to oversee each block.

The *Lindblad Explorer* was still lying at anchor, and it was impossible to maneuver around the chain in order to give us lee on the port side since it was easy to lose the anchor holding ground in that kind of weather. The best would have been to pull up the anchor and stay adrift. Hence, the open lifeboat was lowered with the sea facing the bow, and I knew that each man tried to prepare himself for the absurd voyage. I was far away from happy, and there was no great joy in the moment when Bosun released the davit winch brake and the boat swung overboard into the stormy sea down below.

It was dark, and we gradually approached the surface of the sea with the engine running, and the lifeboat swung like a door knocker against the ship. The waves grew bigger, and then, suddenly, we plunged into the sea and smashed into the hull, and we were afloat. Just then, as I pulled the automatic release, without warning, a huge wave reared up out of the darkness and lifted the bow up. I thought, *God have mercy on us all.*

We were all drenched by the wave, when Tevita shouted at me, sitting at the tiller, "Peter, watch out for the swinging block!" His warning came too late, and in the next second, everything went black before my eyes, and I felt an incredible pain in my frontal bone as the block hit me between my eyes.

A moment later, I was back to reality, feeling blood on my face while trying to use all my skills to hold the lifeboat away from the ship's side as we pitched two meters up and down like an elevator in an attempt to avoid being smashed to pieces on the ship's hull. Finally, we were free.

I ordered the crew to be on standby forward to grab the gangway platform once we approached this one. Over the walkie-talkie, I called the *Explorer* to send the eight Argentineans down to the gangway platform for a quick boarding since I predicted that it would not be easy to keep the big lifeboat alongside the platform. I was right about that.

As we approached the gangway in the wildly pitching boat, I screamed into the wind and signaled to Ketoni to throw the gear in reverse. When we came within reach of the platform, I was barely able to keep control of the boat while the crew put out the boat hooks.

Then something suddenly went wrong. We lost control of the boat, and we were blown away from the platform while the crew tried to hang on with the boat hooks in an iron grip. They stretched out their arms to the maximum not to lose the grip, but they were unable in the high sea; hence, there was nothing to do but to make a new approach. To my irritation, there was no sign of the Argentineans yet in the gangway hall, which caused me again to call the second officer over the walkie-talkie, saying, "What the fuck is going on? Send the guys down to the platform!"

His reply made me more than furious: "Peter, it looks like they are scared of the pitch-black night and the rough seas out there."

I didn't know what to say. I was speechless about the entire situation and the ruthless sea conditions while the bow rose up on top of the next wave and the boat dove down. My confusion was greater than ever.

Gradually, the minutes crept by, though there was nothing that indicated the Argentineans made their way down the gangway platform. I hesitated to approach the gangway again until I was sure I could see the guys standing on the gangway, as it was too dangerous to be close to the platform while waiting for nothing to happen.

Now, seated at the tiller and waiting for the Argentineans, we suddenly collided with a solid, unseen wave; the water opened beneath us; and the bow dipped and swayed to the pulse of the sea. Again, all of us were soaked, and the unmistakable taste of salty water went down my throat. I grinned at Tevita and said, "My mom told me not to get my feet wet. I am going home."

The temperature had fallen perhaps fifteen degrees due to the wind-chill factor since the wind had increased. The air was freezing cold, and we all began to regret the mission as we were caught by the full violence of the wind while spray filled the air. However, there was more than enough to keep our minds occupied with the pitching lifeboat and the snow now whirling around us. I brought the boat as close as I considered safe outside the gangway while I again called up the *Lindblad Explorer* with the walkie-talkie, asking them what was going on with the Argentineans.

The second officer said, "They are all assembled in the main lobby, but they are giving us the impression they are scared to death to walk down the gangway to the lifeboat."

I was silent. I had no response to that.

Then, suddenly, somewhat after one o'clock, I saw them all walking down the gangway with horror in their eyes. I was only ten meters away from the platform but in very rough seas. I shouted to Ketoni, "Dead slow ahead!" as I tried to maneuver toward the gangway platform. "Good God, this is a nightmare!"

With God's help, in all our might, we managed to come alongside the platform while the elements seemed to go berserk. Three times, the boat was lifted up and hurled toward the platform as we all tried to keep the hull off the platform, which we only barely managed.

Trying to make myself heard again over the wind, I shouted to all of them, "Jump down quickly, you fools!" while the waves lifted the platform with a loud bang that shook the entire gangway. They all jumped into the boat in a state of panic and landed on top of each other at the bottom of the lifeboat flooring, and then I shouted to Ketoni, "Full ahead!"

In haste, the engine went up to its maximum revolution, and we heard the engine sound above the wind. We shot forward, plunging into the horrible pitch-black night with all the Argentineans lying higgledy-piggledy on the floor and crying while the bow of the lifeboat plunged in almost every wave. I was surprised at seeing those big guys crying.

I sat in the stern at the tiller as the spray burst over the bow and swept across the dark forms of the men huddling in the bottom of the boat. I wondered about the bad mood that had developed among us. I felt an important mission had been given to me: to bring those guys back home and get back on board.

Tevita was standing close to me since we had an agreement that we would assist each other with the tiller and the steering when needed. The job of the helmsman was to hold her as close as possible up against the wind as we sailed. This required constant vigilance, and it could hardly have been more unpleasant, facing the breaking seas and the intense wind from the side.

Meanwhile, the big searchlights of the *Lindblad Explorer* pointed the way for us toward the base, and the snow whirled in the glow of the searchlights. We had a handheld halogen searchlight powered by the lifeboat battery to spot growlers and whatever ice was ahead of us. The night was black, and we had to travel some 1.5 nautical miles until we were able to go around the outer rocks before we could change the course toward the small concrete pier that was the landing place.

None of us knew what to expect when we entered the open sea of Antarctic Sound. Our primary concern was the ice, but we didn't know really where it was, since the air was full of ice-cold spray that limited our visibility and also crystallized our thermal jumpsuits.

I shouted across the boat, "Keep a sharp lookout for growlers and ice!"

We were worried the ice conditions behind the corner and the open sea of Antarctic Sound could prevent us from approaching the small bay and the pier due to the easterly wind pushing all the ice toward Hope Bay and Esperanza. Our anxiety had a solid basis in fact. We felt insecure since visibility was close to zero due to the heavy snowfall and the sea spray that enveloped us.

Tevita and I sat together on the transom, trying to maneuver the big lifeboat away from the ice, and we were concerned about the crying Argentineans on the floor. They were weeping, some quietly and some loudly, and screaming to each other in Spanish, and they said prayers at the bottom of the floor, saying, "*Madre de Dios, por favor ayudame. Me no gusta morir aqui!*" (Please help me. I don't want to die here!).

Those were the unhappiest hours in my life, and fate seemed determined to thwart us, but if we were supposed to get those guys ashore, then we had to get our act together. The wind was picking up, the blizzard raged on, and the snow found its way inside the boat and to all of us. To bolster the courage of the Tongan crew and myself, I shouted into the wind, "Very well done, boys! We will make it!" but I could see they were exhausted by the cold.

By then, it was after two o'clock, and I felt the pier was from there to eternity, though it was not that far away.

Our progress was creeping at best, when the lookout in the bow shouted, "Ice! A growler straight ahead! Change the course!" I cranked the tiller hard over to starboard— so much that Tevita was nearly torn from his seat on the port side. We barely passed the growlers. The easterly gale screamed on, showing not the slightest sign of fatigue. A few minutes later, the boat rose to a particularly high sea from a wave that passed with weighty majesty beneath the lifeboat as we tried to judge the sea in the darkness. Suddenly, we were in the ship's searchlights, and the boat shone wetly from spray like brilliant electric sparks. It was now snowing heavily, and the temperature must have been far below zero. By then, we had a foot of water inside the lifeboat, and I shouted to the crew to start to pump out the water with the fixed mounted pump or bail it out if the pump was stuck from frozen ice.

The Argentineans shook at the bottom of the floor, and horror was clearly seen in their faces. Our thermal jumpsuits were icing up, and looking at my chest, I saw a one-inch red layer of ice covering the jumpsuit from the constant soaking in the brackish saltwater and from the blood on my face. Tevita said, "You look terrible!"

Furthermore, the spray combined with the snow to freeze into a mushy coating over the inside of the boat and on the heads and shoulders of the men. With the wind blowing at forty to fifty knots an hour and an air temperature of probably -15 degrees, the wind-chill factor was extreme and meant that a few minutes' exposure would numb and exhaust a man. I had an agreement with the *Explorer* that I would call them every fifteen minutes to make sure all of us were safe. As I sat in the stern, I could feel my hands begin to freeze. I had lost feeling completely in both hands. When fumbling with my radio in order to contact the *Explorer*, I accidentally dropped the radio onto the floor, into the oily bilge keel. What a disaster! Now we had no contact with the ship, and Tevita looked at me with accusatory eyes that said everything. I knew exactly what he thought.

I shouted to him, "Tevita, I have no more feeling in my hands! I have to put my hands under your thermal jumpsuit to warm them up!"

With force, I pulled down his jumpsuit zipper, and to my surprise, I saw he only had a T-shirt underneath, but I didn't care. I quickly put both my hands against his warm body, and he suddenly screamed as if stung by a wasp and said, "Peter, what the fuck are you doing?"

I shouted while the wind screamed to new heights, "Sorry, but you are my only chance to warm my hands for a while!" He finally agreed, and I kept my hands there until I got the feeling back.

Time dragged on. The wind furiously blew as the surface of the water was torn into foam, and the wave tops were ripped off and blown downwind. Making slow progress, we came closer to the Antarctic Sound and the open sea; the boat was lifted violently to the succeeding waves. Periodically, the waves burst over the boat, and some, like huge, slippery black sea monsters, drenched us. The conditions on board were miserable, and all of us were frozen and half stiff.

Our passengers at the bottom of the floor looked at us with suspicious eyes as Tevita and I tried to clear our eyes frequently from the salty water. We had faced the wind for an hour and a half, and our eyes refused to function properly; we found it difficult to judge distances, which was now very important. The rest of the crew were sitting on the floor behind shelter as much as they could with the Argentineans, with their backs facing the wind.

There was now plenty of ice around us. Large pieces of glaciers that had tumbled into the water floated on the surface. I waved and shouted to Ketoni, "Slow down more!" since I was not sure if we could safely navigate among the ice with the speed we had kept so far. The speed was the key factor. The last thing we needed was a penetration of the lifeboat hull.

Siua was lying in the bow, trying to control the searchlight, which became weaker. He was probably more soaked than anybody else on board, but so far, he hadn't complained much about his responsibility, though he was also covered with ice.

The immediate goal was now to find the point where we had to change the course to the southeast toward the station, but it was not easy. We drove slowly. Tevita and I debated how long it would take us to reach the turning point due to the poor visibility. Looking at the amount of ice around us, we worried about whether the ice conditions around the corner and in the bay might prevent us from approaching it. If we'd had our radio, then the ship could have informed us when it was time to turn, since I knew they were following us on the radar as much as they could, but I also knew we disappeared on the radar screen among the ice.

Our worries became quickly justified when the lookout in the bow shouted, "Plenty of ice ahead!" I swung the boat southeast, parallel with the ice, to search for a new opening toward the Antarctic Sound. In my inner self, I felt we had to continue for a few minutes more until we were sure we had reached the outer rocks that marked the corner of the bay.

Off to the right somewhere was the base. There were no lights to be seen from the buildings, which could have helped us a lot. Just after three o'clock, I played it by ear and altered course toward what I believed was the bay and the pier. The visibility became better, and the wind came now from the side, when all of a sudden, we saw some small lights from the station, which gave us a bearing toward what we thought was the pier area. I estimated we had some two cables to go to the pier. The cross sea on the port beam was the worst it had been, and through it all, the voice of the wind shrieked as we had never heard it shriek before. The spray broke continuously over, and all of us were as wet as we had ever been. The remainder of that night and our distance left to the pier seemed to be a never-ending story.

One of our Argentinean guests suddenly panicked. In Spanish, he shouted and screamed while our crew tried to calm him down. The rest of our passengers were sitting quietly, looking sometimes anxiously over their shoulders for land.

The wind now remained steady out of the east with occasional squalls to almost forty knots. We had hardly any more power in the handheld searchlight, and the darkness was complete but sufficient to discover that the bay was nearly clogged with ice floes and patches of brush ice mixed with growlers. It was a moment of disappointment. For several minutes, all of us stared without speaking at the ice ahead of us. How could we possibly penetrate that? Slowly, we continued forward with the wind on the port beam, pushing the ice. We looked ahead into the night with salt-rimmed eyes for the shadowy image of headland. I tried to make myself heard above the wind in shouting, "Try to look and listen for breakers pounding against the cliffs!"

I had a strange feeling that we could face problems while sailing through the shallow parts with underwater pinnacles on each side, and the visibility could hardly have been worse. The stars were blotted out, and snow continued to fall and was swept across the surface of the water. The navigational conditions were more than miserable now, and we crept with slow speed, pushing the ice, as Siua, in the bow, pushed the ice away with the boat hook. The sound of the wind howled above us together, and the confused sea ran wild while we strained every nerve in hopes of seeing the concrete pier.

It was a weird situation and a time of eagerness, expectation, and grave unspoken doubts. It seemed an occasion for excitement, even jubilation, that we almost had made it to the concrete pier, but we knew we might well be looking in vain. If the rocks and cliffs were there, then the pier should be seen any minute, we knew.

As we slowly approached, the sea began to calm down due to the ice floes. The ice gave us shelter. Then the deep rumbling sound of breakers reached us off to the right, and an occasional fountain of bursting spray shot skyward in the light of our dying searchlight as the ice rasped against the hull. The whole complexion of things suddenly changed. There was ice everywhere, mixed with dangerous growlers rolling in the sea. If the pier was blocked with ice in combination with the sea breaking over the landing area, there could be no thought of a landing, not there at least, for the boat would not have lived ten seconds in those breakers and that ice. It was something we didn't deserve—a needless cruelty. The landing area lay probably just in front of us, and all of us had to see it, especially our eight suffering Argentinean guests. Now that the journey was almost done, I shouted, "Pull out the boat hooks, and try to push the ice away from the hull!" I thought to myself, *this is a nightmare!*

So far, there was no sign of the pier itself in the darkness. I knew the pier well from before, but now it seemed I had forgotten what was to the left and the right of the pier for a potential landing area somewhere else instead. I clearly heard the breakers on the starboard side as well. We were close to becoming stuck in the ice floes, and the wind showed no sign of exhaustion.

I was motivated to do whatever was necessary to get the job done in the finest possible way, but how? My thoughts raced, and for a brief second, I thought of Shackleton's way of getting a group through a crisis, which I had read in the book *Shackleton's Way*: "Don't be afraid to change your mind when you see your plan isn't working." I thought, *If I show the logic of my changes for the better, then whatever I come up with, the crew and the Argentineans at least will know it's for their own safety.*

Danger is one thing, but danger plus extreme discomfort for a long period is quite another. Most people can put up with a bit of danger—it adds something to the challenge—but no one likes discomfort. Our discomfort on board was immense since we were all soaked with saltwater and freezing, and some were scared. I felt like a leader in hope—or did I?

I wanted to try different solutions, but what? I didn't want to feel that we'd neglected to try something that might have worked, so I said to Tevita, "We have about one cable to go"—bear in mind that one cable, or one-tenth of a nautical mile, was a lot under those circumstances—"but I think we have a problem. What do you suggest we do?"

Tevita said, "We continue through the ice, pushing the ice away with the boat hooks!"

I was possessed by an angry determination to see the journey through no matter what, and I told Ketoni, "Dead slow ahead," since we had ice contact, though no impact so far. Furthermore, I told everybody, including the Argentineans, who needed to be kept busy anyway, to use the oars and boat hooks to push the ice away from us.

Slowly, we made progress. The lifeboat moved forward while everybody pushed the ice. I remembered there was an underwater pinnacle just one hundred meters from the pier, and now I had no clue where it was. Also, I didn't know about the tide, if it was high or low. The tide down there is a maximum of some 1.5 meters.

We twisted the boat and struggled our way through the ice for nearly half an hour more with stop-and-go progress. Everybody knew that the boat was not built for those kinds of conditions, but since the impact of the ice was not too bad due to the continuous ice contact, we somehow continued.

Finally, there was the concrete pier, fully visible. The battle was half won, and I felt we were going to succeed. The Argentinians shouted in happiness. As soaked as they were, they stood up in the boat, showing their appreciation that the nightmare had finally come to an end. The odds against us had been great, but we were winning, even though our progress was painfully slow. The situation around the pier was exactly as we had predicted, and it was obvious we could only reach the pier by using lots of force and with willpower since the ice was packed around us. The easterly winds had compressed the landing area with lots of ice.

The wind was incredibly strong, and the boat was still pitching with the waves now from astern. To the right, the waves were pounding against the rocks, and I thought, *Thank God we didn't come too close to those!* For some reason, I aimed for the left side of the pier. There was lots of ice, but it looked as if there was a possibility to get our guests ashore there, even if it meant they had to wade ashore. As far as I could see, there were no other options, unfortunately. It was time for a last desperate attempt to come as close as possible to the concrete pier, so I told Ketoni, "Just very slow on the engine, barely enough to force the boat through the ice."

We managed to come abeam of the pier, and I tried to scream into the wind to Siua to take the boat hook to measure the water depth, but all of a sudden, the bow of the lifeboat unexpectedly touched the ground. Tevita, who was a creative man, told the Argentinians to jump into the water, and they all looked at me questioningly. They must have thought we were not serious as the Tongans pointed toward the water.

They realized we were serious, so they swung their feet over the side of the lifeboat and jumped down into the water. They stumbled ashore with the water over their knees and scrambled ashore one after another. In the light of our dying searchlight, they waved goodbye to us, and I told Prince, "Full astern!" I felt happiness and joy when I saw them all ashore.

It was still pitch black when we started our journey back home. The wind was still screaming in our ears, and I thought, *Oh my God, we have to go back the same way we came, around the cliffs and back into the open sea and the waiting Hope Bay.* I wrote later in my diary, "A more inhospitable place could scarcely be imagined!"

At the same time, our searchlight gave up and refused to work anymore. I shouted across the boat to Siua to go through the lifeboat emergency equipment and look for a torch or torches. I ordered, "Keep a sharp lookout for growlers and ice!"

Siua, who had been lying in the bow the whole time, was wet enough, so I told Sione to do the job on the way back to the ship.

Once more, we were out in the hostile environment, and the wondrous joy that had marked the landing only thirty minutes before was absent now. Hope Bay was for me an unfriendly place, and the sight of it now was ugly. Whatever was ahead in the way of rough seas and more, I knew we would make it back, even though we would arrive at daylight.

I was sitting, as usual, steering the boat, listening to the gale winds, and relying on Sione, who guided me, as we again fought our way through the ice floes. I wondered when we'd see the crack of dawn, and I tried to look at my watch, with difficulty, to see what the time was, but I failed since my hands were too stiff. I asked Tevita if he knew what the time was. To my surprise, he had almost fallen asleep!

I shouted in his ear and shook him. "Tevita, for heaven's sake, wake up! What are you doing?"

He said, "Sorry, Peter. You look vely bad in your face."

Later on, I became aware of what he meant.

I was more than furious about he almost slept. I was tired as well, but I had to have patience.

Finally, they found a torch, but unfortunately, it was weak since nobody had checked the emergency equipment for a long time. It was typical! An hour more at least, and then it would all be over.

The gale screamed on, showing not the slightest sign of fatigue. The spray continued to break over the boat but out of the starboard side. The boat had a coat of ice inside and outside, and all of us had a thin layer on our jumpsuits. We were all stiff and cold. Sione lay faithfully in the bow, soaked with saltwater, scanning the water's surface ahead of us for ice, while the rest of the crew huddled on the floor, except for Tevita.

We used a slow speed since growlers and chunks of ice floes were around. The gusts increased in violence and became so strong that we could hardly talk.

A few minutes later, we went around the outer rocks, and we set the course toward the *Lindblad Explorer*. The snowfall suddenly stopped, and in the distance, we could see the deck lights of the vessel. What a relief!

The ship's crew were scanning the water in our direction with their powerful searchlights, but we were still outside their range. We were now surfing with the waves from behind, and steering was difficult. The growlers were difficult to spot since they were behind the waves, but somehow, we were able to navigate among them. After a while, we were caught in the light of the searchlights, and night turned into day. We were fully illuminated and felt in better spirits. The rest of the voyage passed without incident.

At six o'clock, we finally arrived. The laborious work remained to connect the boat to the davit blocks simultaneously on the first attempt when the boat was pitching up and down. I shouted across the boat to tell everybody what to do. In my mind, I went through the operation several times, so I was sure about what to do.

As most of the deck crew on board watched our approach, including the captain, while standing on the boat deck, I shouted, "Dead slow ahead!" The blocks swung dangerously and wildly to and fro, and suddenly, we were right under the davit, all trying to catch the swinging blocks. Those were some exciting seconds! The lifeboat pitched heavily in the high waves, and I watched the deck crew handle the blocks fore and aft as they tried to connect them.

Then, suddenly, finally, we were hooked to the blocks, and a shock wave went powerfully right through the hull when the boat became airborne for a few seconds as the waves passed by. I thought the lifeboat fittings would be ripped off, but they weren't. Finally, we were on our way up to the boat deck and safety, and I felt relief. I took Tevita's hand and said, "Thank you, my friend, for all your help."

He said, "Peter, you're my friend, but you look terrible in your face."

I said, "What do you mean by that?"

Tevita said, "Go look at yourself in the mirror!"

Once we were level with the boat deck, the captain stood ready with an open bottle of Chivas Regal whiskey and mugs for all of us. He poured the whiskey into our mugs and said, "Thank you, Peter, for what you did. We all know it must have been a nightmare out there, but you made it." We said cheers to each other.

I was proud of what we had just accomplished, and we seemed to be a wonderfully happy family. Despite the discomfort and uncertainty, we'd had, there was an undercurrent of pride among the lifeboat crew. From my side, it had been a big challenge and a true nightmare.

During the past five hours in the stormy darkness, everyone had come to look upon me in a new light, mostly because of the demanding skill I had presented in handling a lifeboat in rough seas with lots of ice.

In my inner self, I knew that the horrible, wild lifeboat story in Hope Bay would fade away in the future. Yet I did what I wanted to do, and something drew me forward. Coming to my bathroom, I looked at myself in the mirror, still with a layer of ice on my jumpsuit. I couldn't see my skin since my face was black from the soot of the lifeboat engine and was covered with frozen, coagulated blood mixed with ice. I looked terrible, as Tevita had said.

The *Lindblad Explorer* sailed out again from Hope Bay to new destinies and new unexplored areas on the west side of the Antarctic Peninsula.

Chapter 16

Maxwell Bay

IT WAS 1974, AND WE cruised the Gerlache Strait, when Francisco asked the captain politely if we could sail to Maxwell Bay in King Georg Island in the South Shetlands, given that our schedule was flexible. I asked Francisco what kind of place that was, and he said while rubbing his hands, as he always did when he talked, "I was down here in the sixties with the Argentinian navy, and King Georg Island, the largest of the South Shetlands, is notched with bays on the lee side of the prevailing Drake gales and offers ice-free shelves of rocks where people can take a relatively easy foothold. It's a very proper place for beginners."

During the afternoon, we passed a great number of icebergs while entering Admiralty Bay. Some were very large, and one in particular was an overwhelming piece of art for everyone. It was difficult to express the impression it made with its size and its proximity to the *Lindblad Explorer*. It bore a weird resemblance to a man-made castle, all shaped in luminescent ice. The symmetry was strange, almost disturbing. Its square turrets surrounded a flat, smooth, almost regular top. Below, in the center, an arched entrance opened upon a central courtyard of ice. It was a large lump of floating ice.

In another few hours, its shape would have changed, and the likeness would have vanished. Standing on the deck in that freezing solitude and gazing up at those glassy blue towers and through that icy arch, I reflected that it was only by mere chance that any human eyes had happened to see it all. I found it hard to dismiss lightly. As we slowly approached and passed it close to starboard, we all stood amazed. It floated on into the waste of empty sea while we headed for Maxwell Bay.

The captain told me that in all his experience in the Antarctic, he had never seen an iceberg that had made so deep an impression on him.

While we sailed slowly into Maxwell Bay and looked in our binoculars, the most striking thing for beginners and me was that we noticed two stations at the far end of the bay. The bay didn't look particularly blessed by God or honored by men, but we had ahead of us a big group of houses, the Soviet Union's Bellingshausen Base. I was told that

Bellingshausen had always seemed a friendly place. More to the left was the Chilean base Teniente Rodolfo Marsh, also called TT-Marsh Base. In the 1990s, the base changed its name to Presidente Eduardo Frei. While we still sailed slowly toward Bellingshausen, looking for anchor bottom, I was told that on the other side of the bay, on our port side, were the rudimentary huts of the coming Chinese Great Wall Base for the future.

It looked as if the houses had been slapped together on frost-bound gravel built on stilts. Francisco told me while we scanned the two bases with the binoculars that this was an effective method of preventing snowdrifts during blizzards, as the snow-bearing wind was allowed free passage under the buildings. Furthermore, I could see among the buildings several snowmobiles parked in disorder, as if they had newly been abandoned, and a sign that pointed toward Moscow, saying it was 15,200 kilometers away. The Russians had no clue we'd arrived, nor did the Chileans.

We dropped the anchor in Ardley Cove, giving out four shackles in the water, with 0.2 cables from Diomedea Island and from the starboard side land. Every one of us was full of expectation since we felt the Russians would pay us a visit later that afternoon, and we knew there was plenty of vodka available. However, all of a sudden, the engine room informed us that they desperately needed a ball bearing, which the Russians probably could provide; hence, our Polish electrician, Anton, who spoke Russian, was assigned the mission to find a ball bearing at the Russian station.

Francisco and Anton went ashore together in a Zodiac, and Francisco tried to negotiate with the Chilean base commander to coordinate our passengers' visit to that station. Meanwhile, all of us were having a nice time in the lounge, waiting for Francisco's return and update about the day's program.

After several hours of waiting, we heard nothing from Anton, nor from Francisco. Unexpectedly, we heard a small helicopter, and the passengers and I looked out the windows to see what was going on. The tiny helicopter had a transparent glass cockpit. It turned out to be Chilean, and they started to hover just outside the port side of the lounge windows. Amid the noisy sound of the hovering helicopter, we saw Francisco sitting on the left side, waving to all of us in the liveliest way. It was obvious he was slightly intoxicated from alcohol; hence, we knew why he was so late. It was not really the proper way to return to the ship late as we waited to start to land the passengers.

However, from his serious waving, we understood that he wanted us to lower the Zodiacs and bring the passengers ashore. So we did, and Francisco flew back to the TT Marsh station. When the first boat came ashore, I was told over the radio that the Chileans were assisting our passengers at the small concrete jetty, welcoming everybody to their station. Yet there was no sign from Anton, whose mission was to get a hold of the much-needed ball bearing and return with it to the ship. We felt he probably already was part of the Russian base team, drinking vodka and dancing with them.

Anton also looked forward to visiting the nearby Polish station Arctowski on the island when our cruise schedule permitted. He felt kind of at home there, as he was able to talk in his native tongue, and his English was poor. He was good in German, and I mostly talked Swedish and German with him.

We all loved him dearly, and we all knew that after Anton's visits ashore to the east state stations, we would laugh ourselves to death at his innocent impulsiveness when he was drunk; he was so polite that one could almost get annoyed with him, and he beat his heels together when he greeted somebody. Unfortunately, he occasionally became the victim of almost merciless joking about his person due to his politeness, but he had his jokes too.

He was unique among the officers with his aristocratic look and his goat beard, and he was older than most of the officers. The strange thing was that nobody could find him when he was needed, because he sneaked away. The only way to find him was to call him over the PA system, to everybody's embarrassment.

Consequently, Anton had gone ashore to find a ball bearing, but we also knew that he wanted to go ashore to collect fossils and, most of all, have a blast with the station personnel, drinking and dancing with them, whenever possible. He deserved it since he was a hardworking gentleman. He had a real party when he visited his fellow countrymen at the Polish Arctowski station, but he was sometimes happy enough with the Russians.

When he felt there was a potential possibility to get a drink on one of the bases, he would put on his German Tyrol hat with the plume on the side and say, "I'll go ashore for a while to see if I can find some fossils." The plume-covered hat on his head was a clear signal to us that Anton was open to some fun. As we all knew, the Russians down there presented great hospitality, which meant a glass of vodka to the incoming guests, whether they were passengers or officers.

While all those events took place ashore, I was on board due to my upcoming watch from eight to midnight.

Suddenly, Francisco radioed from shore that we would stay there until midnight, and we would have twelve Chilean guests coming on board at 1900 hours for cocktails and a subsequent dinner. When I came up to the bridge, Tevita told me, "Peter, I was ashore, and Anton was dancing Russian dances and playing guitar on his braces!" Tevita was always inquisitive about things, but I became suspicious after what he told me due to the ball bearing that was needed.

I wrote the following in my diary:

> It was a wonderful evening, and the stars were twinkling from a clear blue sky, when we could hear on board the *Lindblad Explorer* the tones of singing people ashore. When the Zodiacs started to come back from shore, we heard laughs and singing from extremely happy passengers and singing people in the crafts. The first boat arrived with a bunch of happy passengers all under influence from the Russian vodka ashore. In one of the last incoming Zodiacs, Anton arrived, sitting only in his uniform shirt, playing on his

trouser braces and playing trumpet with one hand in his armpit, though it was very cold outside.

Our Tongan crew at the platform were forced to jump down into the Zodiac to prevent some passengers from falling into the water backward in their drunkenness, and they had to assist Anton up the gangway as well. To the relief of our waiting engineers, Anton proudly showed the needed ball bearing, along with a huge bowl of Russian caviar.

In those days, the officer on watch also assisted on the gangway platform, even though he was on bridge duty, but somehow, it all worked out.

The twelve Chilean guests finally arrived with a great tumult, as well as some Russians. Francisco came last on board with the Chilean station manager, and in the lounge, he grabbed the microphone with difficulty and warmly welcomed the guests on board. Anton had lost his aristocratic manners and was now, to everybody's surprise, dancing solo a Russian Cossack dance on the dance floor. The Russians joined in, and the American passengers applauded.

Though I was on watch, I could still sneak down to the lounge to participate in the wonderful event with the Chileans, the Russians, our passengers, and the Swedish officers. Everybody was dancing together. In those days, the rules were not as tight as they are now. That was my first evening experiencing the close relation between officers and the passengers and Antarctic base personnel. The evening was an absolute delight, and at midnight, we said goodbye to our guests. Then the *Lindblad Explorer* heaved her anchor, bound for the Antarctic Sound, the wild area.

At midnight, I left the bridge watch, taking my mandatory safety round in the ship, when I met John Green from England in the lounge. He was, as usual, drunk at that time of the late evening and the only person left sitting close to the beautifully shaped bar that was a copy of the hull of a pirate ship, with huge guns pointing toward the bar when it was closed.

He was a remarkable man with a gray beard, and he was an enterprising character and always found seated close to the bar and surrounded by ladies for some reason. His special trait of character was to greet all the incoming people late at the bar lounge. He sat at the end of the sofa close to the bar, pulling up the corners of his mouth and saying, "Hi! Come join us!" The bar waiter, Leif, and the bartender, Roland, also called Macki, ran the bar until the last guest left, drunk the whole time.

John Green was loved by everybody on board, and he was the most amusing man one could have found to talk with, but he was, unfortunately, addicted to alcohol. His nights ended at approximately 0400 hours and sometimes even later. However, still, he was always the first one to be manned and ready at the Zodiacs at 0800 hours, waiting for the Zodiacs to be lowered from the upper deck in the crane hook.

I will never forget his answer when I once asked him about his days and nights in Antarctica and how he had muddled through all his days down there in the past. He said,

"In all the world, there is no desolation more complete than the polar night. It is a return to the Ice Age—no warmth, no life, no movement. Only those who have experienced it can fully appreciate what it means to be without the sun day after day and week after week. Few men unaccustomed to it can fight off its effects altogether, and it has driven some men mad. I loved it all in all as long as I was there."

We had some seventy miles to the Antarctic Sound, and the pack ice was probably waiting for us somewhere south of Zele Rocks. The next morning, there it was: we saw the pack ice edge in front of us. The captain had obviously decided to go slowly throughout the entire night so he could be on the bridge when we met the pack ice. Like most of the passengers, I had never seen polar pack ice before. I was tremendously impressed by it, especially the excitement of dodging large floes. We passed a number of large icebergs, some of them more than a quarter mile square, which presented a majestic sight as they rode the swell with the seas breaking against their sides and leaping high into the air like surf pounding against cliffs.

The action of the sea had worn huge ice caverns in many of the bergs, and each breaking wave produced a deep booming sound as it rolled into one of the ice-blue caves. For one hour, we sailed along the edge of the pack, looking for a way through, but none could be found. Finally, we found a suitable passage through.

The *Lindblad Explorer* twisted and struggled her way through the pack for nearly three hours, making stop-and-go progress. Frequently, she was barely able to push her way through, and sometimes she was stopped altogether.

Though the pack ice in every direction appeared to stretch endlessly to all sides, it abounded with life in the open areas between the pack ice strings. Humpback whales and killer whales pointed their noses above the surface of the ice to look for whatever prey they might upset into the water.

In spite of our disappointing progress in the ice, the sun shone from a clear blue sky, and the decks were filled with passengers. Hope Bay was some fifteen nautical miles ahead of us, and we slowly but surely made our way through. Sometimes we were surrounded on all sides by dense, old multiyear ice floes, yet more often, we found only brittle, young ice in our path, and we could race ahead toward the indigo-colored water just beyond. Dead ahead, the dark streak of so-called water sky held the promise of a large patch of open water. The pack ice was almost through with us. We made slow progress, and suddenly, we had clear dark water stretching toward Hope Bay, and then we finally were through the pack ice.

We continued with full speed. At noon, we sailed into the bay, which was full of ice, and we made it without any problems.

Chapter 17

Downhill Skiing in Hope Bay, Antarctica, and Stuck with Both Anchors

WE SAILED INTO HOPE BAY on February 17, 1975, in the early morning hours, looking for the usual shallow seventeen-meter anchor position with a brisk wind present. The captain decided to drop both anchors to avoid dragging over the night, but that could cut both ways: in strong winds, the ship could start to drag both anchors, so they were crossing each other, and consequently, there was a potential risk they could be tangled together. When the anchors were down, he said, "That's it; now we stay here until tomorrow afternoon since the base personnel are invited on board, and let's hope she will not start to drag tonight."

However, during the night, the wind picked up to force 7, gusting to 9, but the anchor position was still fairly okay. The vessel was swinging heavily around the anchors.

The next morning, the weather was calm, with a blue sky, and Antarctica was showing its best face. I looked up toward the wonderful snow-covered mountains beyond the station, and I was suddenly taken by the idea of going for a downhill skiing tour from the 1,705-meter-high Mount Flora, or at least close to it. For me, it would be something extraordinary.

I wrote in my diary:

> I asked the second mate if he wanted to join me for this possible adventure. The second mate was a very quiet person, and in general, he had some retiring manners, but he happily agreed to my offer, so off we went. I said, "If we are lucky enough to come close to the peak, we will have about two to three thousand meters of downhill skiing back to the base."

While walking from the landing site, we saw five strings of husky dogs tied up in chains. The Argentineans were the only people who still used dogs down there among the various stations in Antarctica, and our passengers were booked for a dog-sledge tour in the icy, open landscape.

Our plan was to ask the station personnel if they could bring us up toward Mount Flora with a snowmobile, or as high up as possible. We knew that if they agreed to this, then we had to walk for another thousand meters upland so we could reach the highest part of the mountain.

It was a true challenge, and we decided not to tell anybody about our plans; otherwise, somebody would most likely freak out.

There were several red-painted buildings around, and we had no clue where to go or whom to ask to borrow ski boots and skis. We aimed for the biggest building and knocked on the door. An Argentinean guy dressed in an orange thermal coverall opened the door and looked at us questioningly.

Since neither of us spoke Spanish, we had some problems in explaining ourselves, but at last, he understood the reason we'd come. Luckily, he agreed to help us with our mission because we were both ship officers. He showed us where the skis and boots were to be found, and then he left to bring the snowmobile.

While he prepared the snowmobile, we tried on our boots and skis. They were not really meant for downhill skiing but were acceptable according to the existing circumstances, and both of us were ready to go. As happy as two schoolboys, we took off, sitting on the open-sided wagon, looking uphill for the approaching Mount Flora.

Coming closer to the point where the snowmobile couldn't take us farther, we could see that we had to ski down on a crusty snow. It was more ice than snow, and we knew that once we started to ski, we would go downhill with the speed of a missile on the crusty snow.

Both of us were experienced downhill skiers from the European Alps, but this was different from the Alps in Austria.

We had been driving for thirty minutes, when the snowmobile stopped, and the driver said something that we understood as "This is the limit. No farther with this vehicle." So we jumped down from the wagon, and we showed him our appreciation. We shook hands with him, and then he left us.

I told my friend, "That's it. Now we'd better start to walk upland." He gave me a look that could have killed. We started to climb the steep snow-covered slope.

I was in the lead with a brisk pace, and we estimated there was an hour and a half to walk in our heavy borrowed Argentinean boots with the skis on our shoulders until we reached the possibly highest part.

For the first thirty minutes, we trudged upward without a pause, and we soon began to feel the strain in our legs. Fortunately, the slope leveled off a little bit. The sun was shining, and our eyes started to suffer from the bright snow underneath us, because we were not used to this, and we had no sunglasses. I thought about what Francisco would have said if he'd known what we were doing. However, since there'd been no objection from the station personnel, I felt better in my inner self, and I felt like an Antarctic explorer for a short while.

We were both fit, and the weather was good, so we continued to walk upland, struggling to the top, and then we paused for five minutes. We also knew that walking too high up could be dangerous with regard to crevasses, as the driver had warned us.

As we looked downhill toward the base, the buildings were like small dots, and the scenery was spectacular, even though a bitter chill had come into the air. We had covered about 1,500 meters, and we were almost there.

We continued to walk on a steep slope, looking sometimes downhill and uphill and to the right. We saw an increasing number of crevasses, which made us concerned, but we stayed away from them. They were like a warning sign for us to be more careful, but still, we continued for a while. I suddenly spotted a crevasse off to the right, and looking ahead, we saw other crevasses in our path.

I could see that my friend did not smile anymore, nor did I, since we both could feel the strain more and more in our legs, and the sight of the crevasses made us stiff and caused us to stop and think. We decided we had finally reached the highest safe altitude for a wonderful ski tour downhill. Mount Flora was still up there, but we had walked higher than we first had thought we should.

We felt a special kind of pride, though many people would have called this a foolish thing to do. But when we looked down over the wide-open icy, snowy landscape, it was like being in a beautiful wonderland, and we felt rewarded for our efforts. The view from the top was an awesome sight, and we were stunned at what we saw. The sky was blue, the hills around us were like huge monuments, and the cold had increased, or perhaps we were beginning to feel it more. However, our eyes were suffering more from the bright snow that surrounded us, so we were better off taking it by the horns. We gave ourselves ten minutes' rest before we started the awesome way down.

The Argentinean skis were not easy to adjust to our comfort, but we made the best we could out of it for that kind of downhill skiing. It took a little more than ten minutes to get ourselves organized before we were ready to kick off. Even after such a brief rest, our legs had stiffened so that it was painful to straighten them, and we felt awkward when we moved them again.

I was ready, and I asked the second mate if he was prepared for our reward. He shouted, "Yes!" and then we took off down toward the base.

We had incredible speed from the beginning on the icy snow, and it was difficult to control the skis. For a moment, I couldn't see anything because I was snow-blind for a while. For a few seconds, I had no idea where I went. I knew the crevasses were around, and for a second, I thought, *where are they?*

The wind shrieked in my ears as we went down. We screamed—not in terror necessarily but simply because we couldn't help it. The sound was squeezed out of us by the mountain pressure in our ears and against our chests. Faster and faster we went—down, down, down.

Finally, we came to a flatter level, and our speed began to slacken. A moment later, we came to a halt. We were breathless, and my heart was beating wildly. We found ourselves laughing uncontrollably. Our laborious fifteen-minute walk upland had turned into a breathtaking triumph!

We were now almost halfway down. We looked up at the top where we had started from, and it seemed so far away. Then we kicked off again for the remaining part and the last challenge. Down again we went, and again, we screamed with happiness while the white snow whirled around us. After ten minutes of skiing, the ice-hard surface grew softer and became more like snow. To my horror, I could see that the glacier to the right fell sheer into the sea.

I shouted to my friend, "For God's sake, turn more to the left toward the buildings! The glacier is falling steep down into the sea!"

Before disaster struck for us, we turned, since our speed was now extremely high, and down below, I could see that the passengers were pointing at us.

The red-painted buildings came closer and closer, and suddenly, we came to an abrupt halt in a snowbank just outside one of the buildings. We were safely back down. The first person we saw was Francisco standing right in front of us, asking while rubbing his hands what we had been up to.

Like two guilty schoolboys and tired to the point of exhaustion, we explained. I said, "Well, we have been skiing down from just below Mount Flora. We thought we would become the first European downhill skiers on the Antarctic peninsula.

I could see Francisco was close to an outburst. He said, "You have been doing what?" Like schoolboys who'd gotten their shares, we thought it was better to be quiet now, and we remained quiet. Our snowmobile driver happened to pass by, and he just shook his head when he saw us, and we knew that Francisco had told him something we didn't want to know.

It was one of the finest days I ever had. It was a pleasure to be on that remote, hidden continent. Apart from our skiing tour in Hope Bay, the bay itself has always been for me a special place, though the weather gods sometimes gave us unpleasant surprises that I will never forget.

On February 18, 1975, I wrote in my diary,

> The following day, our passengers had a morning excursion until noon, and then we were supposed to sail. At noon, I was ordered to go to the forecastle and start to heave up the anchors.

To my horror, I saw that the two anchors were tangled together with seven shackles on the port side and eight on the starboard side. I thought, *how can we possibly get them back on board?* They were so tangled together that I didn't know what to tell the captain, who was standing on the bridge. Furthermore, our depth under the keel was now twenty-five meters instead of the usual seventeen meters we used to have. I said to the captain over the VHF radio, "Captain, I think we have a problem, and you'd better come down here. I believe you will not like what I see."

The captain heard the intonation in my voice, and in less than thirty seconds, he was down watching the disaster over the bulwark. Nothing was said for half a minute since we were both speechless. Now our only hope was that the weather gods were in our favor since it would take us at least two days to untangle the anchors, but how could it possibly be done?

Goran, who was at the time the chief officer, was called out to assist. When he saw the chains twisted together, he said, "What the fuck is this? I don't believe my eyes!"

Time was of the essence. On board we had two marine biologists, Soames and Jeremiah, who were professional scuba divers from England and the USA. At the time of this writing, Soames has been one of the foremost responsible persons for many underwater movies filmed in San Diego. Born and educated in the United Kingdom, Soames always has had, from his earliest years, an absorbing interest in the natural world. He earned a bachelor's degree in biology and later specialized in marine biology during his postgraduate studies. Early in his career, he began leading expeditions worldwide and lecturing on subjects of natural history and historical and anthropological interest. In the course of a decade, he led more than a hundred expeditions to remote parts of the world, from pole to pole. Subsequently, he worked as a scientist and administrator for the Australian government, setting up marine parks along the Great Barrier Reef. During that period, he published many articles in popular science journals and trade magazines, and he has been a contributing author to many books.

Jeremiah was a marine biologist and underwater photographer. He spent his youth in Hawaii and Puerto Rico. His photography career began with Des and Jen Bartlett and Ron and Valerie Taylor from Australia.

In the late 1970s, Jeremiah developed a flexible suit of armor for divers to wear while working around sharks. The suit often is referred to as a metal-mesh shark suit. Jeremiah later on specialized in human–shark interactions and manufactured advanced protective gear for professional, commercial, military, and qualified sport divers who must work or dive in hazardous conditions.

The captain said, "Let's find the ship's structural drawings for the forecastle and the shell expansion plan over the same," since our plan was to pull up both anchors onto the forecastle deck and there start to untangle them. But we had no idea if our forecastle deck could take the load of fourteen tons of chain, including both anchors, so we wanted to analyze the dimensions of the underlying deck stringers and frames before we sent down Soames and Jeremiah.

We came to the conclusion that it was a hazardous mission, but there were no other options, and the deck stringers could perhaps take the concentrated load of the chain coming up. Soames and Jeremiah then dove down in their dry suits to the anchors, which were at a seventeen-meter depth, with two six-millimeter wires, which they connected to the anchors. Then we slowly started to pull them up. My own notes say,

> Toward five o'clock in the afternoon, we had both anchors above the surface. As the hours passed, by sacrificing all our deck and engine crew power, we finally had them both lying on the deck, but still, all the chains were hanging outside. We were now maneuvering, and the bridge watch was distributed among us officers.
>
> It was now three o'clock in the morning of the first day, and we still had to land the chains up on the deck as well, which gave rise to a strength born of desperation since we were in competition with the time.
>
> As the first ship down here, we had no set schedule, but Francisco was rubbing his hands more than usual and gave us all the impression that he was close to a nervous breakdown. It was now more than twenty-four hours since we had started, and by a piece of luck, the weather gods were still with us, and both chains were finally landed on the forecastle deck, which seemed to hold the load.

The laborious and time-consuming work remained to untangle, shackle by shackle, the 450 meters of chain. Throughout the night and the next day, we worked nonstop. We had to ignore the tiredness we all felt. Slowly but surely, we made progress. We were able to clear ten meters of chain per hour, and the weight had to be distributed proportionally over the entire forecastle deck area before it could be brought down into the chain lockers.

Our strong Tongan crew, who took the worst punishment, were an incredible help, and they did not one time complain of exhaustion, even though we were in day number two in our attempt to lift up the chain.

As our work continued, the second day slowly passed by as the light began to fall, and high in the sky was a ghostly pale white image: the light of the moon shining through the clouds and reflecting up from the glacier in the far end of the bay. Goran and I worked side by side, sometimes sharing the bridge watch.

At last, on February 3, at six o'clock in the morning, forty-two hours after we had started, we had untangled everything. Shackle after shackle had disappeared into the chain locker, but we were not yet there, and on top of everything, there were dangerous signs of deterioration in the weather. The wind rapidly started to pick up.

Two hours later, the wind had risen almost to gale force. Hope Bay was far from beautiful now. We still had a big pile of untangled chain lying on the deck, and the *Lindblad Explorer* began to pitch in the easterly wind coming in from the Antarctic Sound.

Throughout the morning, the wind continued, growing stronger to seventy knots, and the surface of the sea was torn into foam while the temperature dropped far below zero.

The wind-chill factor was now decisive, and toward noon, the forecastle deck began to ice up.

Within an hour, the deck was frozen into a solid mass, so some crew were assigned to beat the ice off the deck, all the while fighting with the remaining chain. Noon, one o'clock, and two o'clock passed, and we had been working for forty-eight hours.

At six o'clock, the entire chain was down in the locker, and by the time we were finished, it was close to dusk, and the crew were utterly exhausted and wet. Some of the crew had had no sleep for more than forty-eight hours, and the hard work had drained their bodies of almost the last vestige of vitality.

The *Lindblad Explorer* finally sailed out from Hope Bay into the stormy Antarctic Sound, and I said a silent prayer to never come back to Hope Bay since too many strange things had happened there in that godforsaken bay.

Chapter 18

Prince Bernhard of the Netherlands

On February 8, 1976, it was brought to light that Prince Bernhard, the husband of the Dutch queen Juliana, had been accused of taking bribes from US aircraft maker Lockheed Corporation Aviation. To get contracts worldwide, Lockheed gave out bribes, some of which were received by Prince Bernhard from the Netherlands.

Prince Bernhard was well known as the crown jewel of the Netherlands' industry, and the Dutch government and Parliament appreciated his work to open and create new markets abroad for Dutch industry. However, he asked Lockheed for commission for a business with marine aircraft.

During an investigation into bribes in 1976, the director of the American aircraft factory Lockheed declared that Lockheed had paid Prince Bernhard $1 million with the intention that Prince Bernhard could use his position to recommend Lockheed planes for the Dutch air force and help Lockheed.

Prince Bernhard was concerned about the production of planes in the Netherlands. When the scandal broke, he denied the accusations against him and said he never had received money from Lockheed. A few months later, per a report of the Commission, Judge Donner ruled that Prince Bernhard had received $1 million. He had shown accessibility for indecent desires. Prince Bernhard then declared that he would break all his contacts with the air force. Furthermore, he would stop all his functions in business because Queen Juliana threatened to resign.

Since he was a chairman of the Bilderberg Group with David Rockefeller, Fiat president Giovanni Agnelli, Henry Kissinger, and James Wolfensohn, he was forced to resign in 1976 due to the Lockheed bribery scandal. The Lockheed scandal also shook Japan, and seventeen persons were suspected of corruption.

Prince Bernhard was never prosecuted for taking bribes, and on August 26 of the same year, he resigned from his royal duties. The scandal caused considerable political controversy in West Germany, Italy, the Netherlands, and Japan.

On August 26, 1976, a censored and toned-down yet devastating report on Prince

Bernhard's activities was released to a shocked Dutch public. The prince resigned his various high-profile positions as a lieutenant admiral, a general, and an inspector general of the armed forces. He resigned from his position on the boards of many businesses and charities, the World Wildlife Fund, and other institutions. The prince also accepted that he would have to give up wearing his beloved uniforms. In return, there would be no criminal prosecution.

The scandal was hard on Prince Bernhard, so he decided to go to Antarctica on the *Lindblad Explorer* to get some peace in his life, with the hope that the scandal would fade away. He landed at Ushuaia Airport in December 1976 in a Dutch royal Learjet, which he flew himself, along with many invited earls from Europe, to do an Antarctic cruise with the *Lindblad Explorer.*

The plane was parked at the small airport in Ushuaia. The officer on board the *Lindblad Explorer* stood on the deck, watching, as the plane touched down. The party embarked and got all the attention on board. The prince got the luxury suite, which was the cabin of the cruise director.

A couple hours after the eighty passengers had boarded, we got underway, leaving Ushuaia, the most southern town in the world, through the Beagle Channel with Prince Bernhard and his aristocrats standing on the port bridge wing, enjoying the glossy, calm channel. Everybody was in good spirits, and the prince enthusiastically followed the bridge procedures. It was obvious he was excited about the cruise.

He was a silent person and appeared to be a humble man, and his aristocratic German way shone through. He rapidly became friends with the ship's officers, and soon he was having lunch in the officers' mess room, conversing with them while the officers' mess room waiter, Selin from Ecuador, served them, going through the dining room with his serving tray of drinks from the bar. He did so with the knowledge of the passengers in the dining room.

Prince Bernhard was careful with his physics and did daily exercise on the upper deck, once in a while with the ship's staff. Prince Bernhard often sat on the aft deck alone, reading a book, and once in a while, he walked around, keeping a distance to people. He seemed always to be deep in thought. Every evening, he placed his shoes outside the cabin door for shoe polishing, and every morning, when he opened the door, nobody had polished them, because the housekeeping staff was not accustomed to that.

Everybody knew Prince Bernhard wanted to keep a low profile after the Lockheed scandal; hence, his party enjoyed themselves every day in the lounge until late in the evening. His party permanently occupied the round table on the port side of the lounge, and one could imagine he was trying to overcome his Lockheed worries through laughter and jokes with his fellow earls. Many of the ladies on board chased him, including the Swiss female owner of Bata Shoes.

The next morning, we had Cape Horn behind us, and the Drake Passage ahead of us was the calmest I had ever seen on several voyages.

The crossing of the Antarctic convergence, where the cold water of the Southern Ocean welled up against the warmer water of the South Atlantic, was of great interest to Prince Bernhard. The bridge officer on duty took the sea temperature every hour to figure out when we entered the cold water from Antarctica. At two o'clock the following afternoon, the sea temperature dropped quickly three degrees, and from then on, we announced, it was only a matter of hours before we would sight the first icebergs. Over the PA system, we announced that the first person who spotted an iceberg would be the lucky winner of a bottle of champagne.

Prince Bernhard continuously stood on the bridge, scanning the horizon with his binoculars for icebergs. The same evening, one of his earls spotted an iceberg on the southern horizon; hence, it was announced he was the lucky winner. As the ship altered course toward the tabular-shaped iceberg, we were welcomed to Antarctica by light-mantled sooty albatrosses that dove across the ship's bow, and the prince was delighted to watch them.

The master handed the bottle of champagne to the earl during the evening recap in the lounge, and a special dinner followed in the sparkling, luxurious dining room at the captain's round table.

It took two and a half days to reach the Boyd Strait, and the first stop was Hannah Point on Livingston Island in the early morning, which was an excellent place to observe wallowing southern elephant seals, fossils, and Antarctic terns. The prince went ashore in his high boots and a red *Lindblad Explorer* parka with his friends faithfully accompanying him.

The party returned happily on board after some two hours and were in a good mood. The *Lindblad Explorer* weighed the anchor and sailed south to Deception Island, which was only three hours away. We arrived at Pendulum Cove, drifting in the tiny bay, which had volcanic ash on the shore and in patches up the hills. There the passengers had a one-hour swim and bath in a hot tub of volcanically heated water. The water temperature frequently reached 40 degrees Celsius. Outside that area, the water was so cold one couldn't spend more than a few seconds in it.

The prince went ashore to have a brief swim and became the most southern royal swimmer in the world. Since there was a frequent shuttle service between the shore and the ship, he quickly returned on board with a happy face and was greeted by the Tongan gangway crew. That evening, he shared a bottle of champagne with his earls to celebrate his bath and swim in the hot tub.

The next place of call was Hope Bay, or Esperanza, as it was known by the Argentinians, who maintained there a full military base with husky dogs, even though that was specifically forbidden by the Antarctic Treaty. Because Argentina claimed that part of the Antarctic Peninsula, visitors' passports were stamped by the Argentine Army with immigration stamps into Argentine territory. That was the only place in all Antarctica where that was enforced.

When Prince Bernhard went ashore, the Argentinians lifted their eyebrows when they saw his passport.

Hope Bay is a beautiful place undoubtedly when the sun is shining on the impressive Mount Flora, where I, the previous year, had gone downhill skiing from an area close to the mountain.

On that cruise, the *Lindblad Explorer* visited numerous places in the Antarctic Peninsula before heading for Drake Passage and, ultimately, Ushuaia. Prince Bernhard disembarked in Ushuaia with a big smile and then took off from Ushuaia Airport in his plane, flying via Greenland to the Netherlands.

Chapter 19

The Enchanted Islands, the Galápagos, and Diving in a Cave that Almost Took My Life

AFTER THE COMPLETION OF THE Antarctic season, which ended in the beginning of March 1974, we cruised along the beautiful Chilean coast as the first expedition cruise ship ever in the inland sea waters of Chile toward the Enchanted Islands, the Galápagos.

In the beginning of April 1974, we made six cruises in the Galápagos Islands, sailing from Guayaquil in Ecuador, where we had six turnaround days. The islands are some six hundred miles west of Ecuador. Since Darwin's time, the Galápagos have remained relatively unmodified by man. Like Antarctica, they have been afforded natural protection from customary scars left by man. Through the establishment of a national park and the Darwin Research Foundation on Santa Cruz Island, the hope was kept alive that the plants and animals would continue to survive in their original state. Tourism in the Galápagos had to be done from a ship that covered the scattered islands and allowed the passengers to disembark in small boats, which also included our ship crew. In a way, visiting the Galápagos has had more impact on me than visiting Antarctica. The Galápagos have a tremendous feeling of peace and make one feel as if he can communicate with the animals.

The scuba diving was a thrill and a marvelous experience in that underwater world with a visibility of two hundred meters. We always cleared into the Galápagos Isla San Cristóbal (Chatham), and then we sailed straight north to Tower Island (Genovesa), passing the equator, where King Neptune and his court paid us a visit with a marvelous equatorial ceremony. The island is one of the most northern islands in this archipelago. Tower Island, or Genovesa Island, was named after the Italian city of Genoa, in honor of Christopher Columbus. Referred to in English as Tower Island, it is a shield volcano in the Galápagos. This island is as well-known as Bird Island, which was named for the large and varied bird colonies that nest there.

On April 6, 1974, I wrote the following in my diary:

> In the very early morning, we dropped the anchor in Darwin Bay in Tower Island, which is the most northern island in this archipelago. The program for the day said that at 0800 hours, the first group goes ashore to climb Prince Philip's Ladder, which is an extraordinary steep path that leads through a seabird colony full of life up to cliffs that are twenty-five meters high, and then the passengers would go across to the eastern cliffs, where the focus was mainly to see the abundance of the male frigate birds and to see red-footed boobies, Nazca boobies, swallow-tailed gulls, and storm petrels, and indeed, the island was the perfect place for scuba diving due to its clear water.

The diving is excellent there around the year, and it's one of the best places to see hammerhead sharks, whale sharks, mantas, and eagle rays. Schools of hammerheads are common there all year long. Sometimes the conditions can be rough for scuba divers, and a diver is far from any help.

I had recently been training in the ship's swimming pool to learn to scuba dive with the first engineer, Hans, who was a former Swedish Navy diver. He taught me every day for a week the basic scuba diving rules in the pool and how to deal with situations if worse came to worse.

Since all the scuba diving tanks were occupied by our passengers, the only tank left was a small one of seven liters, which I used. I was thrilled to, for the first time in my life, fulfill my dream of seeing the secret underwater world, and I was prepared for my first dive.

One morning, after my night bridge watch, the chief engineer, Ake, and the chief mate, Goran, decided to go for a cave dive and asked me if I wanted to participate. They had heard there was an exciting cave good for diving. The cave was approximately fifteen meters of depth. I joyfully agreed to participate.

I was told there was one tunnel down and one going up on the back side of the cave. I, however, never had a chance to see all the hammerhead sharks, whale sharks, mantas, and eagle rays on my first dive because I was more or less immediately introduced to a dangerous, ridiculous dive—and it was my first dive ever after the swimming pool introduction on board. The morning turned out to be a disastrous brand-new underwater experience.

The policy was "Passengers first," and when they all had gone ashore, the crew were next to go. We had ten Zodiacs on board, and by manipulating Francisco, we managed to get a Zodiac for our own pleasure for a while that morning.

Walking down the gangway, wearing my white T-shirt, I had no idea that morning would turn out to be the devil's dive for me. Cave diving is an easy way to die; it is one of the most challenging and potentially dangerous kinds of diving. Oh my God, what a stupid idea, but I didn't realize that it was a risky dive.

When all the passengers had left, the three of us took off to the northern side of the islands. Frigate birds hovered above us. We knew that to attract females, male frigate birds would blow up their bright red throat pouches as females passed overhead. The sky was full of frigate birds.

We dropped the anchor at the entrance of a small, narrow passage with crystal-clear water. The chief engineer told me they would go first since they had torches and I had none, and they would wait for me down there. The cave was approximately fifteen meters in depth. The five most recognized cave-diving elements are as follows:

1. Training
2. Guideline
3. Depth rules
4. Air management
5. Lights

I had zero knowledge of these five rules, and still I dove down.

Furthermore, I carried on my back an oxygen tank of seven liters only—good for some twenty minutes—and on top of that, I had no diving skills. It was from the beginning a suicide dive.

I was still in my own little world when sitting on the gray Zodiac pontoon, fiddling with my straps, trying to quickly catch up with the other two guys, who were already by then halfway down. I knew I was late, but they'd told me they would wait for me inside the cave since they had the torches. I trusted them, and when I was ready, I jumped down into the clear water with my seven-liter scuba tank on my back.

I easily found the entrance to the cave, which I entered. It was a kind of tunnel that took me down to the cave. A few minutes into the dive, I found myself inside the cave, and there was no sight or light from the torches of my friends. In that moment, every muscle in my body froze in horror because I knew I was trapped in a pitch-black cave. My worst fear was coming true, and I was not ready to handle it. Getting lost inside a cave is a powerful fear. I could not believe I was trapped in a cave with minimal oxygen available.

I felt around, trying to find the opening with my hands, but wherever I put my hands on the walls, I felt only huge lobsters and no exit out. A million questions went through my head, and it seemed an eternity passed. I tried to figure out how much oxygen I had left, and something in my brain said, *don't breathe too much.* I figured I had about fifteen minutes' worth of gas, but panic slowly rose in my body, as I feared having barely any gas left, and still, I couldn't find the way out.

As my fear rose, I damned the other two guys for not waiting until I had reached the cave as well. Claustrophobia and disorientation began to affect me. I was in deep trouble.

There was no light. The darkness that surrounded me can't be described. I was not able to see my hand in front of me. It was a horror that took its toll on me. My eyes strained to find the way out, but I failed. I couldn't believe I was trapped in a cave, and I asked myself why I was unable to find the way out.

The lobsters on the cave side bothered me and scared the hell out of me because I felt them wherever I put my hands. Dozens of different plans came into my head in my attempt to find a solution to survive that nightmare and find my way out. I thought about how young I was and wondered if that was where my life would end, in that cave. What a horrible death. There was virtually no visibility. Sometimes I could see a little bit more, and several times, I had to feel with my hand what was up and down by feeling the oxygen bubbles ascending. I asked myself why I had no visibility since the water in the Galápagos was crystal clear and caves were less susceptible to wind and currents. The answer came soon.

As I was slowly moving and fiddling around in the cave, I by accident saw a tiny ray from the sun slightly up to the left. Though the ray was tiny, I grabbed that ray with the speed of a missile, and I found the way out.

Ascending to the surface—some five meters in a cave tunnel and an additional ten meters to the surface—felt like an eternity. I quickly ripped out the double hose regulator from my mouth to breathe fresh air at the surface, and I praised God I had survived.

A look at the oxygen meter showed I had air for only approximately five minutes left. In five more minutes, I would have died.

The Zodiac floated in front of my eyes like a blessing. The chief engineer and Goran sat on the pontoon, asking what had happened to me. I had no answer as I climbed into the Zodiac since I was still in a state of panic, and my body shook as I finally sat down on the pontoon. Thinking about what I had just experienced was terrifying, and the enormous stress I had encountered erased some of the shocking details; hence, I was unable to speak with them, but I knew I would never go cave diving again.

I spent a lot of time afterward going through in my mind why I had gone on the dive. I had been close to running out of oxygen in the cave and not making it back alive. It was a miracle I'd survived. After the dive, analyzing my memory of the incident did not help me to understand what had happened. I couldn't believe I'd made the dive without a safety line. It was just unbelievable.

The lesson was learned: there are no shortcuts to cave diving, only shortcuts to the grave.

We pulled up the anchor, and I drove back to the *Lindblad Explorer* in silence.

Chapter 20

Diving with Hammerhead Sharks outside the Devil's Crown in the Galápagos

THE DEVIL'S CROWN IS A crater located northeast of the coast of Punta Cormorant in Isla Floreana.

The depth outside the crater ranges from six to twenty-four meters, while the inside depth reaches only three meters. The Devil's Crown is a great place for observing manta rays, schools of fish, octopuses and other reef species, and hammerhead sharks.

On April 12, 1974, we arrived at Isla Floreana for a full-day program. We dropped the anchor to the west of Punta Cormorant at the designated anchor spot.

At Punta Cormorant, there is a landing beach where the sand on the beach is tinted green due to the presence of green olivine crystals, and there were lots of sea lions and a lagoon with a large number of pink flamingos. Post Office Bay provided visitors the opportunity to send postcards home without a stamp via the more-than-two-hundred-year-old post barrel.

Lars-Eric had hired a freelance photographer from Stuttgart, Germany, who was a commercial photographer and a pioneer in producing documentary movies. On the morning of our arrival, the photographer asked our first engineer, Hans, who was a professional diver from the Swedish Navy, if he would volunteer to make a dive just outside the Devil's Crown and film the hammerhead sharks with his sixteen-millimeter underwater camera, which was a huge, clumsy apparatus weighing lots of kilos. To my delight, Hans asked me if I wanted to participate in the unusual dive, assisting him if the hammerhead sharks turned out to be too curious during the approximately twenty minutes of diving and filming. I gladly agreed to get the diving experience. We knew sharks were potentially dangerous wild animals that were difficult to predict accurately. The late Jacques Cousteau, who was many times with us and in the Antarctic, said during one of his lectures, "The only predictable thing about sharks is that they are unpredictable."

Both of us knew the risks as we sat on the Zodiac pontoon together before we descended into the crystal-clear water. Prior to the dive, we rehearsed signs and body language to communicate in any eventuality that could occur some twenty meters down below with those beasts. I felt I was in good shape, though I felt it was kind of a shaky dive, and I hoped the dive would not lead to a fatality with whatever was down below.

From the Zodiac, we only saw some turtles. I was thrilled when we jumped backward from the Zodiac into the crystal-clear water, and as soon as the water closed over my head, I thought about what I was doing and about the sharks down below.

Hans had the clumsy, big sixteen-millimeter film camera, and I was armed with a broomstick to push the sharks away if needed. In an effort to remember what happened down below, I had my small Kodak Instamatic camera, but the camera turned out to be no good due to the water pressure. Luckily, Hans had his Nikon camera with him.

I was thrilled as we slowly descended and hit the sandy bottom with our knees. We both had twelve-liter oxygen tanks, which were good for approximately thirty minutes. As we stood on the sandy bottom with our backs toward each other, looking at the crystal-clear surroundings, we saw not one shark. It was an empty, marvelous underwater world with a sandy bottom underneath, some coral, and nothing else.

Suddenly, a hammerhead shark appeared from nowhere, and we immediately focused our attention toward the lone big, peculiar shark. We had a mission: to film these monsters. In case of close contact with them, I had my broomstick. The Lindblad Travel Service from New York needed a PR movie to present the Galápagos' underwater world.

Unexpectedly, in the distance, we saw hundreds of the gigantic hammerhead sharks pop up just like that. We stood tightly back to back at the sandy bottom with seemingly endless 360-degree visibility, excited about what was going to happen next—or were we facing disaster? The sharks circled closer and closer around us as Hans filmed with the clumsy movie camera, and I wondered if we were safe down there in Devil's Crown. I was down there in a place where no one could find me if things went catastrophically wrong, and just the name gave me goose bumps as I stood twenty meters at the bottom, waiting for something terrible to happen, such as one of our hands being bitten off in a rare attack. Hammerheads were not considered particularly dangerous to humans, but why else would they have circled around us?

We knew hammerheads were aggressive hunters, though they did not actively seek out human prey. They are defensive and will attack if provoked, and we surely did not provoke them. One of the sharks suddenly made an attack and missed me by just inches as I fumbled around with my broomstick and forced my stick into the side of the shark. I found myself continuously pushing the beasts away with my wooden broomstick as their side fins touched our bodies, and to my delight, they kind of withdrew. Still, I felt we were condemned with the unpredictable and intrusive sharks as we tried to please the photographer from Stuttgart.

Hans, who was standing tightly behind my back, filming, told me with his body language by elbowing me in the side to push a beast away since the shark was too close and dangerously curious. Given that I had no depth-gauge meter, he pointed at his wrist and his depth-gauge meter, stating that the time we had spent in the Devil's Crown was soon to expire. The clock was ticking, and we slowly—back to back, as usual—rose to the surface. But we did not anticipate that the sharks would closely rise with us all the way to the surface; therefore, I found myself still pushing them away downward with my broomstick as we slowly rose the twenty meters to the surface and the safety of the Zodiac.

The sharks followed us all the way from the depths as we came closer to the surface, and we knew that the sudden violence of a shark attack would be a terrifying experience for us. For a split second, I thought, *Diving with these beautiful, dangerous creatures should only be done by professionals.* None of us were really professionals, though we knew a lot about the behaviors of the sharks. Close to the surface and the Zodiac, the sharks became more aggressive, and we both panicked, screaming to each other while trying to get the big, clumsy gray camera onto the Zodiac pontoon. We felt the sharks' fins touching our legs, and at any time, we expected that one of us would scream in pain when a shark bit us as we saw them swimming around at the surface. When the camera was safely on board, both of us practically flew on board as the sharks circled closely around our Zodiac.

Chapter 21

Diving Down to the HMS *Bounty* at Pitcairn Island

TWO HUNDRED TWENTY-SEVEN YEARS AGO, on April 28, 1789, twenty men of the British warship HMS *Bounty* mutinied against their captain, William Bligh, and took over the ship. She was rated by the admiralty as a cutter, the smallest category of warship. This is probably the most famous nautical mutiny in history. It has been the subject of countless books, and the term *Captain Bligh* has passed into our language as a synonym for a tyrannical, overbearing authority.

In the late 1780s, the British navy was made up of more than six hundred ships of various sizes and types. Yet the admiralty must have considered none of them suitable for the planned breadfruit expedition. For that purpose, a ship had to be found that could be converted to a floating greenhouse. Carrying capacity in relation to size was the main criterion.

Six merchant ships were considered, and the admiralty chose the *Bethia*, which was new, having been built two and a half years earlier at Hull. She was a three-masted, full-rigged, snub-nosed ship of only 215 tons' burden and had so far been used only for coastal trading. The Navy Board bought her on May 23, 1787, for £1,950 and, on the suggestion of Sir Joseph Banks, renamed her *Bounty*. She was refitted, and the bottom of the hull was sheathed in copper plate to protect the wood from teredos and other wood-boring worms, a new and expensive feature. The procedure had first been tried in 1761.

The *Bounty* was incredibly small when one considers her mission. She was ninety feet ten inches long, with a beam of twenty-four feet four inches and a draft of eleven feet four inches. She had no superstructures; all accommodations and facilities were below deck. Her three masts varied in height from forty-eight to fifty-nine feet. There were three yards on the fore and mainmasts and two on the mizzenmast. Under the bowsprit, there was a figurehead portraying a woman in a riding habit.

The nine members of the *Bounty*'s crew who eventually settled on Pitcairn Island, the Pacific paradise, will forever be associated with the ship, whose remains still lie there to this day.

The *Bounty* sailed under command of chief mutineer Fletcher Christian into the bay called Bounty Bay. There were twenty-eight people on board: Christian, plus eight other former *Bounty* crew men; twelve Tahitian women, some of whom were married to the Britons; six Polynesian men; and a baby. Christian chose Pitcairn because it was an obscure island on the British charts, believed to be uninhabited, and he thought the chances of the British navy finding them there were nil.

Christian and his men took everything useful off the *Bounty* and then scuttled the ship and set her on fire. It sank there; its wreckage still lies at the bottom of the harbour at a depth of some twenty meters.

The Pitcairn Islands are a loosely grouped handful of tiny islands in the remote South Pacific, farther from any continent than any other inhabited island. The islands and Pitcairn are the last British colony in the South Pacific and the most isolated British dependency, apart from Tristan da Cunha in the South Atlantic Ocean. The rocky main island was settled by the infamous mutineers of the HMS *Bounty* and their Polynesian companions from Tahiti.

The story of the *Bounty*, with its incredible mixture of adventure, violence, and mystery, had long fascinated me, and now I was heading toward Bounty Bay.

I wrote on November 15, 1977, in my diary,

> Sailing from the west through the entire South Pacific islands, we suddenly saw this famous island of Pitcairn rising slowly out of the sea, and it gradually took on the shape of a bowing island with the white of the breaking seas.

Most yachts approach Pitcairn Island westbound from the Galápagos, Easter Island, or South America. Given that Pitcairn Island lies just outside the normal southern boundaries of the southeast trade winds and tropical storm zone, it is an ideal place to visit before the season for French Polynesia, offering reasonably easy and quick passages to the west. When I first visited Pitcairn Island in 1977, I was captivated by its beauty and its history.

We passed close to the Young's Rock, watching the rocks and the island from the north, as we headed for Bounty Bay and Adamstown, which was uphill to the east of the island.

Prior to our arrival at Pitcairn, one year in advance, we had announced our intended arrival. As we now slowly approached Bounty Bay, looking for a safe anchor bottom, to our surprise, suddenly, longshore boats appeared in the huge breakers that rolled into the bay; thus, they pitched up and down and disappeared behind the rollers until they were out in calmer seas, heading for us. We could see the huge swell and breakers breaking into Bounty Bay in our binoculars from the bridge as a possible obstacle for our passengers' Zodiacs when they approached the surf and the inner bay at some stage.

Once the longshore boats were close to us, they waited until we had anchored up, and then they approached us, pitching slowly up and down in the swell, keeping themselves away from our hull.

From the bridge wing, I stared at the boats down below, and my first impression was that there was a friendly atmosphere. They all waved to us, looking up toward the bridge wing in happiness, since our ship had long been expected to arrive at Pitcairn Island. Every upturned face from the boats wore a smile. I was captivated by what I saw, as were my fellow shipmates. We asked the islanders in the boats about the customs and immigration rules, but they referred us uphill to Adamstown and the public hall house, where one of the *Bounty*'s anchors was on display.

The purser went first ashore with a Zodiac driven by a staff member, passing the rough breakers safely with the ship's documents in a waterproof bag, to clear the ship into the island and stamp all the passports. Though Pitcairn was administered by the council and a commissioner on New Zealand, the clearance was made there. Once the clearance had been obtained, the purser radioed the *Lindblad Explorer* to say the passengers were free to go ashore.

To pass the treacherous breakers with safety, the standard procedure was to wait while keeping a constant watch for the right type of wave approaching from behind and then speed up, surfing along ahead of the breakers into still water in the inner bay. It was an exciting experience. For safety reasons, each Zodiac had only eight passengers when passing the huge breakers.

As the passengers came ashore, they walked slowly up hills on a tiny, sandy path that wound its way up toward the main square in Adamstown. When it was my turn to make my way ashore with the first engineer, Hans, we asked some on Pitcairn about the location of the *Bounty*, but they were unclear as to its exact location. Anyway, they gave us an idea about her location (in the 1970s, there was no GPS position available; hence, everything was pure assumption). A Mr. Young suddenly approached us from Pitcairn Island. He was a descendant of a *Bounty* mutineer, and he offered to dive with us to show us the approximate location of the remnants of the *Bounty*.

As the afternoon dwindled, the first engineer, Hans; the second engineer, Talufa; Rob, a marine biologist from Rhodesia; and I made plans to go for a dive with Jerry Young in an attempt to locate the remains of the *Bounty*. The Pitcairn residents had told us to anchor up the Zodiac beyond the surf on a depth of three to five meters, giving us some landmarks to find the wreck site. Unfortunately, there was no time for a reconnaissance dive due to our short time available. We knew there were lots of currents by the significant difference in the tide-water range calculated by the harmonic constants, which was the accurate way to figure out about the tide-water range in those days. The HMS *Bounty* had been burned by the mutineers, and its wreck was exposed to the full ocean swell and current; hence, it would be mere luck if we could find her.

Off we went on our secret dive mission in Bounty Bay. We took our visual cross bearings from predetermined landmarks given to us by the residents, and then we anchored up the Zodiac on a depth of some five meters. I was thrilled, and all of us were equally excited when we dove in pairs, armed with a crowbar for all eventualities. Who knew what we would discover? I dove with Hans.

Coming down in the clear and shallow water, we searched everywhere for the remnants of the *Bounty*. We knew she was somewhere around, but where? Suddenly, out of the blue, we found some remains of her spread out over a coral plateau, heavily encrusted. With a huge portion of luck, Hans saw the ribs of the *Bounty*, which was unbelievable.

We knew the remains of the *Bounty* had lain undisturbed on the sandy bottom until 1957, when a National Geographic Society diving expedition led by Luis Marden had located them. To my knowledge, the *Bounty* had been resting in peace since Luis Marden located the remains in January 1957, until we discovered the remnants on that dive twenty years later in 1977.

We waved to each other to come share the awesome spot, and when we were all assembled above the ribs, we were stunned while looking at the *Bounty*'s coral-covered bones. Trying to whisk the coral sand away as much as possible in an attempt to see her ribs, we then saw the incredible remnants of some ballast blocks, which were scattered throughout an area between large rocks. They were partly buried in the sand, but one could still locate them. As we slowly and carefully searched and crisscrossed the sandy bottom, part of a cannon was suddenly visible in the coral sand. It was barely visible, but it was there—an astonishing discovery that we kept as a secret among ourselves. The *Bounty* had only four guns and ten swivel guns on board.

Digging in the coral sand and whisking the swirling sand away, we suddenly saw a special type of rectangular coral measuring some fifty by fifty centimeters. It caught our immediate attention and made all of us excited, as it was so different from anything else submerged in the sand. We felt it was something beyond the ordinary and knew we were above the remnants of the HMS *Bounty*. As we brushed the sand away, we became speechless, as we could see there was a clear pattern of the ribs of her remnants.

We felt that under the coral was the copper plating covering her underwater hull, and we used our crowbars to free with force and lots of work a piece measuring some twenty by twenty centimeters. Why we did so was to some extent unclear to me, but Hans was determined to get his hands on that piece. As we worked our way to free the piece of coral, we figured out it was indeed a part of *Bounty*'s copper plating.

We were aware that this was an illegal dive, though it was 1977; therefore, we made minimal disturbance to the site. We knew we were looking at a world-famous heritage and, therefore, could touch nothing. However, we broke the rules. Holding the coral piece in my hand, knowing the copper plate was underneath, while trying to keep my position steady above the site and against the current, looking at the historic wreck was an undeniably incredible feeling. We then slowly returned to the Zodiac, bringing with us a twenty-by-twenty-centimeter copper plate covered with coral.

Back on board, Hans, after following all the rules of the art and using all possible cleaning methods, finally showed us the copper plating. I could not believe what I saw. The same evening, Hans sat in the lounge, breaking off small pieces of copper plates and giving them to the passengers. What a remarkable day and evening.

Chapter 22

Ushuaia and an Absurd Voyage
in the Beagle Channel

COMING BACK FROM ANTARCTICA AFTER crossing Drake Passage, we headed for Ushuaia in the Beagle Channel in Tierra del Fuego (the Land of Fire) in the southern part of Argentina. It was February 1975.

Ushuaia was our turnaround port and was one of the strategic staging posts where international flights could repatriate our passengers and bring in new ones, but such ports of call offered only a hint of an ordered pattern. Since we were in Antarctica for about four months, for the austral summer in that hidden continent, Ushuaia became for us a home port that we all loved dearly. The population of the town was no more than approximately three thousand inhabitants. In 1975, that wonderful town was still a pioneer town under colonization, and one easily got the feeling that the town was a subject for a southern gold rush.

It's surrounded by some impressive mountains, which are partly snow-covered year-round, and will charm you in the sunshine, chill you in the rain, and take your breath away at the slightest provocation. The air there is incredibly unpolluted, and in the windless nights, the air is a prism, and the Beagle Channel is a mirror. At the time of this writing some thirty years later, the air is still uncontaminated.

Visitors to the Ushuaia almost always flew in via Rio Gallegos from Buenos Aires and then to Rio Grande in Tierra del Fuego and traveled by bus from Rio Grande to Ushuaia, which took some six hours.

In the early 1970s, there were not many tourists to be seen on the streets, except for a few backpackers who stumbled off into the few shops. It was still a hand-to-mouth business, and tourists, especially foreign tourists, hadn't quite caught on yet. Trucks and cars rumbled off, loaded with children and junk. People greeted each other on the street as though they had traveled just two miles from the town rather than a couple thousand miles from another continent. On gusty nights of the summer, when the wind blew wildly off the Beagle Channel and the rain assaulted the waterfront as the lights of Ushuaia gleamed wetly through the rainfall, it felt as though you were arriving somewhere noticeably remote and oceanic, barricaded against all the mountains behind by the stormy seas from Drake Passage a little bit farther from the channel.

The hundred or so people in Ushuaia probably nearly fainted at the sight of the *Lindblad Explorer* arriving alongside their new pier in their town. There was just one main street, which was paved and bisected the town in the upper part and lower part, as the town had grown up on the hillside. The land to the north of the street was a lot steeper than the southern side. There were barely any trees to be seen in the town, except when one looked up toward the hills; then the land exploded in rich vegetation and forests.

It occurred to me that the forest up there was exactly the kind of forest that appeared in grim tales of mythology that included half-human creatures I had heard about as the familiar wolves and witches of my childhood.

However, a wonderful atmosphere rested over the entire town. Bear in mind that we called on Ushuaia more or less every fourteen days during the north European winter season from early November to late March, which was the summer season down there. But in the month of December in Ushuaia, when Christmas was standing outside the door, the town gave everyone a feeling of affection and a true Christmas feeling that was rare to find anywhere else. Whenever one walked on the main street, one could smell the wonderful scent of wood smoke coming from the small number of steak restaurants, each of which had a fireplace at one end of the room. The atmosphere in the restaurants was romantic, and the places were enchanted.

Ushuaia had something we looked forward to and always had during our overnight stays in those years: fresh king crabs, locally called *centolla*, at Tante Nina's restaurant. Tante Nina was a special lady; she was of German origin, and she helped us with all kinds of problems we had. She guarded the sailors' money when needed.

Upon our arrival in Ushuaia, after the passengers had disembarked, the hour of freedom finally came. Coming back from Antarctica, after battling the unpleasant and harsh weather conditions in the Drake Passage, we all went ashore like a unified family, and each of us felt it was something we deserved.

Staff, officers, and crew went ashore to enjoy the delicious, sought-after centolla dish. In the 1970s, king crab was already under a unique protection in the Beagle Channel, but there in Ushuaia, it was one of the main dishes.

The staff always joined us whenever we went ashore in Ushuaia, and it was a joy to be together at Tante Nina's small centolla restaurant on the main street, where we could sit down, recapitulate the experiences from the last cruise, and make new plans for the upcoming one. Tante Nina, the owner of the restaurant, was more than pleased to see us visiting her place, and now and then, she gave us a welcome drink: the mandatory pisco sour, which was a blend of two-thirds pisco, one-third lemon juice, a bit of sugar, and egg white shaken with crushed ice. Five or six of them can drop an untrained drinker to his knees. Take my word for it. She then would serve us the best centolla she had, along with a good Argentinean white wine.

However, in February 1976, pilotage in the Beagle Channel suddenly became compulsory, as Argentina claimed ownership of the islands of Picton, Lennox, and Nueva, which created the Beagle Conflict, a border dispute between Chile and Argentina and the scope of the maritime jurisdiction associated with those islands. The conflict brought the countries to the brink of war in 1978, and the Argentine port of Ushuaia, located on the north shore of the east Beagle Channel, had no direct free way to the Pacific Ocean through Argentine inshore waters.

The *Lindblad Explorer* had been sailing undisturbed up and down the channel without a pilot on board until that season. The problems between the two countries persisted and grew gradually bigger, and there was conspicuous tension in the Beagle Cannel, which was especially noticeable in the nighttime, when we sailed in the darkness either outward or inward bound. Frequently and suddenly, we found ourselves escorted for a while by one or more blacked-out torpedo boats coming rapidly from nowhere, from either Chile or Argentina. They stayed with us for a while and then took off as quickly as they'd come, like fast ghost boats. They played with us a game.

It was strange to see what was going on in the Beagle Channel. As we navigated at the beginning of the Beagle Channel, close to Isla Nuevo, Isla Lennox, and Isla Picton, with the ongoing dispute, we never actually know for sure if we sailed in Chilean or Argentinean waters, and the reporting system was for us a burden and confusing. To please them both, we reported our arrival and departure to both the Chilean and the Argentinian military commands.

In 1977, when the tension rose to its peak, the Chileans transferred a major part of their navy down to the southern part of Chile, with all the torpedo boats hidden behind the islands in case a war broke out. The bridge command on board the *Lindblad Explorer* could feel the tension building.

However, as the tense affairs continued between the countries, the *Lindblad Explorer* was the only foreign cruise ship in the waters that continued faithfully to sail undisturbed in and out of the Beagle Channel. Each time we entered the channel, we faced more penetrating questions from the southern Chilean military command situated in Puerto Williams, close to Paso Mackinlay.

A few years later, the prolonged dispute was passed on to the International Court of Justice in the Hague in Holland after the pope tried to resolve the differences between the countries but, unfortunately, failed to solve the problems. War was not far off, when the boundary dispute suddenly and swiftly was solved in the Hague with a judicial decision that ended up benefitting Chile.

However, before the territorial dispute was solved, we were instructed suddenly by the Argentinean authorities to pick up accordingly an Argentinean pilot close to Cabo San Pío to bring the *Lindblad Explorer* to Ushuaia and vice versa. The suddenly instated rules were to put pressure on Chile because Argentina partly claimed the pilot rights to the Beagle Channel for vessels calling on Ushuaia. Both countries deployed military forces, moving to the brink of open warfare with a frenzy of diplomatic activities. That was the most dangerous phase of the Beagle conflict.

For us, there was nothing to do but cope with the new rules, whether they now came from Chile or Argentina. We were later told that due to our new and frequent presence as the first cruise ship in the Southern Hemisphere and the Beagle Channel, we played an important role and partly were a reason for the new and sudden pilot problems in the area, because tourism in Puerto Williams and Ushuaia was a new and fast-growing business. Therefore, the pilot question became a subject in the Beagle Channel.

On the night of February 15, 1976, at 2300 hours, approaching Cabo San Pío, we waited excitedly for our first announced pilot from Argentina to board, though we knew perfectly well how to bring the vessel all the way to Ushuaia and through the narrows of Paso Mackinlay, which was, at the narrowest part, no more than three cables, or five hundred meters, wide.

Unexpectedly, we saw a blacked-out black-painted torpedo boat coming in from the starboard side, and the prevailing thought on the bridge was *This can't be true. Why is a torpedo boat bringing the pilot?*

The boat came alongside, and the pilot boarded. When he came to the bridge, the captain wished him welcome on board, but we were quickly brought down to earth when we saw him, as this first official pilot was no more than a drunken fisherman with a brand-new, shiny cap full of gildings.

He looked like a retired navy admiral; he wore a white knitted pullover with big holes on both elbows, and he smelled so fishy that one got the impression he had been dragged up from a cargo hold on a fishing trawler in his drunkenness. Nevertheless, he was our pilot, and as such, we politely had to hand over the control to him. The vessel was due for Ushuaia first thing the next morning at 0700 hours, which meant the speed was adjusted for that ETA (estimated time of arrival).

At four o'clock the next morning, I entered the bridge for my sea watch. The second mate, who was the outgoing officer, instructed me to keep a watchful eye on the guy, and then he left the bridge. His advice turned out to be wise. I stood with my coffee mug in my hand, watching the odd pilot's behavior. I became skeptical about the guy, and in silence, I watched the pilot as we slowly approached the narrows of Paso Mackinlay.

After I had finished my coffee, being sufficiently awake, I saw that our course was ten degrees wrong as we approached Punta Mackinlay. It was supposed to be well on our starboard side, but it was not. Mackinlay Point was dead ahead, and the underwater rocks were only a couple cables ahead of us in our course line.

Trying to follow the newly established pilot rules, which meant being polite to the pilot, turned out to be a difficult task. I long-suffering stood watching and waiting patiently for a course change given by the fishing admiral, as he was for me, but nothing happened.

The fishing admiral was sitting peacefully in the bridge chair, and on top of that, his head occasionally nodded off. He was unaware of what was going on ahead of the ship.

I thought, *I'll give him a few more seconds to react before going into action.* Ultimately, I had to break the Argentinean pilot rules in the Beagle Channel, as disaster was closing in. My judgment of our acting pilot was null and void, and besides, my blood was reaching the boiling point.

Tevita, who was at the helm, was looking at me with begging eyes that said, "Do something," so I ordered Tevita loudly and clearly, "Rudder port ten degrees."

Obviously, the pilot, or the fisherman captain, as he probably was, felt immediately our course change since he was close to falling off the high chair, and then he came with heavy objections to my actions. To my understanding, he had no clue how serious the situation was and where our actual position was. A brief look in advance at the calculated tidewater situation from the harmonic-constants tables for the area showed that it was low tide, which meant additional caution was necessary for a safe passage. I doubted our pilot was at all aware of that. My conclusion was that it was impossible he knew about the approaching danger, so I continued to navigate myself.

As we were now in the middle of the narrows, heading for the next point, Punta Esposo, keeping a parallel index of two cables off to the starboard side from that point, which was still about four cables (seven hundred meters) away, the fishing admiral became suddenly hostile for incomprehensible reasons.

As a twenty-eight-years-young man, my Spanish was at the time not the best but was sufficient to understand his wrath and his highly sophisticated swearing in his own language, which he now practiced toward me, and it became too much. He continued to swear like a trooper, and I was convinced he must have felt himself bypassed. Furthermore, our pilot insisted he should be in charge of the remaining voyage and continue to navigate the *Lindblad Explorer* through the narrows and toward Ushuaia.

As I bypassed him, giving Tevita direct helm orders, he started to interfere by giving him new commands that caused Tevita to become confused about the situation. At that stage, I had already made up my mind, and I considered the mission of our pilot or whatever he was, including the newly instated Argentinean pilot regulations, terminated on the bridge with immediate effect until we arrived at the Ushuaia port.

I took it for granted that our pilot had an instinct for self-preservation and knew when he was defeated since I thought he must have been aware of his grave mistakes. Obviously, he was not that kind of a man, so my biggest problem was how to somehow persuade him to leave the navigation to me for the rest of our voyage. After all, he was drunk!

In our second round, during the tight navigation, it unfortunately came to blows. I became convinced that the fisherman admiral's glory was probably hurt, since he placed himself in front of me, insisting that he was still in charge and giving orders to the helmsman. I realized that haste was now important, given that his actions were totally unacceptable to deal with as we approached the narrow part.

money in an Argentinean bank. The sum had not yet been mentioned. I was deeply surprised and confused about the news, and so was the agent.

It was incredible that I was sitting there as a negotiation object while the lawyer was clearly squeezing money out of Broström, along with the smiling, corrupt police commissar. Furthermore, we never got to know the name of the lawyer, which was hard to believe in that tangled skein. I was pleased to hear that the company in Gothenburg was more than supportive in the peculiar situation. I guess they didn't want me to breathe my last breath in an Argentinean prison, because it was well known that the junta in those days were experts in astonishing the world.

The agent left and promised to come back if there was any news. As nightfall came, I was more than tired, and I looked with suspicious eyes at the barrack bed in the corner. As no other options were available, I fell asleep with a smelly blanket covering my body and without a pillow.

In the early morning hours, after a sleepless night, the guard offered me a cup of coffee and nothing more. I received no news during the morning. I just sat looking out the small window with steel bars, waiting for some positive results from somebody.

Due to the conditions in Argentina in the 1970s, there was no doubt many lawyers were always on the hunt to attack the dignity of whomever they could for profit. They discovered rapidly one who had become unpopular for one reason or another, and they acted in the blink of an eye so they could be rewarded with money. The family members of lawyers, when they realized exciting things were to happen, quickly and immediately reported this to them with the hope they could themselves get some money out of it. It was an ill-will circle.

Even though to my knowledge, as I was told, a counter allegation was filed against the unknown lawyer, he immediately hit back by saying, "If the money is not paid out, then the prisoner will remain in custody!" Presumably it was believed he was a man of power.

Behind the desk in the Ushuaia police station sat a mustachioed police commissar in his mid-fifties, smiling and rubbing his hands, convinced I was an easy prey. He was probably right, and it was apparent he was updated about what was going on, based on the many phone calls to his room. I damned myself that my Spanish was insufficient to be able to understand his phone conversations.

A number of cases like that had probably taken place in the past in that country under the government by the army, and my case was an easy one since there was a cruise ship alongside in Ushuaia due to sail the next day to Antarctica. They knew well that the *Lindblad Explorer* couldn't sail without a minimum number of manning officers on the bridge, and I was one of them.

In the late afternoon, our local agent came back, this time accompanied by the smiling police commissar. He said, "Would you like to hear the good or the bad news first? Progress has been made, my friend!"

A spark inside me ignited my temper, and I was all for immediate action, so I turned my attention toward the pilot, instinctively grabbed his left arm, and faithfully escorted him with force from the bridge. I had to drag him over the doorstep out to the open bridge wing and the fresh Beagle Channel air outside, which I believed he was in a great need of, all while he was pointing his finger at the gildings on his cap, telling me he was the pilot. I closed the bridge door from inside with a subsequent bang and locked it.

Due to the circumstances, I called the captain immediately and informed him of the reason for my actions. He said, "It's okay. Just continue as usual to Ushuaia." Upon hearing his words, I felt relieved because he'd defended my actions.

As the pilot all of a sudden found himself outside the bridge door, I believe he must have felt extremely upset, because he was knocking so much on the door and the window with both hands that I thought he would break the glass, which would mean even bigger problems, so I gave him a smile due to the entire episode. In my opinion, the pilot was running off the rails. Tevita was laughing so much that he almost choked. I told Tevita, "Stop laughing, for heaven's sake! God damn it, don't upset the pilot more than he already is. I might face big problems once we arrive in Ushuaia." I didn't know that my assumption would turn out to be justified. The bridge became once again peaceful, which was a blessing, and after a while, the pilot disappeared, and who knew to where?

At 0700 hours, we went alongside the berth, and I continued with my mandatory duties, when I suddenly saw from the bridge wing our pilot hurrying ashore. I thought, *there is mischief brewing in the wind.*

At nine o'clock, when I was standing in my shower, I suddenly heard knocking on my bathroom door. I couldn't believe somebody had had the courage to enter the cabin when the door was closed, since there was an unwritten rule about privacy in the cabins. Suspicious, in the midst of my shower, I opened the door just little bit and found myself looking into a rifle barrel carried by a threatening army soldier. Stunned, I said, "What the heck are you doing here?" I must have said something more since the soldier behind the rifle then pressed the barrel up against my stomach, which caused me rapidly to calm down. I was speechless, and apparently, he was a man of few words. After such an astonishing experience, I knew now for sure why the pilot had hurried ashore; as I had suspected, he was revengeful.

Then an army officer appeared from behind my bathroom door, along with the fisherman pilot, who suddenly stepped forward and placed himself safely behind the back of the soldier. Without any doubt, his nasty joy was evident as he gave me the same smile, I had given him before when the bridge door kept us apart. So, there I was, standing nude in my shower, with the barrel of an automatic rifle pointing toward my stomach. I thought, *this is un-fucking-believable. I should probably never have given him that last smile after he was deported to the bridge wing.*

With a hawkish voice, I said, "This is a foreign vessel with immunity, and you have no right to be here without written permission from at least the Argentinean junta or whoever they are!" I was fuming and trying to control myself, but I quickly figured out that none of them understood my English.

It was indeed a peculiar situation. I decided to step out from the shower, but before that, I kindly asked them for permission to dress myself. I believed I would then be escorted to an uncertain destiny. It was not a surprise to me when I was told we would go by car to the police station to investigate the pilot's accusations toward me.

On the pier, there was a waiting military jeep with an additional escorting soldier sitting comfortably in the rear seat. I was brutally told to sit down next to the soldier, and of course, I was trying to analyze my situation, feeling worried. At the police station, I was taken into a room with a huge sign on the door: Commissary. There I was introduced to a mustachioed policeman who must have been the commissar. He looked at me from behind a big table with a big smile. The local agent arrived as well.

The pilot, in his eagerness, without warning, started to talk immediately in Spanish to the commissar and insisted I had committed a crime against the Argentinean pilot rules in the Beagle Channel by kicking out the pilot from the bridge, which probably was the nearest approach to the truth that I could figure out. I gave my situation a good thinking, and I thought, *what a miserable drama I ended up in!* It was easy for me to pick up his accusations, even though my Spanish was poor, but to my surprise, the commissar told the pilot to keep his mouth shut.

Later on, I was authorized to speak, and I told them the truth. I told them their accusations toward me were wrong, in my opinion, even though I knew I had not much to put up against these people. I protested emphatically against the pilot's pathetic reason for why I was there. I clearly informed the police commissar of the reason for my actions: the pilot had ended up on the starboard bridge wing because he had undoubtedly been under the influence of alcohol and had jeopardized our navigation and the safety of the vessel. Unfortunately, the commissar didn't listen to my words, which was amazing.

Then our local subagent suddenly confronted the police commissar but was firmly told to stay out of it, as he had not been involved.

The agent lapsed into a nervous silence. To my astonishment, I was suddenly informed through the agent that I was to be detained until further notice. I informed the police commissar, staring and pointing my finger straight at his eyes, that I was unwilling to accept that, but my response only brought a smile to his lips. Oh boy, I was indeed in South America. The agent left, and I was eventually escorted to the cell where I would stay, and God only knew for how long. A more inhospitable place could scarcely be imagined!

As the hours dwindled away, two unknown people from the Ushuaia authorities unexpectedly paid me a visit and asked me questions in limping English about the story, but I refused to make any comments since I thought it was better to keep my mouth shut. They, however, continued to explain to me some things with the hope that I could understand their message. Their message was that for some reason, they suspected something illegal with the story, and then it suddenly occurred to me instantly that they, in their poor

English, were trying to tell me that the entire situation smelled of heavy corruption from Buenos Aires at a higher level. They informed me that it was possible the higher level in Buenos Aires was a lawyer who for unknown reasons had been informed by someone in Ushuaia about the situation; hence, he'd become involved because he could smell money without delay.

In the afternoon, the phone was obviously going hot in the police commissar's room regarding my case, because I could hear him talking since, I was not too far from his room. It was clear to me that the unknown lawyer in Buenos Aires demanded money for my release through the police commissar in Ushuaia, and the fee they demanded was beyond reality. I thought, *Oh my God, what a mess!*

While the sun was setting over the mountains and splashing Ushuaia and the surrounding mountains with warm colors, I was sitting in my prison cell, looking out through the steel bars at the passing pedestrians. I thought perhaps they were heading for Tante Nina's famous centolla restaurant. In my dreams, I ate king crabs with a bottle of Chablis white wine, which I had been looking forward to. I had no clue that in that moment, the Swedish ambassador to Argentina became involved in the remarkable story, which meant fast actions took place behind the scenes.

As money was obviously involved due to attempted blackmail, the situation finally ended up on the ambassador's table in Buenos Aires. Our female agent Astrid in Buenos Aires had contacted the Swedish embassy and the Broström group in Gothenburg, who had management of the *Lindblad Explorer*, about the dilemma.

Astrid was everything for us, assisting us with all kinds of matters and needs, and she was a big help in that delicate case, which had been completely blown out of proportion.

As all parties involved outside the town of Ushuaia could see, the police commissar had rapidly smelled money, and for that reason, he'd alerted the lawyer, who was more than cooperative. The situation smelled of corruption from miles away! How could the lawyer otherwise have been on the ball about a story that took place thousands of miles away from Buenos Aires? It might be left an open question, but it was assumed that the lawyer was a friend of the police commissar.

Corruption was in bloom in Argentina in the mid-1970s, and regrettably, it had affected the ship and me. I found myself in a bizarre situation still with lots of details to be resolved including whether or not I would spend the night in that jail and, if so, for how many days I would be there. I still didn't know the outcome of my imprisonment. However, it looked like it would culminate in that way. For the first time, I doubted I would leave that godforsaken place in the near future.

After some ten hours in the jail, I became undoubtedly worried in thinking about my future, whatever it meant. While my mind was distracted with that, I suddenly received a visit from the local agent, who told me that the Broström company in Gothenburg was discussing the matter with the Swedish ambassador and the agent in Buenos Aires, who in turn was negotiating with the lawyer on behalf of the company to deposit the requested

I said, "In what kind of way? I'd like to hear the good news first."

He said, "The good news is that you can leave the jail tomorrow if the conditions are met—that is, the bail must be paid tomorrow before the late afternoon. If not, you will continue behind the bars. And the bad news is that the police commissar says he will move heaven and earth if these conditions are not met."

The agent said the matter had been vigorously debated in Buenos Aires for the last hours, and there was no way around but to pay the predetermined sum to the lawyer. When I questioned the agent about how much money we were talking about, he said, "He demanded an astonishing sum of thirty-one thousand dollars," and once again, he pointed out that if the money had not been deposited in a designated bank in Buenos Aires by tomorrow afternoon, then I would accordingly remain behind bars for an unknown period of time. I turned pale when I heard that.

The next problem was that our new incoming passengers would arrive by late afternoon tomorrow, and we were then supposed to sail at 1700 hours for Antarctica. The police commissar continued to sarcastically smile, and I bet he understood every word the agent had told me.

No progress was made that day, as expected; hence, I spent my second day and night in that godforsaken prison, waiting and waiting. I asked myself if the company really was prepared to pay the money without my having to pay it back. I understood that the company was keen to get me out, which made me more than grateful.

Later, it was verified that the Swedish embassy in Buenos Aires had declared there were no other options than to muddle through with the corrupt prevailing rules in Argentina, though it was illegal.

After two nights in the Argentinean jail, I was finally allowed to walk out from that nightmare, and I walked down the street to the berth and the *Lindblad Explorer*, bewildered with questions in my head and pleased I was worth $31,000. From a distance, I could see that Tevita stood at the gangway as an AB on watch. When I arrived, he looked at me, which caused me to say, "Why on earth did you laugh at the pilot when he was behind the bridge wing door? One of the reasons I ended up in jail was because you couldn't control your happy-go-lucky life!" I felt I had to say that, though I knew it was not really his fault.

For the next coming hours, I became an object of attraction for many people due to the remarkable event.

The next morning, I was told the money transferral was still a topic of discussion in Sweden. At least the captain was cool when we discussed the matter, but a big portion of extraordinary luck was needed before the deadline expired, which was in the late afternoon. Still, there was no quick formula to the problem in the near hours. Afterward, I wrote in my diary, "I feel myself worried about the afternoon. Are they going to pay the money or not? I can only wait patiently." After all, one blessing was that Broström in Gothenburg was trying hard to prevent the ship from being detained with regard to the safe minimum certificate, which required one master, one chief officer, one second officer, and one third officer. Hence, they were eager to get the situation sorted out and to avoid the vessel's being detained and my returning to the jail.

At three o'clock in the afternoon, there was still no positive news from the agent in Buenos Aires. For me, the clock was ticking, and it did so too fast, in my opinion. I was convinced I shortly would have to return to that godforsaken prison. As the hours dragged by, my misery deepened, and I thought never had there been a worse afternoon in my life.

Finally, somewhat after five o'clock, the local agent came with some wonderful news: the money could be transferred—but not until tomorrow sometime.

My first thought was *What is the lawyer going to do, since he clearly dictated the terms through the police commissar?* However, the police commissar agreed that I could stay on board, but the vessel was not allowed to depart the harbour until the money had been deposited.

As the next morning was dwindling away and throughout the afternoon, the captain eagerly waited for confirmation that the $31,000 would be deposited in a bank in Buenos Aires. Fury was rising among all of us, and I was about to lose all hope, when, at five o'clock, there suddenly was a message from Astrid that the money had been transferred and would be available the next day. We all heaved deep sighs of relief, but it was not over yet, as there was a four-hour time difference between the two continents, and the lawyer had made it clear that he wanted to be sure by verifying the transaction the next morning. I was more than happy.

To my astonishment, adding to the sweetness after the last events, the radio operators, Jack and Ove, had made arrangements that evening with the agent to rent a timber lodge up in the mountains for the crew to enjoy a barbecue prepared by a couple gauchos, who would bring whatever local girls they could find, in order to give appetite to life in the lodge. I thought it was a fabulous idea since we apparently had one more night in Ushuaia due to the circumstances.

A bus was rented to bring as many of the officers, staff, crew, and local girls as possible. A formal announcement was unnecessary since news of the upcoming event spread like wildfire among everybody.

Off we went in the bus. We stopped at a dependable place to pick up the girls. I had no idea who the organizer behind this was, but the girls just popped up, and I had no objections!

Shortly, the road started to narrow as it climbed. We were told the bus ride would take close to an hour since it was a narrow gravel road. Everybody started to sing on the bus, and the increasingly out-of-tune singers unsteadily passed a bottle of whiskey back and forth and shouted out songs of obscenity while the walrus-moustached driver laughed with delight.

We stopped for five minutes, as somebody had to urgently urinate, while the declining sun for a moment bullied its way through the clouds, and several shafts of celestial light fell across the landscape so that the Tierra del Fuego Mountains seemed like Eden. Eight hundred feet below, I could see the Beagle Channel shining like a mirror while many of us were urinating and laughing.

There were small tea-coloured streams coming down from the higher regions, and the surrounding trees, covered with light moss, looked for the best place to steal what was left of the sunlight from nearby competitors. One tree dominated that section of forest—a great, straight-trunked giant that rose above all the others like a monstrous stalk of broccoli. A kind of warm, organic fog steamed up off a tea-coloured stream to one side.

We continued the bus ride, and half an hour later, we arrived at an inviting timber lodge enveloped by the wonderful smell of a wood fire. The crowd in the bus tumbled out with the girls clinging to us. Also, with us was a small blonde stewardess from Finland, who was an attractive girl. She was married to our wine steward on board, who was a nice and quiet man. Unfortunately, he was unaware that his wife had become the mistress of another person on board.

We were met by a gaucho on horseback. He wore a poncho and a wide sombrero hat. We also saw a barbecue table with a big, open grill stove surrounded by kerosene lamps, fully loaded with the most delicious grilled Argentinean beef steaks one could have imagined, which were ready to be handed out to all of us. I thought this was for sure to sugar the pill after all the problems we'd had.

A pisco sour welcome drink was served amid soft Argentinean music in the lodge. The girls were soft and had a seductive way of behaving, and there was an unmistakable feeling of adventure hanging in the air. They were there to please us, so they did. Somebody suddenly sneaked away after a while with one of the girls so they could be undisturbed for a while, and he returned relaxed with a smile on his lips.

The stars were twinkling in the sky, and the air was intensely clear, with purity that was perfect except for the smoke coming from the grill, which whet our appetites while the stars shone from a crystal-clear sky, along with the shining moon, making the place romantic. One of the gauchos was singing and playing melancholic, poetic Argentinian music on his guitar. The girls were affected by the incredible atmosphere, and they sank into the arms of our happy-go-lucky officers and crew.

As the night steamed, everybody became more than slightly intoxicated, and once in a while, one could see a couple dancing slowly, tightly together, hugging and kissing each other under the twinkling stars, and then they'd disappear behind the corner or a tree outside to have sex.

At two o'clock in the morning, the vote was unanimous: the sweet hours were over, and it was time to board the bus for the one-hour ride back to the *Lindblad Explorer*. Our walrus-moustached driver was sleeping, unconcerned in his best dreams, on the first row of seats with his legs spread out. He was brutally awakened by the sound of laughing girls and singing crew members who walked unsteadily into the coach. Pleased with the surprising and wonderful experience, we all fell asleep during the bus ride to the ship.

Now, as I write this some twenty-seven years later in Iquitos, Peru, where I live, reading my old notes from this absurd voyage in the Beagle Channel, during which I ended up in jail, the incidents are still fresh in my mind, including the magnificent time in the mountain lodge.

We knew the following days at the end of Drake Passage would become grey and misty, with ice crystals adrift in the air, and I tried to convince myself that the night in the Ushuaia prison was just a godforsaken dream that had never happened.

At least I knew that the next time we went to Tante Nina's centolla restaurant, there was more to recapitulate.

When I returned to Sweden some months later and visited the company, the facts were presented for me about the money transfer to the lawyer in Buenos Aires.

Chapter 23

Papua, Indonesia (West Irian Asmat Region), Headhunters, and Unfriendly Welcome and Adoption in West Irian

THE ASMAT REGION IS THE shallow estuarine landscape of southern West Irian (Irian Yaya), the old Dutch New Guinea, which is part of Indonesia. Even today these arcane stone-age people are dangerous, unpredictable, and still engaged in tribal vendetta and ritual headhunting.

In 1973, the *Lindblad Explorer* came for the first time to Indonesia and West Irian, cruising around the enormous archipelago of islands for six months in a row. The ship always called on West Irian, also called Western New Guinea, and the missionary villages of Asmat and Agats. In 1976, she would continue to cruise in that exotic part of the world for the coming years for about three months each fall, with turnaround days in Bali and occasionally Darwin, Australia, to repatriate the passengers.

However, in the fall of 1976, some changes were made in the itinerary since

the idea was brought up that we should visit the remote headhunter villages in addition to the traditional Asmat and Agats villages. The idea was greeted enthusiastically by everyone, but as it turned out, the changes also gave some of us some new and unexpected adventures with risks involved.

The Indonesian authorities told us that not too far from the missionary villages of Asmat and Agats is a small river to the southeast leading to the two villages: Biwar Laut and Basim.

Basim is south of Biwar Laut and some eighty kilometres south of Asmat and Agats.

On September 5, 1976, we departed Kai Besar in the Kai Islands in the Arafura Sea, which is west of Dobo in the Kepulauan Aru Islands, toward the Basim village with a waypoint approximately twelve nautical miles outside the river delta on the coastline, which was swampy due to its shallowness. The Arafura Sea is an extremely shallow area and tidewater dependant.

Lyall Watson, our expedition leader at the time, was a South African botanist, zoologist, biologist, anthropologist, and ethologist and an author of many new-age books, among the most popular of which was the best seller *Super nature*. Watson tried to make sense of natural and supernatural phenomena. When he talked with the Swedish officers, he often used the word *lagom*, which had no real equivalent word in English and meant more or less "moderate."

Lorne Blair, born in England, was a resident of Bali for thirty-five years. He was a lecturer on board the *Lindblad Explorer* in the Indonesian islands in the 1970s with his brother Lawrence. They made documentary films together and made the documentary series *Into the Ring of Fire*, in which Lorne filmed and photographed peoples who have since become endangered in their habitats and cultures. Some cease to exist as they were documented at that time fifty years ago. The Emmy-winning documentary series of the same name, *Ring of Fire*, is a first-person account of the adventures of English brothers Lorne and Lawrence Blair as they explore the rich cultures of the Indonesian islands.

On August 6, 1995, Lorne Blair unexpectedly died just three weeks before his fiftieth birthday. He died in a hospital two days after having broken his leg by falling into a hole on the sideway in Legian. Possibly the cause of death was emboli or a heart attack.

Lawrence Blair was an anthropologist, author, explorer, and filmmaker. With backing from Ringo Starr of the Beatles, they departed London's Heathrow Airport with two still cameras, a tripod, two sixteen-millimeter cameras with underwater housing, a tape recorder, a small Honda generator, a five-minute sun gun for night filming, and a pocket-sized slide projector. Their film stock and equipment comprised nine-tenths of their luggage, and without any insurance or filming permits, the Blairs flew into the steaming metropolis of Jakarta. Their plan was to practice a form of guerilla ethnography: to record the lives of the planet's least contacted tribal peoples, eating their food, speaking their languages, and sharing their lives. Among Indonesia's seventeen thousand islands were lands of real living kings and queens, Komodo dragons and pirates, cannibals and headhunters, mystics and magicians. Both filmmaker brothers were amazingly lucky to come back alive from their numerous expeditions.

Lyall Watson had decided that instead of going to Biwar Laut, which was the most inaccessible village, we would arrive unannounced in Basim to inform them of our presence because our schedule would only allow us to visit one village per day since each visit was a full-day program, and the village we'd visit according to the day's program would indubitably be taken by surprise. Unfortunately, we could not visit Biwar Laut as another day of exploration.

There was no time to waste, and as per the policy, we had to make a pre-visit trip to Basim with a small six-person Zodiac to give them fourteen days' notice in advance prior to our scheduled arrival—with the customary gifts that would act as bribes in an attempt to please the head-hunters. It was going to be a challenge and a risky mission since we were aiming directly for Basim without informing them of our arrival. Basim was just to the south of Biwar Laut. None of us had been there before, and the head-hunters had no idea about our presence in the area. They were unpredictable, and the public opinion was that they were still head-hunters, and some of them had never seen a white person before. We were concerned about suddenly arriving there and taking them by surprise, and the Indonesian authorities had already explained their concerns about our visits to those hidden tribes and told us to be careful about our bold venture.

Also, the approach to anywhere on the West Irian coast was not done with simplicity from a navigational point of view. In the 1970s, this demanded some skill since there was still no GPS, and the entire coast consisted of low, swampy vegetation with no real peaks or high landmarks to use as a reference point for the radars to achieve a more accurate position to the final waypoint when approaching a river entrance. An astronomical position received from the sun, stars, or planets the evening before was a blessing, and after that, it was all dead reckoning.

From that last fix, if we were lucky to get one, we sailed to a waypoint, taking into account the setting of the current, and furthermore, the tidewater calculations for that coast had to be done in advance with the aid of the harmonic constants. Without doubt, we were skilful when using all these methods simultaneously on our final approach; though our last fix had been received the previous evening, the error to our destination was at the most no more than plus or minus 0.5 nautical miles. Being some twelve nautical miles away from the assumed coastline, the radar picked up the weak, swampy land contours, and a better position could not be obtained.

The climate there is tropical, and humidity is a fact of life; even the dry months get a minimum of fifty millimetres of rain, and it takes six separate categories to describe the variations in rainfall there. The wet season typically runs from December through March, fuelled by the intertropical convergence zone, a junction between air streams originating in the Northern and Southern Hemispheres. The ITCZ passes over West Irian and Papua New Guinea twice, seeming to lag behind the sun's movement. As it passes southward, the island is hit by north-westerly monsoonal winds. Nearly 80 percent of the island is jungle forest. Lowland swamp forest predominates, with a canopy that can reach as high as forty meters, often matted by strangler figs with huge crowns and thick, merging aerial roots.

Sheltered under this canopy are palms, woody vines, climbers, masses of ferns, orchids, creepers, and a profusion of other plants. Along the southwestern West Irian coast are mangrove swamps and coastal forests. Inland in the lowland plains of the rivers are broad freshwater swamps overgrown with cane and swamp grass. There are more than seventy species of snakes there. Seven land snakes and all the sea snakes are venomous, and the insect to be terrified of is the malarial mosquito.

However, the people of this coast—the nationals, as they are called—are a fascinating, diverse group who still live much as they have for thousands of years. Although practices such as cannibalism and head shrinking are said to have been wiped out today, in the 1970s, they had not been wiped out. The head-hunters lived in a world of mud, water, and wood, and the Asmats were an enigma. Fierce warriors, head-hunters, and ritualistic cannibals, they also were great artists, carving some of the most beautiful and sought-after primitive art on earth, which was one of the reasons for our visit there in that godforsaken place.

On September 7, 1976, I wrote in my diary of Basim,

> Yesterday just before sunset, we dropped the anchor with very little water under the keel without seeing land at all, nor in the radar because of the very low, swampy land some twelve nautical miles away, because we had no more

than three meters of water under the keel. We spent the night peacefully at anchor under the tropical sky in the Arafura Sea with an impressive sunset.

Somewhere toward the swampy coastline from our anchorage position was Basim, an unfriendly village—hence the warnings from the Indonesian authorities.

Lyall Watson, Lorne and Lawrence Blair, a translator from the government, a motorman in charge of the outboard, and I, as a volunteer driver, took off toward the assumed entrance of the village in the early morning at 0600 hours. The Zodiac was loaded with gasoline tanks and a spare outboard engine to enable our safe return, as well as gifts for the head-hunters. We were sat on gasoline outboard tanks that covered the floorboards, and luckily, nobody had any desire to smoke.

We had a pretty good check of the location of the entrance river to the village. It took us approximately an hour and a half to enter the river. At the entrance, we slowly navigated upriver to Basim. I felt a weird feeling in coming to that godforsaken place, and I felt it was a hostile world. Ahead of us, we saw the village and the highly situated, narrow, swampy walkway planks that led toward the village. We arrived at low water; hence, it was difficult for the guys to climb up some two meters to plank. Nobody greeted them as they walked toward the village carrying the gifts. I remained seated in the Zodiac with the motorman, waiting for the others to return.

I felt strange and became concerned because there was just something wrong about the place, something weird. Hence, I climbed up onto the wooden planks with the hope of getting a better view of what was ahead of me. Lyall and Lorne were not to be seen, which made me even more concerned. I decided to walk some hundred meters more, knowing Lyall and Lorne Blair were somewhere ahead of me—probably in one of the huts, negotiating—when my eyes all of a sudden saw a dead head-hunter lying on the ground with an arrow through his body. I saw several more lying stone dead in strange positions. Apparently, a war had taken place between that tribe and another closely related tribe in the area.

I witnessed an old world, and it was a frightening experience. The headhunters had no clue the times were changing. Astonished by the sudden discovery of the dead corpse with an arrow right through his chest, I thought in my inner self, *this poor warrior probably was harmless.* At least that was my belief. Suddenly, I heard screaming in the distance, and I saw Lyall Watson, Lorne Blair, and the translator come running from the village on the wooden planks in an extreme hurry, shouting and screaming. I immediately understood things had in one way or another derailed, and the situation had become serious; consequently, I ran back to the Zodiac on the half-rotten wooden planks.

As I ran for my life, I thought, *I hope this will not be my last few minutes of my personal life, and I hope I have time enough to escape this horrible place with Lyall and Lorne to tell the story about what happened here today.*

I ran as fast as I could, hearing clearly the noise behind me from Lyall and Lorne and the scary sound of the locals as I tried to focus on where I set my feet without falling through the planks. I finally jumped down into the Zodiac, shouting on the way down to the motorman, "Start the engine, for heaven's sake!"

Behind Lyall, Lorne, and the translator, a bunch of screaming females and head-hunters followed, throwing all kinds of rubbish at them. Lyall was trying to protect his head with his arms. No more than five meters separated them when they all made a desperate jump in panic into the Zodiac from the wooden planks above. They almost landed on top of each other. It was a blessing nobody got injured from the jump.

The outboard engine was already in reverse gear as the nationals in grass skirts threw cassowary-bone daggers and everything else they had in their hands at us, shouting and screaming in their native language. It was obvious they still maintained a fierce warrior image. It was a wonder they did not use their bows and arrows to kill us. The sound of the forty-horsepower Johnson engine was a blessing to hear as we took off toward the river and the open sea.

What a nightmare we just had experienced. Lyall and Lorne were deeply upset and traumatized by the incident, which almost had cost them their lives. We arrived at noon back at the ship, facing thousands of questions from everybody since we had given the ship a brief explanation over the radio about the incident. A shaken Lyall Watson assembled everyone in the lounge and gave them the full story.

Lunch was then served, and the ship moved slowly north up along the coast toward Asmat and Agats.

We spent the afternoon sailing across the shallow water of the Arafura Sea separating Aru from the present coast of West Irian (Indonesian New Guinea). The rich waters abounded with dolphins and sea snakes. We anchored up in five feet of water as the sun dwindled in the tropical sea.

The following morning, it was an early wake-up call at five o'clock, and after an early breakfast at 0600 hours, we went along at low water conditions like a task force with seven Zodiacs and two open lifeboats in swirling rain toward the invisible coast of Asmat and Agats. We had a lifeboat emergency radio, water, and provisions sufficient for an adventurous full-day journey for a hundred people, as well as spare outboard engines and medical equipment. It was a long journey, and the rain would not stop, as if it were saying to us, "This is what the Asmat swamps are really like." We estimated we had about two hours' drive in the open sea toward the mangrove-filled, swampy coast and an additional forty-five minutes' drive upriver to the isolated stone-age village called Owus in the Asmat and Agats area. Thus, we would arrive approximately at ten o'clock in the morning.

The picture below shows the original chart we used to find the Asmat and Agats region.

I was sitting at the tiller as a boat commander in lifeboat number three with Tevita, as usual, next to me, looking over the twenty passengers' heads at the wide-open Arafura Sea ahead of me without any sign of land ahead. The outboard mechanic, Ketoni, was, as usual, in charge of the engine. In the 1970s, we indeed did real expedition cruising, literally discovering the world.

We had been driving for an hour, and I was carefully watching the magnetic compass, which hopefully would take us to the assumed river entrance somewhere ahead. I knew there was a current, but I was not sure how strong it was or its direction. Hence, I looked over my shoulder at the propeller water in an attempt to see some kind of a drift, but it was not easy to figure out. There was a good atmosphere among the passengers; they were all chatting and full of expectations for the adventurous upcoming day, and rightly so.

One of my passengers, an elderly man who was a veteran of World War II and had fought with the Japanese in Guadalcanal, suddenly said, "Crocodiles can be found here everywhere. Ask any of my friends who were down here with me. As we waded in the shallow, swampy rivers, suddenly, all of us heard a heart-piercing scream from a soldier who unfortunately disappeared into the mouth of a crocodile. The only thing left to be seen was the blood." There ensued a profound silence in the boat after that!

It was a peculiar feeling to sit and chat with the passengers in a lifeboat for two hours and listen to the monotonous sound of the engine in the wide-open Arafura Sea while looking at the muddy brown water that surrounded us. They were all of an exceptionally different character; some knew better than others about things, and some were noticeably scared. The seven Zodiacs surrounded us as a task force. I had in my boat the emergency transmitter with a foldable five-meter-high antenna to stay in touch with the *Lindblad Explorer* every second hour of the day, as per the agreement. Ove, the radio operator, was in charge of the radio communication and the assigned hours of transmission.

Suddenly, far away, we could see the contours of land ahead of us, and all of us were tense, given that we were deeply in doubt about whether we headed in the right direction. Keeping the drift of the current fresh in mind hopefully would lead us to the river's mouth. Loudly, I suddenly made an announcement: "Ladies and gentlemen, as you know, we are all in the same boat with the same goal: to find the entrance to the river's mouth. Therefore, I encourage you all to lift your binoculars and look for the entrance to make sure we are heading the right way."

They all instantly used their binoculars, and once in a while, someone shouted, "I see something over there! I see something!" Spirits were high on board the lifeboat on that outer edge of the hot Arafura Sea.

We were heading for the mud-stained river entrance, which we only knew existed theoretically on the sea chart. The land slowly came closer, and after half an hour, we could clearly see the mangrove forest, but there was no sign of the entrance.

Less than half a mile off the coast and at ten o'clock on the port side, one of the ladies suddenly shouted, "I see the entrance—and something is moving over there behind the trees! Oh my God, there they are—the head-hunters! I don't believe this!"

Upon finally reaching the coast, we altered the course toward port and the entrance since we had been drifting toward the south with the current, and we found ourselves only approximately 0.2 nautical miles (two cables) wrong in our calculations, but we did find the mouth of the river—and the head-hunter's had found us!

As we approached the river's mouth, suddenly, with startling rapidity and from the middle of nowhere, at least twenty-one fully manned war canoes came out of hiding in the forest; surrounded us; and launched into a noisy frenzy of bones, feathers, and paddles around our Zodiacs. The reception was impressive, and we were glad they were welcoming us and not seeing us off. After the demonstration of power, the canoes turned, secure in their dominance over us, and latched on to our craft to tow us far up the narrow river to the village of Uwus in the Asmat and Agats region.

It was a totally different and almost frightening experience to be in the midst of some 150-armed men in full war paint and regalia. Furthermore, they clearly demonstrated that they could elicit far greater speed from their canoes than our Zodiac task force. More and more canoes came out to us as we progressed slowly upstream with our cumbersome tails until we reached Uwus. We counted more than fifty canoes.

It was a different experience to find ourselves so close to the head-hunter's, which was precisely what they were. The men stood in their canoes in full war paint and war regalia.

Tevita gave me querying eyes, and I suddenly thought about Michael Rockefeller, the twenty-three-year-old son of Nelson Rockefeller, who had disappeared in 1961 under menacing mysteries in the stone-age world of the Asmat and Agats cannibals. I felt strange when thinking about it. Michael Rockefeller had been there to collect carvings and artefacts from the various tribes in West Irian. As a matter of fact, Nelson Rockefeller came in person to the *Lindblad Explorer* for a cruise as we were doing six adventurous expedition cruises in 1973 between Bali and West Irian in an attempt to figure out partly what had happened to his son. Michael's disappearance is one of the enduring unsolved mysteries of the twentieth century.

On November 11, 1961, Michael Rockefeller led a small expedition along the treacherous cannibal coast of New Guinea with anthropologist René Wassing. Heavy seas swamped their trading raft in the Arafura Sea. The raft he had constructed was a platform built on top of two dug-out canoes, with an outboard motor for power. Outside the wide mouth of the Asewets River at dusk, the ocean waves capsized the raft. They salvaged some of their belongings and spent the night safely on the inverted platform. The Papuans abandoned the raft and swam for shore.

After a night adrift and clinging to the remains of his raft, Rockefeller set out to swim some twelve miles to shore with empty fuel tanks lashed to his back to keep him afloat, leaving Wassing with the fateful words "I think I can make it." He was never seen again.

Despite a massive air and sea search, no trace of Rockefeller was ever found.

Seven years later, Milt Machlin, editor of the adventure magazine *Argosy*, was approached by a nefarious Australian smuggler named Donahue with the startling question "What would you say if I told you I saw Michael Rockefeller alive not ten weeks ago?" Did this mean Michael had somehow survived among the cannibals in the wilderness of New Guinea? Donahue claimed that while on a trading venture in the Trobriand Islands, a thousand miles east of where Rockefeller disappeared, he and an associate visited a remote village on the island of Kanapua. There a white man with a long red beard hobbled out of a small hut on two badly healed broken legs, squinting through the cracked lenses of his glasses, and croaked the words "My name is Michael Rockefeller. Please help me!"

Could it have been that Rockefeller was still alive in 1968, held captive by headhunting tribesmen? Then the smuggler slipped away into the night. Machlin was determined to find Michael with the cryptic clues given to him by Donahue, including the name of an island that wasn't even on the map. Milt Machlin set off for New Guinea to discover the truth for himself and to find Michael Rockefeller dead or alive.

Why did Michael, the privileged son of Nelson Rockefeller and successor to one of the world's great fortunes, journey to a place where his name and wealth meant nothing—to the cannibals of Asmat? Rockefeller's expedition was intended in part to acquire some of the extraordinary carvings, *bis* poles (ritual totems), decorated skulls, and other artwork created by the Asmats. However, by driving up the price of human skulls with steel ax-heads and massive quantities of tobacco, did Michael inadvertently provoke headhunting raids and thereby become the architect of his own death? Or did he simply drown in the Arafura Sea on his long swim to shore? Could he have been eaten by sharks or crocodiles that infested the waters?

As we slowly drove upriver in the world of the head-hunter's, in the area where Michael Rockefeller had disappeared, I thought, *Perhaps he disappeared in the Anchunep village close to us.* I decided it was not even worth contemplating his fate.

The isolated cannibalistic culture and forgotten society soon came into sight. It was unreal as we listened to their monotonous "Uooh-uooh-uooh" in tempo while they forced their canoes toward us. All of them were partly nude, and they all wore feather headgear and full regalia. It was frightening to see them, and we felt defenceless. One lady started to cry in fear when the war canoes rapidly surrounded our inflatable Zodiacs and hitchhiked with our lifeboats and Zodiacs, clinging to the hulls or pontoons, touching our arms and skin. It was a bizarre and frightening experience.

I was astonished, and so were the rest. Ove, the radio operator, said, "What the heck is this, Peter? I don't believe my eyes!"

I said with a tone of fear, "Ove, I fucking don't know. Try to make contact with the *Lindblad Explorer* to tell them we are still alive."

I felt bizarre and scared when I suddenly was accompanied at the tiller by a head-hunter who sat next to me and stared right into my eyes with his shifty eyes, touching my tan skin. It scared the hell out of me, and he had a bone through his nose. Others had bones through their noses as well. Furthermore, he smelled as if he had been dug up from a rotten tomb. Later on, I was told their bodies were smeared with urine and pig fat. What a body lotion! At the time of this writing, I can still smell his odour.

The lifeboats and Zodiacs were now crowded with smelly head-hunter's sitting on the railings between every passenger, touching them. Looking at the scary warriors, I had to pinch myself on the arm, so I knew I was not dreaming what I was witnessing. They were sitting on the Zodiac pontoons, touching the passengers' skin and bodies; it was obvious they had never before seen any white person. Under the hot tropical sun, the passengers used the traditional sunscreen lotion, which caused the head-hunters to touch their creamy bodies even more. Their curiosity made us all scared, and rightly so since we had entered a world none of us could believe existed.

To the monotonous sound of the loud lifeboat engines and the tones of the seven Zodiac outboard engines, we passed the narrow river mouth, which barely could accommodate one lifeboat. Manoeuvring the big lifeboats was not an easy task, especially with an escort of nude head-hunter's sitting everywhere, some with their penises visible, staring into our faces. It was a horrifying experience.

The canoes were sophisticatedly kept alongside the Zodiacs since they got a free lift from us. Sometimes the load was uneven, which occasionally caused a Zodiac to shear quickly over to the other side of the narrow waterway with the jungle hanging over their heads. This made the passengers concerned and caused complete disorder for a while. The last thing we wanted was for the passengers to get scarred, but they were definitely scared, and so was I.

It was not an easy task to tell the head-hunter's what to do with their canoes in that situation to re-establish order for a safe, continuous passage upriver to the village, which was still an hour ahead of us. I thought, *My God, we have these stone-age people sitting next to us, and still one hour remains to the village.* I had never seen such a thing before, nor had anybody else among us. As we sailed upriver, we saw many head-hunter's walking nude along the river with their bows and arrows.

Ove was in the process of rigging the high antenna in the boat, trying to make radio contact with the ship, so I told those in my lifeboat that we unfortunately had to stop the engine for a while to obtain some silence and stay adrift in the river for a couple minutes as we tried to tell the vessel we were safe and still making our way upriver to the village. Tevita told Ketoni in his own language to stop the engine, and the silence became noticeable. The sounds from the jungle were overwhelming from every direction. The electric simmer of insect life was so pervasive that it seemed to have a tangible effect on everyone. The head-hunter's had no idea, of course, what was going on.

When the five-meter antenna was rigged and the frequency was on five hundred kilohertz (the equipment was tuned in), Ove called, "*Lindblad Explorer*, this is lifeboat number three. Do you read me?" Everybody was silent, including the head-hunter's, as Ove manipulated the radio knobs.

Suddenly, on the other end, Jack responded, "Boat number three, this is the mother ship, *Lindblad Explorer*. Jack. Do you read me? Are things okay with you?" I doubt the head-hunters had heard a talking box before!

When the *Lindblad Explorer* knew everything was fine with us, the radio equipment was switched off, and we started the engine, which again drowned out the sounds of the jungle as we resumed our voyage upriver deeper and deeper into the swampy, narrow, muddy river with the head-hunter's in their canoes, clinging on to us with their smelly bodies. What a destiny this was.

Mrs. Grace Anderson, Nelson Rockefeller's private secretary, an attractive lady in her fifties, was sitting next to me. Grace was from Lincoln, Massachusetts, and she was overwhelmed and excited by what she saw. She was a repeat passenger who frequently came back to the *Lindblad Explorer* to see the world with the chief engineer, Gote from Sweden, since she was in love with him. They were lovers, though Gote lived in a happy marriage in Sweden with his wife, so they kept their beautiful love story secret. They met frequently on board in all the remote corners of the world, where they kept their love story going on, and they lived together as a married couple on board. Neither was in a hurry to return back to his or her respective home.

Grace was the most beautiful lady I ever had seen. She was a lady full of grace, like her name, and full of charm. She and Gote complemented each other well. Their love story affected all of us. Each time she left the ship, it was a sad story as she walked down the gangway wherever she went ashore in the world. When she put her feet on the ground, she turned around, and tears fell from both as they slowly waved goodbye to each other.

The isolated cannibalistic culture finally came into sight. After another hour of driving upriver, behind the last sharp turn to the right, suddenly, out of the blue, we saw smoke over the treetops from a village somewhere in front of us, though it was still obscured by the bush. In excitement, I watched some more head-hunter's walk along the riverbank in ankle-deep mud with a black sniffing pig in front of them, carrying their bows and arrows in their hands, looking suspiciously at us. I stared at them, fascinated.

We had just about three hundred meters left, and the river looked so narrow with the jungle hanging tightly over us like a roof that the rays of the sun could barely come through.

We had only about three hours' time at our disposal in the village before the tide started to fall again, when the waterway would become just a narrow ditch that indubitably caused our lifeboats to get stuck in the mud. I got creeps in my body when I thought about what would happen if worse came to worse and we had to spend the night in that muddy, forgotten place with mosquitoes and God only knew what else.

As we approached the only possible landing place with hard mud, I told Ketoni, "Full ahead," to get the bow as high up as possible in the mud. A fair length of rope was taken ashore and tied to a black ironwood tree so that even a cyclone would not have been able to rip it off. Due to the shallow water condition and the limited time we had in that godforsaken place, I told everybody with a loud voice that they all had to be back in three hours' time, since the tide was rising again, and we had to be able to pass the bar outside. I was dead serious about that. To confirm how much water there was, I forced the ore down into the water, and to my astonishment, there was just about two feet of water (i.e., the lifeboat was at that point resting in the mud). In my inner self, I said a prayer that we could make it out safely back to the sea. I had a copy of the harmonic-constant graph with me that told me what was going on with the tidewater.

All the responsibility was in my hands for a safe journey back. After bringing them safely there, I felt I needed to smoke a cigarette, which I did with reflection.

There we were while the entire village—some two hundred people, I gather—lined up, staring at us in front of and close to our two lifeboats. They were all more or less nude, both men and women. Also, the mosquitoes greeted us. The men had feather headgear or some kind of fur hats, and they smelled of urine and pig fat, which covered their bodies. My nose was filled also with the smell of rotting vegetation.

I told Tevita to stay and guard the lifeboats, and I gave a last quick look down at the doubtful water level before I stepped down onto the muddy shoreline. As we stepped ashore, they watched us and touched us as we passed by. We hurried along one after another, feeling guilty that we were there passing over their muddy shores, sometimes walking in ankle-deep mud, toward the village.

In the village, several hundred women and children were waiting with drums already warmed up over small fires so that the lizard-skin timpani were properly tuned to give us a resounding, body-twisting, ear-splitting Asmat welcome. Everyone was painted and stripped down; the carvers were out on sago mats, carving; the dancers were dancing; children were singing; and everyone was on display. They had grass skirts, cassowary-bone daggers, and safety pins in their ears. We stayed until everyone had run out of film. We couldn't have had a better day.

The village consisted of nothing but mud-and-bamboo huts with palm-frond roofs and walls made of old planks without doors. All the huts were on pillars—I guess because when it was raining, the entire place was drenched in water; hence, the soil consisted of mud. We had gifts with us to please these stone-age people. One could feel a danger hanging in the air, and in our inner selves, we felt that ritual head-hunting was going on inside the huts.

Occasionally, some brave ones came and shook hands, and then they quickly walked away. It was a forgotten world. Some of us offered them a cigarette, giving them also the matchbox, but they didn't know how to light the match. Somehow, I managed to trade my spare T-shirt for a bow and six arrows. The bow was made of black ironwood and was almost two meters in length. The arrows were an impressive work made by skilful hands. As the passengers mingled with the head-hunter's, they traded as much as they could—everything from human bones to stone axes.

When I walked around in the village, I came across a narrow path of wooden planks that dwindled into the jungle. I became curious and wanted to see where the path ended up. Without thinking, I set out on my own, walking the path, and I found myself outside the village. Maybe it was foolhardiness, but I continued to walk.

I hurried slowly, and I came into the forest, walking on the narrow wooden planks that floated on the muddy swamp. What I did was stupid, considering what had happened to Michael Rockefeller. I knew if I stepped outside the planks, I would be standing up to my knees in mud, which caused me to walk steadily on the planks. I thought I must not walk too far from the rest of the group, but the mystery and the unknown ahead of me made me continue to walk farther away from the village and the passengers. Ahead of me, the planks ran straight for a good one hundred meters. There was nothing but mud and dark jungle to the left and right of the path, with lots of fallen trees and a horrible smell, all tangled with one another. It was a little bit scary, I thought. The mosquitoes started to bother me, and I hoped the malaria pills we had taken would prevent me from getting malaria if there was any there. I walked on top of wet, muddy soil.

I felt I was out of my mind for walking alone and away from the others, so I stopped for a while, looking backward, asking myself if I should go back, but somehow, I went on walking. I was in a state of hypnosis amid the sounds of monkeys and the other sounds from the jungle. The village was already behind and had vanished behind the dense vegetation. As I was thinking about what could possibly go wrong there in my aloneness in a place our Lord had forgotten, ahead of me, a big black pig suddenly came into sight from nowhere and stared at me before it vanished again into the bush.

I carried on walking, and I felt my heart anxiously beating in that strange world of the stone-age people. I thought, *I must be out of my mind for doing this*, but I kept walking. I could smell smoke as if from an open fireplace, and it smelled as if somebody were cooking. I heard a scream come from somewhere behind the trees in the direction of my path, and I thought I ought to find out what was ahead of me. Being in the world of the head-hunter's, it occurred to me that maybe somebody had been killed and was on the way to being eaten. Who knew? It was for me to figure out what was at the end of the path.

I could see a few huts farther on as I approached, and then I saw three almost-naked natives standing close together in their bast skirts, side by side, and they stared at me with great astonishment in front of their hut, watching me as I slowly walked toward them with my bow and arrows in my hand. Their eyes were black, and their bodies were partly covered with white paint, which was a contrast. All three of them had bones through their noses, and they looked as if they could easily have boiled me in a pot. They had no hair on their chests or on their arms. Their mouths had a red colour—I guessed they were chewing some stimulants.

When I was right in front of them and close to the hut, I lifted my arm to greet them, but there was no reaction from their side. They continued to stare at me, and the inspection lasted two minutes. They were motionless like statues, and then suddenly, to my surprise, one of them, the oldest one, touched me on the shoulder, which made me worried. I started to regret my lone discovery walk. I thought, *how stupid could I be, walking alone over here by myself?* Then the other two touched me as well, feeling my skin. No one else was to be seen. I felt somehow, they were friendly, but I thought about what to do if things went wrong. I undoubtedly would have to run for my life on the swampy planks, hopefully without an arrow hitting me from behind.

Suddenly, five or six women, all naked, came out from the hut. They obviously had been hiding behind the door openings and observing the elderly man who had touched me first. Apparently, he was the chief of the big hut.

A woman who looked younger and less ugly than the others took me by the hand and led me into the shade of the hut and toward an open fireplace in the middle of the hut, where some men sat. I understood I was told to sit down in front of the fireplace. I watched the breasts of the younger ones, and they were far from my taste; though they were younger, their breasts hung down like leather bats. The other ladies followed, and they all sat down around me. It took a while for my eyes to adjust to the darkness, and when I could see something, I saw they all had placed themselves in a circle around an open fire in the middle of the floor, and some were around me.

When I finally could see something in the flaming fire, I was taken aback. The hut was made of a palm roof and walls of ironwood mixed with mud. I also noticed a turtle shell so huge that a man could have lain down in it. They all sat down on the floor in a circle, and with gestures, they told me to sit down with a younger woman, the one who had led me into the shade. Next to me on my left, she set her hand on my leg. She had long, thin, rough-skinned fingers that were scarred and wrinkled. There was also an elderly man who must have been a medicine man, because he had a lot more feathers and odd ceremonial objects around his neck than the others did. There was something cooking over the fireplace in a big pot. Then a bowl of strange, hot liquid started unexpectedly to circulate among all of them. My instincts told me it was made of chewed jungle fruits mixed with saliva and going through a fermentative process that gave a level of alcohol. I had heard before about that weird liquid, which was common in West Irian.

After a person in the hut drank, he mumbled a long string of words and handed it over to the next person, who did the same. With horror, I saw the wooden bowl coming closer to me. Finally, it was my turn, and I was invited to drink. I looked down into the bowl with discomfort at the viscous white liquid, and I saw that everybody was staring at me. I guess they stared at me since they knew it was a mysterious liquid to me. I apparently hesitated for too long, as my new friends pushed me to drink, saying something that I understood as "Drink."

I could only blame myself for ending up in that kind of a fate because I had outstripped myself from the passengers and walked away into the unknown, which was something only fools did. I must have been one of them. I was clearly challenging my destiny.

In addition, the crew and Ove had no idea where I was, which made my situation scarier since I had no walkie-talkie with me. Looking at my new friends, who were nude and terrifying-looking cannibals, I found it safer to drink as I was told; otherwise, there was a possibility I would perhaps end up in a boiling pot. I grabbed the bowl, closed my eyes, and took a sip.

After I swallowed the sludge, I was close to throwing up, and I could barely control myself not to do it. I must have made grimaces because they looked intently at me. I handed the bowl to the young woman at my left, who still had her hand on my leg, and then we were getting along fast, though I didn't mumble any words afterward. My eyes were used to the darkness now, and I could make them out quite clearly. Also, I could see that the medicine man had only three teeth below and two above in front and an ulcer on his left ankle the size of a golf ball, covered with flies. From time to time, he whisked at them, and when they bothered him too much, he dusted the ulcer with ash from the fire.

I felt something was going on, and I sat quietly, watching with great concern to see what would happen next. The young woman at my left still had her hand on my leg, and I did not dare to move it. I wondered why she kept her hand there.

I didn't know what to do or how to respond to the gift given to me. I was lost in that peculiar stone-age world, and I had nothing to give them in exchange, except it suddenly occurred to me that I had a cap on my head. I quickly handed it over to the chief by crawling halfway over the floor like a dog, close to the fireplace, inside the small circle of head-hunters. I must have looked ridiculous. Crawling back the same way to my place, I gave him a smile with the hope that my old cap would please him, which it apparently did. I felt my time was running out, and I wanted to leave the dark hut.

Then one of the strangest things I'd ever seen took place: it looked as though they were talking about adopting me. The medicine man stood up and did a dance of some kind right next to the fireplace with rattles in his hands, dancing as if he were in trance. I was enchanted by what I saw. I thought, *the only thing that is now missing is they will impose me to have sex with the young woman to my left*, who was still holding her hand on my leg with the rough fingers full of scars. My thoughts stopped there.

Amid the bizarre ceremony, which meant I was somehow in progress to get a new family, I suddenly thought about the state of the tidewater in the ditch where we had parked the lifeboats. Suddenly, the chief of the hut said something that caused the young woman at my left to snatch my arm and then slowly force my head and mouth toward her right black leather-bat breast and nipple to suck it. My first thought was *This is the end of my happy-go-lucky life on this planet*. I was trapped, and I had no chance to escape from the situation, which was unreal. I felt my blood pressure rapidly go up because I had put myself in a strange situation that I couldn't predict, control, or know the outcome of. I thought, *If I suddenly run, with their knowledge of the bush, it wouldn't be any sort of fun having them after me*.

The situation that had been, in the blink of an eye, forced upon me was a nightmare. Good words were now at a prime. I couldn't avoid it; I felt that if I wanted to see the lifeboats again and the world outside that place, I was better off sucking her nipple, so I did, while she kept her hand behind my neck. Was I dreaming? No, I wasn't; I was sucking the nipple of a female head-hunter as I was duly told to. I felt it was my only chance to escape the hut alive.

When I finally had sucked her nipple, hopefully to her satisfaction, my mouth had a strange taste. I was pleased it was over, but soon I figured out that I was mistaken, because then extraordinary things happened.

The chief pointed at the remaining four woman and then at me. Apparently, they were next in line to give their breasts for me to suck. I felt there was an undertone of seriousness in his orders. I was lost, and I became scared because I could tell there was no way out of the jumble. I had to do as told to get out alive and leave and run for the lifeboats. I knew the head-hunters were not to be taken lightly, and it was well worth a little embarrassment to get out of there. There was indeed a good thirty minutes to go to the others.

I counted the four women and thought, *oh great God, do I really have to suck all these nipples?* None of the others were young, and they all had severe faces when they looked at me. They looked as if they were between seventy and death, and their skin was almost black. In my inner self, I cried, and I certainly wasn't happy about my fate. It was nearly pitch black in the hut, apart from the flames coming from the open fireplace, which made every face look like a phantom face. I wondered if it was my fate to die there if I didn't suck their nipples.

The chief made me understand, with backup from the medicine man with the bizarre ceremonial objects around his neck. They both pointed at a woman and then at me, and the medicine man went down on all fours, showing with his body language that I had to creep on my knees in front of the fireplace from where I sat to the specific woman he pointed at. I felt peculiar. Well, I was twenty-nine years of age and in a perfect health, so I did as I was told. I thought if my friends in the village had known what I was doing, they would have declared me to be out of my mind. Anyway, there was no way out of it; I had to comply with my situation, whether I liked it or not.

I crept slowly over the floor toward the assigned head-hunter woman, looking from down below at her horrible nipples that awaited me. In all probability, she was to become my second mother out of the five. I must have looked amusing as I approached her with a frightened feeling in my body. The others were silently watching me. I felt I was going to need God's help to get through this without facing any problems since I was by then involved in a pretty serious ceremony.

My head was full of thoughts, and as far as my experience went, I knew I was an idiot for walking alone to that place by my own free will and ending up in a nightmarish situation I couldn't escape from.

Her nipples tasted horrible. It took me no more than three seconds to do it, but there were three more to do. I then crawled over the floor to all of them, and one by one, they felt my lips on their nipples. I could have paid a million dollars for a glass of water. When it was done, I stared all around, waiting for approval, which I obviously got from the chief. I guess he must have accepted my way of sucking all the nipples. I thought I was dreaming, and one thing was for sure: I was out of my mind.

It was strange. I glanced toward my new family with a bitter taste in my mouth from all the nipples I had sucked. I had the right to feel pleased with myself. My mind had triumphed over matter, and in my inner self, I congratulated myself for being adopted by a pure headhunter family, though my mouth still had a strange taste.

I felt from that moment that I was indeed adopted for good in that bizarre world of the headhunters. We sat around the little fire in the middle of the hut, and from time to time, the flames lit up our faces. We looked silently at one another, and they all inspected me from head to foot. The chief then suddenly left. He came back and sat down opposite the fire, and to my surprise, he held a stone ax in his hand, which he gave to me. I was stunned and, of course, happy to receive the ax, which today hangs on my wall in my house.

Unfortunately, I had nothing to give in exchange, and since the clock was ticking for me, I stood up in front of the fireplace and moved toward each one of them, taking their hands in an attempt to say a kind of polite goodbye. None of them said a word, so I interpreted that everything was peaceful, and it was a consolation for me since I wanted to make a peaceful sortie. I slowly backed out toward the bright entrance door, keeping my ax tightly in my hand as I desperately tried to figure out where I had come from. The darkness in the hut made me disorientated as I came outside into the bright daylight. I spotted in the distance the wooden planks, and I quickly took off toward them. I knew I had to walk for a while again on the swampy planks toward my fellow passengers. After a quick walk, in a state of hurry, I finally came back to the lifeboats.

The passengers were still scattered all over the place, and they all were dripping of sweat due to the high humidity. I had spent some two hours on my private excursion, or whatever it was. The clock was ticking, as I knew we had to get all the passengers back within a couple hours, keeping in mind that the tropical darkness came instantly, and then the jungle became pitch black. I wanted to avoid all of us being left alone in the dark in that narrow, swampy black tributary we'd come from earlier. To sail back toward the Arafura Sea in a tight pitch-black river was on God's providence; hence, it was time to call and assemble all the passengers as soon as possible.

Tevita and I left the lifeboat together, walking toward the village, looking for the passengers, and when we found them, we spread the word that they should make their way back to the lifeboats as soon as possible. We knew they all would come back loaded with artefacts and God knew what.

The tidewater was kind of unpredictable. We had our harmonic-constant graph at hand, but still, it was all prediction, and we were under stress, as we felt our departure was much delayed. After a kind of disarray with lots of shouting and telling everybody to get back to the lifeboats and the Zodiacs, we managed finally to get the passengers back, and we made a desperate roll call to be sure nobody was left behind. It was a blessing to know they were all there.

When we were all finally together, off we went with the two lifeboats crowded with passengers sitting together with the sound of the slow-going lifeboat engines. I sat at the tiller, as usual, and looked at the dense jungle passing by while some of us waved goodbye to the stone-age people who slowly vanished behind us. As the tide was now low, I was deeply concerned about whether or not we could pass the shallow bar outside the river entrance.

After a bit of drama in getting over the bar at low water, I was sitting in my own thoughts, when I suddenly saw in the open sea in the distance a small dot far away. I set the course toward the *Lindblad Explorer*, which was somewhere out there and not yet visible. We sailed again on the magnetic compass, when I figured out that that small dot was a human being, a head-hunter standing more or less in the open sea, fishing with a fish-throwing net.

As I wondered why he was standing that far out in the open sea, my back and my white shirt became covered with mud that whirled up from the propeller, and the boat came to an abrupt halt, suddenly making everyone fall forward topsy-turvy. I immediately knew we had missed the tide, and consequently, both lifeboats were now grounded in the middle of nowhere. At least we were lucky to be out of the swampy river before sunset. We were better off being out there, and I thought, *there are worse places to be aground on.*

I checked the water depth with the oar, and there was no more than two feet of water. There was still an hour and a half of daylight, so I said, "Ladies and gentlemen, due to the circumstances, I kindly ask all of you to step out and assist by pushing the lifeboat slowly until we reach sufficient depth of water to continue the voyage safely back to the ship." As a result, everybody took off his or her camera and stepped into the muddy, warm water of the Arafura Sea, and we started to push the big boat. It was a peculiar view to see everybody walking slowly while keeping one hand on the boat. They all talked and laughed, which was a blessing. The water reached up to the thighs on all of us.

After two hours of slow walking, the sun was slowly approaching the horizon, and people started to become tired, when suddenly, the water started to reach our hips. Therefore, I told everybody to step back into the boat with the help of each other. It turned out to be a difficult thing to lift everyone back over the railing.

Tevita and I walked around the boat from person to person, lifting each one of them up, until we both were at the brink of exhaustion. When we finally got everybody back on board in the lifeboat, they were wet but still in a good mood, and we resumed the voyage toward the *Lindblad Explorer*. We sailed again on the magnetic compass due west since we knew she was out there somewhere. We hoisted the huge radio antenna to the emergency lifeboat radio, and Ove called the vessel while Tevita cranked the levels to obtain power.

The ship suddenly broke through on the radio to everyone's delight, and they agreed to switch on the strong searchlight and point it up toward the sky so we could locate the vessel in the dark, tropical Arafura night. All the Zodiacs surrounded us as a task force as we sailed toward the *Lindblad Explorer*. Everybody was by then singing and joking as the deck lights of the ship grew bigger and bigger. We walked up the gangway, and the waiters greeted us with welcome drinks. A truly adventurous day had come to an end.

Chapter 24

Isla Plaza, the Enchanted Island, and Lars-Eric Lindblad Disembarked When a Killer Whale Attacked the Zodiac

ON MARCH 4, 1974, THE ship transferred at the end of the Antarctic season via the Chilean coast to the enchanted islands of the Galápagos. We cruised the Galápagos Islands for two months for the next two years, changing passengers in Guayaquil, Ecuador. On that cruise, Lars-Eric joined us for some four days only before he had to return to his office in New York.

When we arrived at the north of the South Plaza Islands to the east of Santa Cruz Island, as the islands were on our cruise schedule, the sound between the two islands was far too shallow for us to enter; hence, we anchored up to the southwest of the two crescent-shaped islands, which lay just a few hundred meters off the east coast of Santa Cruz.

Some thousand sea lions inhabited the islands, which attracted the top predators of the seas: orcas (killer whales). The island of Baltra was to the north of Santa Cruz and, conveniently, had an airport. Since Lars-Eric had to disembark and return to New York, we made contact well in advance with a reliable local person on Santa Cruz to come pick him up at North Plaza Island.

I, as usual, volunteered to drive the Zodiac, as new events were going on, and that day, one of the Tongan deck crew, Siua, the brother of Tevita, accompanied me for safety reasons. Over the VHF, we heard the boat from Santa Cruz was heading toward our meeting point at North Plaza Island; hence, Lars-Eric showed up at the gangway platform in his best suit with three suitcases. We took on board his luggage, and off we went in the beautiful environment with the soft wind caressing our bodies.

It was supposed to be a fairly short ride to the pickup boat, when we suddenly discovered a pod of dorsal fins quickly approaching—killer whales! We were between the islands when the orcas approached us, and all three of us followed the fins carefully with great concern.

One fin in particular caught our attention since it was heading steadily toward our

Zodiac. The gigantic fin became an immediate threat to us, but it remained to be seen if worse came to worse. It was a terrifying moment to see the orcas aiming directly for our Zodiac, and one of them suddenly dove under the rubber Zodiac. That special orca swam uncomfortably close under our gray rubber Zodiac pontoon. Bear in mind that in the 1970s, the quality of these Zodiacs was not the best. Once in a while, the orca followed close behind us. It was amazing to see that monster, but it was scary, and the huge beast got so close to the boat that at one point, it would have been possible to touch him. He was flipping, spinning, and spraying us right behind the transom of our Zodiac. We knew he was playing with us, but in what way? I wondered if we were going to be his next meal as I tried in fear to estimate the remaining distance to the shallow water and safety ahead of us.

We knew they were sophisticated predators, which was not a consolation. When recapitulating the incident later in the evening, we figured that the Zodiac pontoon's outboard engine must have attracted them for some reason. We asked ourselves why the single orca did this while the rest kept a distance to us. Lars-Eric was pale, and Siua and I were as well. We quickly looked to see which way was nearer to the shallow area.

It seemed our destiny was now in the hands of the evil killer whale, when disaster unexpectedly struck. The whale suddenly turned and headed right toward us close under the surface with incredible speed that scared the hell out of me. I thought he was going to kill us. His dorsal fin, either intentionally or unintentionally, punctured our Zodiac so hard that we heard when the air went out from both forward pontoon sections, and the entire forward part of the boat became crumpled and deflated. We were sitting on the Zodiac floorboards in the water.

Lars-Eric became soaked in his best outfit as the boat rapidly filled with water, and I felt sorry for him. All of us quickly folded up the deflated part over the remaining intact part of what was left of the Zodiac, which was not much. The engine was still okay, but Lars-Eric's suitcases were drenched in water. We were now driving something that barely was afloat, and I was concerned if we could make it to the shallow area and if the engine could last and be kept dry until we were safe. We looked at each other with astonishment at what had happened. We couldn't believe what we just had experienced.

We asked ourselves if there would be another attempt to kill us since orcas were experts at figuring out what was going on. For example, in Antarctica, they repeatedly will try to wave-wash a seal into the water from an ice floe if it escapes and jumps back on.

Perhaps the orca saw us as prey; hence, there would be a second attack shortly. It would try to wave-wash all of us into the water one by one, and then we would be easy prey for the hungry and evil black-and-white predator. What a nightmare, and what a horrifying destiny. What a horrible death it would be to end up in the stomach of a killer whale, I thought.

It was pointless to approach the boat coming from Santa Cruz since it was too far away, and we had to, under those rare, scary conditions, play safety first with the punctured boat;

therefore, we estimated the time and distance to the nearest shore of North Plaza Island as we carefully looked for the location of the orca pod and the next attack.

We looked at the engine to see if it could last until the shoreline since we knew we were sinking due to the water ingress that rose under the floorboards. Apparently, the remaining air compartment had been well punctured. The orcas were closely around, and it was obvious they showed interest in us.

The killer whale had done a good job, and he scared the hell out of us as the boat slowly but surely filled with water. It was now a matter of minutes until we went down. Could we reach the shoreline and safety? We were trapped by the evil killer whale, which once again appeared behind us. With begging eyes, we looked frequently at the deflated Zodiac pontoon's outboard engine, which was now coughing, hoping it would bring us to shallow water before we were all swimming. We hoped we could at least wade ashore with Lars-Eric and his luggage and ourselves. If that was not the case, we knew that female orcas could attack in extremely shallow water while the males stayed outside.

The shaft of the outboard engine was now totally submerged, and to our fear, we saw that the lower part of the engine casing was submerged, and then the engine went horribly quiet as we were still some hundred meters from the shoreline.

I quickly scanned the water surrounding us for the killer whale pods, especially the male with the huge dorsal fin that was directly responsible for our tragedy. We used the paddles and desperately paddled the rubber wreck with submerged suitcases and a scared and upset Lars-Eric. After much paddling and fear, we managed to reach the unfriendly, rocky shoreline, where we intensely waved to the boat from Santa Cruz to come pick us up. We offloaded Lars-Eric's luggage onto the rocky lava shore and waited for the pickup boat to come pick up Lars-Eric.

The boat arrived, and we transferred a wet Lars-Eric and his luggage to the boat. The *Lindblad Explorer* rescue Zodiac picked us up, including the remains of the deflated Zodiac.

Chapter 25

The Grounding of the *Lindblad Explorer* on Christmas Eve 1979 in Antarctica

THE FOLLOWING DRAMA GOT HUGE attention in newspapers worldwide because the *Lindblad Explorer* was on a voyage under charter of Kanokawa Films, a Japanese company that used her as a floating hotel for the camera crew and cast of a science-fiction film called *Virus*. American actors Glenn Ford, George Kennedy, Olivia Hussey, and Chuck Connors and the Swedish Hollywood actor Bo Svenson were on board to film the movie, and the cooperation of the movie was given to the Chilean vessel *Piloto Pardo* and the thirty-five-year-old Chilean submarine *Simpson*, originally the USS *Spot*.

She was probably the first submarine to operate in Antarctica since the USS *Sennet*, which had 1,816 tonnage, entered the Ross Sea with the United States Navy's Operation Highjump expedition in 1946–1947.

Men at the United States' Palmer Station were the first to learn of the movie stars in their neighbourhood. Two Jet Ranger helicopters from the *Piloto Pardo* arrived on December 8 with several Japanese film crew. At midnight, the submarine and the *Lindblad Explorer* arrived at Arthur Harbour, Palmer Station. The sub took on fresh water and fuel, and then everybody settled down to enjoy the brief visit. The Palmer Station personnel were invited on board both ships for banquets and festivities and were also given rides in the *Piloto Pardo* helicopters. Actor Chuck Connors flew over the station and waved to his fellow countrymen.

What happened on Christmas Day 1979 was a disaster. The *Lindblad Explorer* left Paradise Bay in Antarctica, heading for the British Antarctic station Port Lockroy. While aiming for the Neumayer Channel in the Gerlache Strait, she hit rocks on the port side and was almost lost.

At 11:52 a.m., the ship experienced a rough shock that went through the entire vessel. Some passengers and crew claim they fell out of their beds. The radio operator, Jack, fell off his chair in his cabin. The electrician, Anton, and Jack ran to the bridge in only their underpants after a call from the officer on duty alerted them.

The bridge officer on duty on the eight-to-twelve watch was a German second mate who was well acquainted with the sailing procedures and the safe route from Paradise Bay to the entrance of the Neumayer Channel. On that route, no shortcuts were permitted, as the port side of the entrance consisted of treacherous underwater stones. Therefore, a safe distance was always kept when entering the channel from the Gerlache Strait. Coming from the south, there was only one safe navigation route into the Neumayer Channel.

All watch-going bridge officers were well aware of that, apart from the captain, who was new to Antarctica. He told the mate to take a shortcut in sailing out from Paradise Bay toward the Neumayer Channel. The officer refused. He told the captain that he would set the ship on ground if he insisted on taking the shortcut. The captain then told the mate, "I am the master, and I decide what to do." The captain then took over the command from Officer Herman and altered the course toward port and the shallow areas north of Wiencke Island while the mate shouted, "No, don't do that!"

Shortly afterward, the *Lindblad Explorer* struck the rocks at 64°43.5′ S, 63°08.5′ W off Cape Astrup.

Anton, who rapidly arrived at the bridge, asked the captain if he should close all the watertight doors, and the captain responded, "Do it!" Anton pressed all the buttons on the panel, and with bells loudly ringing throughout the ship, the doors closed. Jack, still in his underpants, asked the master if he should send an SOS (Mayday), and the captain responded, "Yes, do so!" The picture above is from the echo sounder after the grounding.

Anton, also in his underpants, ran to his cabin to find his boiler suit. He then ran with the speed of a missile to the engine room because he felt the vessel was in a distress, and he needed to check the situation of the three electrical generators that supplied the ship with electrical power. Anton quickly pulled out a provisional electrical cable from the emergency generator room on the boat deck port side to the radio station to secure the power connection.

To the left is the logbook extract on the bridge from the grounding.

At 1300, the deck crew launched, on the captain's order, all the lifeboats into the sea, and at 1305, over the ship's PA system, the captain informed all the passengers that the *Lindblad Explorer* had run aground, and the situation was under control. Meanwhile, the radio operator, Jack, still in his underpants, transmitted the SOS as the water ingress in the engine room drenched the electrical generators, and the ship went black. The emergency generator started automatically; hence, the radio station could continue to function. To preserve the vital electrical power points in the vessel, such as the emergency lights in the vessel, and to be able to communicate with the world, the radio station needed power, but apparently, there was a problem.

As the power diminished in the ship, the priority was to keep the radio station going; hence, there was a need to shut down the emergency lights in the accommodations. Anton told Jack to go to his cabin and dress himself, which he did. At 1320, Anton and Jack were dead tired, as was Tevita. Anton later said his stomach was in his throat, his heart was racing, and his legs were tired from the frequent running between the engine room and the bridge. He sat in the emergency generator room on the boat deck port side with a Tongan engine crew to keep an eye on the emergency generator. They were freezing under their boiler suits, as the outside temperature was zero degrees and, of course, dropping as the night approached. Anton had only his boiler suit and nothing else underneath. The AB brought them three glasses of cognac, a gift from the master. Anton tried to drink, but he vomited, as did the Tongan crew. They then through the nice cognac glasses overboard, along with the cognac bottle. Before that, they cleaned their oily hands with the cognac. Anton then went to the radio station, as the radio officer, Jack, and the master wanted him to be there instead.

The radio station was apparently functioning, and suddenly, they received confirmation of the transmitted SOS from Australia, South Africa, McMurdo Sound's US Antarctic station, the Russian station Bellingshausen on King George Island, and the Polish Antarctica station Arctowski. After some minutes, they also received confirmation from the Chilean warship *Piloto Pardo* and a Chilean submarine heading for Chile.

First to reach the *Lindblad Explorer* in distress was the Chilean Navy ship *Piloto Pardo*. Three other ships were also asked to assist: the Norwegian research ship *Polar Circle* on her way to the Weddell Sea with a West German base survey expedition, the Soviet freighter *Gueizer* in Punta Arenas, and the Russian high-seas tugboat *Uragan*. The *Uragan* responded and started to talk with the *Lindblad Explorer*. She was apparently guarding a Russian fishing fleet in the southern part of Drake Passage, and they were fairly close to the scene of the grounding, but there was a communication problem, as the Russian could not speak English. Consequently, the captain asked the Broström Company in Gothenburg if they agreed that the *Uragan* should assist the *Lindblad Explorer*. The answer was a direct yes.

Meanwhile, Anton disconnected the power to the radio station and switched on the emergency lighting in the vessel for the passengers while the master held a conference with all the ship's officers. At 1345, the power to the radio station was reconnected, and the emergency lighting in the accommodations was disconnected. On the master's order, they called up the Chilean warship *Piloto Pardo*, asking them to assist. They thanked the Chilean submarine for their help, saying the *Piloto Pardo* would be assisting shortly.

On December 25, not much happened apart from some terrifying noises coming from the keel as the ship moved slightly on the rocks while the radio operator was in touch with the *Piloto Pardo*. At 1650, the *Piloto Pardo* arrived and dropped the anchor about one nautical mile to the north of the *Lindblad Explorer*.

The entire technical engine crew from the *Piloto Pardo*, with divers, boarded with hopes of making some temporary underwater repairs. They made an assessment of the damages, and their response was "Senores, *reparaciones no possible. Barco finito.*" The *Lindblad Explorer* was, according to them, domed. Most of her tanks were penetrated.

The lifeboats transferred all the passengers to the *Piloto Pardo*, along with all mattresses, pillows, and blankets and the entire provision storeroom with meat, sausages, butter, cheese, tins, coffee, beer, wine, and more. The vessel was stripped except for food for the crew remaining on board.

Everybody worked intensively to complete the transfer to the *Piloto Pardo* because she had received a severe-weather warning. At 2000 hours, all the passengers—ladies first— were transferred in orderly fashion, followed by the entire Japanese technical film crew.

None of the American actors were on board during the grounding. At 2200 hours, all the ship's crew, with passenger luggage and crew luggage, were transferred.

Some twenty crew members remained on board, including all officers and two female housekeepers. On December 26, at 0100 hours, Antarctica showed its worst side. A deep, low pressure from the southwest with strong gale force and heavy snowfall caused the ship to move dangerously on the rocks. The increasing wind moved the ship even more while the crew on board heard with fear the sound of the damaged keel plates as the ship moved around in the hard wind with the forward area still on the rocks.

Since the grounding apparently took place in a low tide (the tidewater range in Antarctica is approximately 0.5 centimetres in average), there would be an imminent risk when the tide rose. The vessel would lose stability and could potentially sink. The situation was critical and a nightmare for the crew on board. As the wind blew with a horrifying force, the ship moved, and the keel plates were definitely suffering. The temperature inside the ship was -8 degrees Celsius. Jack and Anton were sitting together in the radio station, comforting each other while they listened to all the doors banging and slamming in the accommodations down below.

It was a nerve-racking situation. They went down to close all the doors, and then it went quiet, besides the horrific sound coming from the keel. Anton said they collected the remains from the passengers, such as stockings, scarves, and gloves, to keep their bodies warm during the night.

One day passed, and the second day, the Russian tug was on the radio. They said in bad English, "Shall we come to you?"

The answer was yes!

The Russians said they had been in touch with Leningrad and told the *Lindblad Explorer*, "We can help you out."

The *Lindblad Explorer* responded, "Thank you. Come here!"

Meanwhile, as they tried to maintain radio contact with the rescue ships *Piloto Pardo* and *Uragan*, the water ingress in the engine room became serious and killed all the electrical generators. The entire ship went black, including every pump. The outside temperature was -8 degrees at night and 0 degrees in the daytime. All toilets were out of function, and no drinking water in the taps was available. The captain said they would have to abandon the ship in the lifeboats. The ship's doctor, who was still on board, came with tranquilizer tablets to calm them down, and he took one pill himself.

Jack shouted, "I have collected all the ship's cash money in a big plastic bag!" Anton attached it to Jack's bare chest using strong duct tape. Jack then helped Anton attach a plastic bag with lots of paper money to his body. On his back was a plastic bag with the book *My Voyages at Sea*. The ship's doctor assisted Anton in taping and wrapping himself up with electrical tape, and then they dressed themselves with whatever clothes they could find.

It was four in the morning on December 27, 1979, and they could not sleep. The entire night, they listened in fear to the ships keel banging against the rocks. He connected the electrical power to the radio station. Jack called up the Russian tug. The Russians said, "Your flag?"

The answer was "Panama, but the owners are the Broström Company in Gothenburg, Sweden."

"What happened?"

"We ran up onto the rocks."

"What has happened to the ship?"

"The engine room is taking in water, and the ship's generators are flooded."

"Has anyone been killed or drowned?"

"Nobody killed or drowned."

"We are heading toward you, but we had to reduce the speed due to the severe weather, and we do not have any appropriate sea charts over the Gerlache Strait."

At 0800 hours, they launched their two remaining lifeboats with approximately ten crew in each. The sea conditions were extremely rough as they touched the water, but they managed to make their way to the gangway platform. At the platform, the boats pitched up and down several meters because they were exposed to the rough seas in the Gerlache Strait. The crew could only jump into the lifeboat when the boat was at the same level as the platform. The first to go were the remaining three girls. Anton, who was not that fit, faced difficulties when embarking the lifeboat, and unfortunately, he hit his right knee with subsequent severe pain. Then they took off in the bumpy Gerlache Strait toward the *Piloto Pardo*, which was somewhere one nautical mile away to the north. Bear in mind that at the entrance to the Neumayer Channel and nearby areas, it was impossible to anchor. Hence, the *Piloto Pardo* was lucky to find an anchor position to the north, wherever it was.

The captain told Anton to keep order in the boat because he was superior and had more experience than the rest of the crew in the lifeboat. The captain then waved goodbye to the lifeboats and remained on board until further notice, as per the rules.

It was a horrible storm, and the two lifeboats pitched heavily, with the wind punishing the passengers' wet and cold faces. The order was to go to the *Piloto Pardo* with the crew. Anton sat at the tiller while the girls huddled together in the bow of the lifeboat for protection against the high seas and wind. Anton went rapidly forward and covered the girls with tarps taken from the vessel for safety reasons. As he did, he told them to stay calm. Due to the heavy sea condition and the sea spray, the water lever rose in the lifeboat. The lifeboat had to approach a huge iceberg to get some shelter and give everybody on board a moment of calm and at least no wind for a while.

In the shelter of the huge iceberg, the Filipino crew started to pump out the water from the boat with the fixed manual pump to keep the water level at a minimum as the girls vomited and suffered.

The stewardess came to Anton, saying, "I must make a pee!"

Anton, who was a genuine gentleman, prepared a big piece of tarpaulin attached to his body, and on Anton's order, she crawled between his legs behind the tarp, which was blowing in the wind, and did whatever she had to do. Then she went back to the bow of the lifeboat. After a while, the two remaining girls were in the same desperate need, which caused Anton to shout, "Girls, now it's time to stop peeing, for heaven's sake!"

One girl, the bar waitress, swiftly responded, "Anton, please do not be upset; maybe my nerves are out of order, but we consider you to be our father in this horrible lifeboat, and we rely on you."

The hours went by, and they were all freezing to their bones. The beard of Anton became like ice taps due to the howling Antarctic wind. At 1200 hours, they departed the shelter of the iceberg, looking toward the *Lindblad Explorer*, if she was still afloat. Yes, the boat was still afloat, and she had a lifeboat alongside.

They arrived at *Piloto Pardo*, offloaded the stewardesses, and started the journey back to the *Lindblad Explorer*. When they came back on board, the captain gave a glass of wine to Anton and asked him if he still had the money attached to his body, which he confirmed.

The Russian tug said they would arrive that day at 2400 hours. Meanwhile, the two lifeboats took lots of damage in the high seas while riding up and down at the gangway platform. At 1600 hours, the remaining crew had to abandon the vessel into a Zodiac and leave all personal articles behind, and off they went to the *Piloto Pardo*.

The Russians' tug, the *Uragan*, had to heave to the north of Dallmann Bay on the evening of December 26, as they didn't have the appropriate sea charts for safe sailing toward the grounded *Lindblad Explorer*; hence, it was agreed that the *Piloto Pardo* would take Chief Officer Goran over to the tug with the relevant chart to bring her down to the *Lindblad Explorer*. The idea was that they would pull her off the rocks with no crew on board because no one knew if she would stay afloat during the operation due to the bad weather in the area, including light snow, poor visibility, and eighteen to twenty-five knots of wind.

Due to the grounding incident, the insurance company, the Swedish Club, hired the Swedish towing company Röda Bolaget for a salvage operation from Antarctica to a shipyard in Chile. The company hired from Cape Town a bigger tug, a supply ship, that was supposed to tow the *Lindblad Explorer* to Talcahuano Shipyard in Chile, and the Swedish Club hired a smaller tug as well to assist with the towing. It would stay behind the *Lindblad Explorer* during the towing operation.

The next day, the Soviet tug *Uragan* pulled the *Lindblad Explorer* off the rocks while the remaining skeleton crew sat in a Zodiac next to her, concerned about whether she would stay afloat or not. They all expected her to go down, but amazingly, she stayed afloat, to everybody's surprise. She was then towed to King George Island by the *Uragan*, close to the Polish base Arctowski, for makeshift repair in a sheltered bay, where she stayed for some two months. The Chilean technical crew, along with some skeleton crew, repaired the tank tops as much as they could prior to the upcoming tow to Chile. Because she was heavily ripped up on the bottom and partly flooded in the engine room, a huge number of wooden supporters were shipped down from Chile and fitted to strengthen the tank top, as she was apparently only floating on the one.

They spent approximately two months on King George Island, making the vessel ready prior to the Drake Passage with the skeleton crew on board, as it was of the utmost importance, she was prepared for one of the world's toughest oceans, where three oceans met. When worse came to worse, the waves could easily build up to some thirty meters of height, which was indeed a pretty good show. The Russian captain of the tug supply ship coming from Cape Town had plans to tow the *Lindblad Explorer* to Elephant Island because he thought there would be more shelter to check the towing gears again prior to the crossing. Goran, however, had objections regarding that idea, saying there were no proper anchor positions around Elephant Island. However, the insurance company and the Russian captain refused to listen to his advice, and they towed the ship to Elephant Island. When they finally arrived at Elephant Island, they figured out they were wrong in their decision, and they returned to the Arctowski base for two days. When they finally took off for Drake Passage, Goran was on board the tug supply ship during the crossing and took photos, as shown below.

Drake Passage was without a doubt the world's stormiest area.

The second engineer, Rolf, volunteered to stay on board the *Lindblad Explorer* during the towing, while the first engineer, Hans, went to the *Piloto Pardo* with the second officer, Leif. The *Uragan* then returned to the Russian fishing fleet.

The *Piloto Pardo* had already departed for Puerto Williams in southern Chile in the Beagle Channel with all the passengers, film crew, and ship crew. The crossing was difficult and took its toll on everybody and everything, including the towing gears. When they approached the Cape Horn area, they did not get permission from the Chilean Navy to sail between the southern island and inland sea to Talcahuano and were directed to sail through Estrecho de Maire and the Isla de los Estados to Estrecho de Magallanes to Punta Arenas.

Coming finally to Punta Arenas, which was located far outside the route to Talcahuano, the tug finally dropped her anchor outside that remote Chilean city. They stayed at anchor for a couple days, resting and checking the towing gear, before continuing through the Magallanes Strait and inland sea toward Talcahuano. The relieve Captain came down to Punta Arenas since he was the head of the towing company Röda Bolaget.

Talufa told me several years later that it was a nightmarish crossing. They faced a rough storm, and they could hear the hull and the keel plates shredding and suffering violently in the rough seas each time the ship pitched in Drake Passage. They slept in fear on board during the crossing, having no heat and a constant fear the tank top would suddenly crack and break down, causing the ship to sink on the spot. Despite all this, they finally arrived at Talcahuano Shipyard, where she was repaired.

She was then sold to Swire Pacific Offshore, a Hong Kong company, and she resumed her expedition cruises worldwide. From that day until she was sold in 1984 to Society Expeditions and in 1992 to Abercrombie and Kent in Chicago, she never experienced any other major problems. In 2003, I brought her to Genoa, Italy, to the inner harbor, where she was put up for sale. Unfortunately, in November 2007, she sank in the Bransfield Strait in Antarctica due to an inexperienced bridge command with inadequate Antarctic knowledge.

Chapter 26

I Was Offered to Become a Ship Pilot in the South Pacific Micronesia

ON JULY 10, 1993, I was lucky to return to the *Explorer*, which was now under the ownership of Abercrombie and Kent in Chicago, in the Keppel Batangas Shipyard in the Philippines, which was some two hours south of Manila. The vessel was under the management of V Ships in New York. It had been fifteen years since I walked on the decks of the Ex *Lindblad Explorer*, and now I was finally back on board. This time, her name was the *Explorer*, and she was laid up in Batangas Shipyard in the Philippines for a three-month refit after she had been taken over by Abercrombie and Kent in Chicago.

The Swedish captain had been on board during the shipyard time, but he left when the vessel was ready to sail when the captain from Germany took over the command, and I was the happy chief officer.

There was apparently not much money available from the Explorer Shipping Corporation in Chicago during the shipyard period, and the CEO apparently did not realize that the vessel was in desperate need of provision via a local ship chandler. Seemingly, he was not paid on time; hence, one day a government official with a black briefcase came to the ship and put a huge yellow patch on the port bridge windows, showing the ship was detained until further notice. It was a peculiar feeling to see the yellow piece of paper with bold letters showing we were detained. I still ask myself how that person found his way to the outer part of our bridge windows. When the official person finally left, we rapidly removed the yellow sign from the window, and we called the Chicago office to tell them what was going on.

Later on, I figured out that the case was settled, and the ship chandler finally got his money.

We were bound for Chile through the entire South Pacific Ocean and all its remote, exotic islands. Our first cruise began in Yap Island in the Caroline Islands and went to Apia in the American Samoa; the second cruise was to Papeete, Tahiti; and the last cruise went from Papeete to Valparaiso in Chile. We departed Batangas, sailing out through the San Bernardino Strait, with the Luzon Peninsula at the port side, for Yap Island in the Federated States of Micronesia, where our passengers arrived for the first cruise.

However, shortly after we left Batangas Shipyard, our food reefers on board ceased to work, and within a few hours, all our frozen food started to melt. We saw disaster quickly coming, so we immediately asked V Ships in New York for a technician from the USA to attend ASAP, but he wouldn't be able to arrive in time before all our frozen food was completely lost.

The ship was for the time being under the management of V Ships in New York, but the owners were Abercrombie and Kent in Chicago. The CEO was the son of an admiral who'd commanded the British naval task force in the South Atlantic during the Falklands War in 1982. He worked out the timetable for the campaign, starting from the beginning and working it to the end. Knowing that the Argentine forces had to be defeated before the Southern Hemisphere winter made conditions too bad, he set a latest date by which the land forces had to be ashore, and that in turn set a latest date by which control of the air was achieved.

Coming alongside in Yap, we tied up in the small container terminal—one ship size—surrounded by Japanese fishing factories everywhere. That gave us some hope because we thought we perhaps could get some professional aid from them, but that was not the case. Meanwhile, the harbor area was full of sharks that surrounded the *Explorer* due to all the blood in the water.

We immediately involved the Yap harbor authorities in the search for a twenty-foot reefer container to hire until we arrived at Apia in the American Samoa. Finally, the reefer container arrived, though it looked like it came from a scrap yard. It was lifted on board onto our forward cargo hatch situated on the forecastle. The sight of the shameful container did not fit into our expedition cruise ship concept, but the reefer container was desperately needed.

Because we were an expedition cruise ship with no deck space for containers, apart from a tiny space on top of our forward hatch seven by three meters on the forecastle, we were not equipped or prepared with any kind of securing or lashing material on board for those kinds of events. Consequently, I left the ship with two deckhands and walked in the harbor area, searching for turnbuckles, wires, and wire clips. We dug in all kinds of metal scraps and piles at the pier where we thought there could be securing material but without any success. Luckily, we managed to get hold of two local policemen driving in a small police car, and we bribed them to drive us to various places on the island in search of the owners of shops that might have the items we desperately needed.

Every shop owner we met was chewing red tobacco with pleasure. Due to the presence of the police, the shop owners opened up their shops one by one, and the three of us rushed in, looking for the lashing material with torches in our hands, but we found nothing.

We gave up, and we became depressed because we knew we had to find something that could keep the container in its position as we sailed in the Pacific Ocean. Finally, we found far away from the *Explorer* a rusty Japanese fishing trawler alongside the jetty, and full of confidence, we boarded the trawler, shouting, "Hello!" We told them our problems and begged and bribed them for some lashing material, which, to our surprise, we finally received.

We couldn't believe our eyes when the Japanese crew on board happily gave us everything we needed, though it was rusty, including wires and clips sufficient to secure our twenty-foot container. We were deeply grateful. We happily paid them with US dollars. After coming back on board with huge smiles, we started to secure the twenty-foot reefer container. We then connected the power cable, and to our relief, the cooling system was running. What a beautiful sound it was to hear the reefer system running.

At 1800 hours, as the sun was setting, we sailed out from the Yap harbor with the green sea marks on the port side and yellow marks at the starboard, doing some six to seven course changes in the fairway between the reefs, until we were safely outside the lagoon. We instantly knew the huge container on the forecastle would cause us stability problems once we were out in the open sea, and we had to alter the course. Each time the duty officer on the bridge had to alter the course either to starboard or to port, he said, "Slowly, slowly come to starboard."

We had a chief sea pilot on board whose jurisdiction was between Yap and Pohnpei, and our first island was the Ulithi atoll.

The following morning, we positioned ourselves outside the reef entrance to the Ulithi Islands, and the pilot was remarkably quiet. He let me do the navigation with the captain as we slowly entered the only reef opening on the east side of the islands. As a matter of fact, I felt he had minimal knowledge of reef navigation; hence, he never made any comments to assist us in our actions whatsoever.

We sailed slowly on a course of 318 degrees with a safeguarding speed through the reef entrance with a minimum depth of twelve meters under the keel, which was a lot, looking carefully at the underwater reefs from the bridge wings to starboard and port side in the clear water, until we were safely inside the reefs. Then we altered the course to 30 degrees and dropped the anchor 0.3 cables from the small village of Mogmog. This was the breathtaking, romantic, beautiful South Pacific I had always dreamed about as a young teenager.

When I was off the watch, I went ashore with the cabin stewardess Sol, a beautiful Filipino woman, and together we walked around the entire small coral island. We went for a swim dressed in our clothes, and afterward, we were covered with fine white coral sand.

On our way back to the landing site, we met females who walked topless, and some were sleeping in hammocks as we gently walked through their domains. Their men chewed constantly on their red stimulants, looking at us. The sun was harsh and burned my skin noticeably.

I was happy to be back in the South Pacific, and I enjoyed every hour of the day. I loved my daily sea watches on the bridge between four and eight, and the captain was in his prime. He was a genuine social master on board. Together we were a good team.

Obviously, the sea pilot—unfortunately, I cannot recall his name—had noted that I was a good navigator. While we lay at anchor in Mogmog, he asked me onto the bridge.

"Mr. Mate," he said, "I have noted that you have a feeling for close navigation between these reefs, and in this respect, I'd like to ask you if you have an interest in becoming a sea pilot for our company in the Federated States of Micronesia, because we are in a need of an additional pilot here."

Upon hearing his words, I was astonished and didn't know what to say.

Furthermore, he said, "You will have your own bungalow at the seaside and your own car at the company's expense."

I was speechless at his offer. I was stunned because I had just returned to the *Explorer,* which had been my dream for a thousand reasons, and now, when I was finally back on board the Little Grand Old Lady, living out my South Pacific dreams, I was suddenly offered a job as a sea pilot in the South Pacific paradise.

Paradise is subjective, but this was true paradise, and I was right in the middle of it. I was flattered. On top of that, I was offered a fairly good salary, and what more could one ask for? Even though I was offered good living conditions, I started to think about my free time. I imagined sipping a tropical drink on my terrace alone while watching the turquoise lagoon and blue ocean behind. I knew that typhoons for sure once in a while hit Micronesia from July to mid-November. Though I was an adventurous person, it did not appeal to me that I probably would have to flee somewhere when all hell broke loose—but to where, since it was a flat island exposed to everything?

I knew if I lived there, one day a lady probably would seduce me and want to have a life and a child with me—and God knew what else. I had a son at home in Sweden, and I did not want to be without him. Therefore, I had a thousand questions in my head, but I knew what the outcome would be if I settled down in the Federated States of Micronesia as a sea pilot.

It was the first time in my life I was really confused, and I felt as if my boyhood dreams told me, *Do it. Accept the offer. What are you thinking about? Just accept!* No, it was not that easy. My son was my everything, and he could not come to me because of his schooling.

I wanted to consult the captain in command about my dilemma because I was in doubt about what was going on regarding the job that suddenly had been offered to me. I had only been on board for some three months, and I hesitated to talk about it, because I saw the hula girls in my mind ahead of me. I thought about lying in my bed as a teenager, looking at the world map hanging above my bed, and dreaming of the romantic South Pacific. Now I was right in the middle of paradise with a sudden new job offer down there. I guess it was my boyhood dream that made me confused.

Well, the chief pilot gave me a respite to ponder his offer until we arrived at Pohnpei fourteen days later.

On August 29, I wrote in my diary,

> Just before sunset, we pulled up the anchor, and we sailed for the Sorol Islands, using a Japanese government chart from 1925 for our approach.

The program for our passengers for the morning included the following:

> Sorol is an uninhabited atoll, though at one time there were several families living there making their living in the copra and fishing trade. We plan to spend the morning on Sorol and one of the outlying islands in the atoll searching for nesting seabirds. We will also have the late morning at leisure to enjoy snorkeling, beach coming or scuba diving.

We approached the island from the north, having the island on our starboard side, and the island was plainly visible on the radar screen due to a sunken Japanese fishing trawler. We kept a distance of 0.9 nautical miles from the reef on our starboard side as we sailed around the southern tip of the reef to the east, sailing slowly until we arrived at the position, where we stayed adrift the entire morning, as the water depth under the keel was 414 meters. During the entire morning, blood from the melting reefer container dripped down into the turquoise water; thus, sharks swarmed around the ship. It was not fun to see.

We had a potential incoming technician from New York, who was supposed to fly in and land at Woleai Island, which was part of Yap State. We had received information that there was apparently an airfield on that island.

We departed Sorol at 1400 hours and sailed for Woleai Island.

In 1944, as the Allied forces closed in on the Mariana Islands, Woleai was heavily fortified by a contingent of 6,426 troops from the Imperial Japanese Army's IJA Fiftieth Independent Mixed Brigade and the Imperial Japanese Navy's Forty-Fourth Base Guard Unit and 216th Base Construction Unit. Wolfe Islet was completely leveled and made into an airfield with a single 3,290-foot runway and 2,050-foot taxiway. A seaplane anchorage was also constructed off the southwest corner of Woleai Islet. The island and its military facilities were bombed on numerous occasions from the end of 1944 until the middle of 1945, driving its defenders underground and isolating them from supplies and reinforcements. Upon the surrender of Japan, only 1,650 survivors remained; the rest had perished from starvation or disease. Following World War II, the atoll came under the control of the United States of America. It was administered as part of the Trust Territory of the Pacific Islands from 1947 and became part of the Federated States of Micronesia beginning in 1979.

On August 30, I wrote in my diary,

> A very exciting day. We are waiting for an incoming service technician to repair our broken-down reefers system on board, and if this was not possible, he had to as well repair our twenty-foot reefer container on the forecastle. We arrived to Woleai Island in the early morning using a US chart of 1944, which was accurate enough for passing Falalis Island on 0.4 cables on our port side leading up to our anchorage position in the west lagoon, which was kind of outside the inner reefs, though it was inside the lagoon and some 0.5 nautical miles from the landing beach. Here we dropped the anchor in a bad holding ground, as it was pure coral bottom. It was a strange lagoon but breathtakingly beautiful. The water was just unbelievably blue and so inviting. Again, that water surrounding our ship hull was full of sharks due to the leaking container.

Over the radio, the locals told us that the landing strip from World War II was underwater, and it was not possible for a plane of any kind to land. They said the middle part of the airstrip was underwater as a consequence of the last heavy rain they'd had. We had our doubts about this, and we demanded to see the airfield with our own eyes because the situation on board was becoming serious, and we were running short of fresh food. Hence, the technician was now desperately needed because we were running out of food on board.

The chief engineer and I decided to go ashore to figure out what was going on with the submerged landing strip from World War II, the only airstrip available for our service reefer technician to arrive on from the USA. It was a situation of emergency for our passengers and crew, because if it turned out the airstrip was full of water and no plane could land, then we were in deep trouble.

We took off with a Zodiac loaded with lots of spare gasoline tanks because the old airstrip was located on Woleai Island, which was some four nautical miles away. We were in the West Lagoon, and we had the reefs ahead of us and a few sandy islands as well. We drove through the reefs until we met some locals in outrigger canoes who were diving for fish. We asked them for a safe way toward the beach and the village, and to our surprise, they spoke English. They told us how to drive, and I felt like Captain James Cook in uncharted waters.

We finally beached our Zodiac on Utagal Island, in front of some palm huts, and some locals slowly made their way down to us, staring at us. We asked for permission to talk with the chief of the islands, and they referred us to Woleai Island, which was some four nautical miles away. We showed them our gratefulness, and we backed out from the beach and started to drive the four nautical miles toward Woleai into the East Lagoon.

As we drove toward Woleai's East Lagoon, it suddenly started to rain. We arrived at Woleai Island, where we again beached the Zodiac while the locals assembled on the beach, looking curiously at us. We were soaking wet in the heavy rainfall that had come from nowhere. The chief engineer and I only had T-shirts on as we walked up the beach while the palm trees slowly waved in the gentle rain. We walked slowly toward the huts and asked for somebody in charge. My glasses were completely out of focus due to the water on my face. It was a strange feeling to stand in my swimming shorts barefoot on the sandy beach in heavy rain with a wet T-shirt, seeing almost nothing. Desperately, I tried to wipe my glasses clean in an attempt to orientate myself. However, my sight just got worse, and I ended up seeing almost nothing.

Finally, after I had made my way toward a hut with a palm roof and become even more soaking wet, a good-hearted person who saw my difficulties in cleaning my glasses offered me a rag to dry my glasses. The rag was not dry, and the world outside was blurred, but still, I gratefully showed him my thankfulness. To our surprise, the rain stopped.

Then the chief of Woleai Island unexpectedly came to us, and we explained to him the reason for our visit. He said in poor English that if we wanted to see the airfield, we were only allowed to do so without our T-shirts on.

I was stunned at that kind of a ritual and demand and looked at the chief engineer. He slowly took off his T-shirt, and so did I. In the meantime, we had to wait for transportation to the old airfield under the palm roofs. Suddenly, after half an hour, an old jeep from the US Army era came. We jumped up, and off we went to the airfield.

As we drove, we occasionally saw wrecked planes, cannons, bunkers, and dumped heavy equipment in the bush from the jeep. The road was muddy and bumpy, and the rain was again pouring down. My T-shirt was hanging on my shoulder. Suddenly, the runway from World War II came into sight in front of us. It was a peculiar feeling to see the old wartime airstrip. I told the driver to drive on the landing strip, which he did, to get a feeling of how much water there actually was.

We lost all hope, as we could see the middle part of the runway was sagging and completely submerged. Furthermore, the landing strip was in bad condition. I measured the water depth, and it turned out to be some twenty centimeters of water, which was too much for the safe landing of an airplane. For the first time in my life, I acted as a person authorized to judge if an airplane could land on an airfield—in that case, a remote World War II airfield.

I radioed over the walkie-talkie to the ship and the captain about the prevailing situation, and I suggested we take ashore a gasoline-driven pump to pump out the water into the surrounding jungle terrain with hopes of lowering the water level for a safe landing, but that would have taken an enormous amount of time to accomplish. The captain sighed into the radio when he heard the verdict. We were running out of proper food on board, and we became nervous because a safe landing for our incoming potential reefer service engineer had turned out to be impossible.

In our misery, we told the driver to go back to the beach, and I was told over the radio there was going to be a barbecue party on an adjacent island, with the local dance team doing a performance for our passengers. That cheered me up; it was a consolation. What a wonderful idea it was to cheer up our passengers and ourselves.

Since Woleai Island could not offer us any vegetables, we counted the days and hours until we arrived at the next scheduled island, asking them in advance over the radio if they could sell some vegetables to us.

As the sun was setting, all the passengers took off to the adjacent beach, along with the galley crew and the barbecue equipment. A barbecue was set up on the beach with an open fire and romantic guitar music performed by the crew band.

At eight o'clock, I went ashore in my white uniform shorts and short-sleeved shirt, and I was met by happy-go-lucky passengers and crew dancing on the beach as the moon slowly rose above the horizon, making the water dazzling. The sea pilot was there as well, and he asked me again, "Mr. Mate, have you made up your mind if you'd like to become a pilot in the South Pacific?"

Looking at the glossy, calm East Lagoon in that gorgeous paradise and hearing the beautiful guitar music from one of our ship waiters, who was singing Elvis Presley's "Blue Hawaii," I told the chief pilot, "Mr. Pilot, we need to discuss this."

The Filipino cabin stewardess suddenly came walking by, and I persuaded her to take a swim with me in that beautiful dream world, a gorgeous, calm lagoon with the moon rising above the horizon. Together we jumped into the glittering water. I had only my white uniform shorts on, but so what?

I was happy to be there in that paradise, though it was just for a couple hours. I thought about my son back in Sweden and how unfair it was that I was there, and he couldn't join me.

Suddenly, the sky grew darker in the already dark night as the moon went behind the clouds, and we felt raindrops falling slowly. It was a warning sign of more rain to come.

Amid sudden, intense rain, the barbecue came to an abrupt end, and all of us rushed to the beach, soaking wet, to the waiting Zodiacs while some crew killed the barbecue fire and then carried the barbecue grill and supplies to the Zodiacs on the beach. As the Zodiacs were almost filled up with passengers, crew, and the galley equipment, some of us pulled the boats, wading, until we had water enough for the propellers.

The moon shone on the water as we drove back to the *Explorer* in a heavy rain while everybody sang, soaking wet. It was true paradise in that breathtaking South Pacific lagoon while the moon was shining. It was like sweet music in our ears, and everybody was stunned at what that part of the globe could offer.

At ten thirty that night, all passengers were back on board, and we pulled up the anchor and slowly sailed out from Woleai's East Lagoon toward Ifalik Island in Yap State, which was forty-five nautical miles away to the southeast. It was an easy navigation out to open water, and we had our premade safe distances in the radar.

I did my sea watch from four to eight the next morning, as usual, and as per my bridge routines, I spent time on the open bridge wing with a cup of coffee in my hand, enjoying the magnificent South Pacific with the moon still hanging above the horizon. I also watched from the bridge wing the blood from our twenty-foot reefer container on the forecastle leaking down into the ocean.

The following morning, at 0600 hours, we arrived at the southern part of Ifalik Island. The lagoon was approximately one nautical mile wide, with Ifalik Island to the east and Flalap Island to the southeast. It was a breathtaking island where the palm trees slowly swayed in the wind.

The arrival chart we had was, as usual, from a sketch— "Survey on a Japanese Government Chart of 1925"—but it was accurate enough for our arrival. We did not have the guts to enter the narrow southern passage sailing into the lagoon; hence, we stayed adrift outside the reef entrance because it was far too deep to anchor up. That morning, the passengers spent some four hours snorkeling inside the reef, and for the brave ones, there was scuba diving at the drop-off outside the reef, with a depth of some fifty fathoms, or one hundred meters.

We took up the anchor at midday and continued to sail to various islands in the South Pacific, including Lamotrek Island, where we dropped the anchor inside the lagoon.

We dropped the anchor on every inhabited island that came in our path, and we were able to purchase some fresh vegetables to keep our passengers happy and keep all of us alive. We begged the locals for vegetables and chickens as much as we could. We did not receive much, but the food kept our passengers happy until we arrived at Truk Island, which was our savior.

On Truk Island, we went alongside at the small commercial berth, which could barely accommodate one ship with our size. All passengers and crew received orchid necklaces upon our arrival.

Because Truk is a diver's paradise, scuba diving and snorkeling were on the agenda for that day.

The day's program for Truk Island said the following:

Quote:

> Disembark for morning Island tour which will include a bus ride. Then transfer to pick-up trucks for a drive thru the jungle to see huge caliber Japanese guns. Those wishing to take a more strenuous hike will take a 10-minute uphill walk, then climb 90 steps to a Japanese lighthouse for a spectacular view. All passengers will be able to enjoy the view from the top of Xavier high school (formerly a fortified Japanese communication center, and currently a Jesuit high school). The tour will also include the Chuuk ethnographic center to view local artifacts and photos of the surrender ceremony, and a stop at the local handicraft center.

Unquote:

I went for a flight in a two-propeller Beaver seaplane to see most of the twenty-five sunken Japanese wrecks in the lagoon from the above with a group of passengers. The technician from New York then finally arrived in the afternoon with all the proper spare parts, and what a relief it was to finally see that shameful, monstrous container land ashore in Truk. Our next problem was that we were unable to get fresh water enough to fill up our tanks. The *Explorer* had a freshwater tank capacity of 204 tons; hence, we had to implement freshwater restrictions on board for everybody, which meant showering together.

We arrived at Pohnpei on September 5, 1993, and the service technician stood on the pier with spare parts for our reefer system. It was by mere luck that we had been able to keep all 160 people on board alive with our limited amount of food.

I also knew that it was now or never in terms of deciding my future life. The chief pilot told me, "Peter, let's go to our office to talk through things. It is in our interest to explain to you what we'd like you to do for us."

When I came to his office, there was the CEO of the pilot association of the Federated States of Micronesia. As we met, he asked me to sit down while he explained to me the technical pilot association's rules and such. I was stuffed with information about the rules when piloting a ship from Yap to Pohnpei.

He said, "We'd like you to be our sea pilot in the Federated States of Micronesia. Our chief pilot has noticed you have the skills needed and a feeling for doing close reef navigation. And of course, you will get a nice bungalow close to the sea in Pohnpei." Yes, he was bribing me, and it was certainly a beautiful bribe.

Upon hearing his words, I was stunned, and I knew I was just seconds or minutes away from signing my life away in a different direction just by saying yes. He looked at my face, eager to hear my response. Saying no was not an immediate option from my side. I contemplated if this was really what I wanted to do, when I was now happy to be back on board the *Explorer*, where I truly felt I belonged. I knew I could fuck up my life completely by saying yes and probably would regret many things afterward, so I got my act together and told the CEO and the chief pilot, "Gentlemen, I am deeply grateful for this job offer, but for a thousand reasons, I cannot accept this." I thanked them for the confidence they had in me, and I walked out of their office, smelling the beautiful air of the tropical island. A taxi took me back to the waiting *Explorer*.

The first South Pacific cruise was finally over, and it had been a nightmarish cruise in many respects due to the lack of food on board, though it had been an exciting cruise. All of us were pleased to see a mobile crane land the container from the forward cargo hatch. I noticed that since 1977 sixteen years earlier, when we'd cruised the South Pacific Ocean with the *Lindblad Explorer*, major changes had taken place in the islands of the South Pacific Ocean.

In the evening, I left the ship with my fellow ship comrades, and we went to a disco. We danced with the local girls, and to my surprise, there were some European ladies as well. Most likely, they came from their sailing yachts. Oh yeah, this was unconditional paradise.

The following day, I met a Swede who was the port captain in Rarotonga in the Cook Islands.

The next morning, we left for Apia in the American Samoa with sufficient food in our reefer rooms for the new cruise to Papeete in Tahiti.

Chapter 27

Trying to Reach the Larsen Ice Shelf in the Weddell Sea

IN 1996, I BECAME THE master of the *Explorer*. The vessel's logbook was already piled up with lots of firsts since she'd made her shakedown maiden voyage in 1969 to Buenos Aires. The *Explorer* was now heading for the Prince Gustav Channel, and I hoped to reach the long-awaited Larsen Ice Shelf.

In February 2000, the *Explorer*'s cruise schedule was given sufficient time to explore the Prince Gustav Channel, ice permitting, which ran between the Antarctic Peninsula and James Ross Island, with options to explore and do something out of the ordinary, such as go toward the Larsen Ice Shelf. Global warming had apparently melted a passage at the southern end of the Prince Gustav Channel; perhaps the time was now right to make a serious attempt to achieve another first for the little red ship, the Grand Old Lady. We passed Gin Cove and Rum Cove on our port side on James Ross Island, and we headed south toward Cape Longing to the starboard side on the peninsula.

The Weddell Sea was indisputably a wild and dangerous area due to the presence of a current and lots of pack ice. The ice was constantly moving in the channel, which was treacherous and could easily cause one to become trapped in pack ice.

There was a Boeing 737 waiting for us at the airport in Ushuaia, Argentina, to bring our passengers to Santiago, Chile, and the USA.

The good news was that an Argentine ship made an annual resupply to Base Matienzo on Larsen Nunatak by following the ice shelf edge when its limit ran between Cape Longing and Christensen Nunatak. The vessel would tie up alongside the ice shelf edge between Christensen Nunatak and Robertson Island, and with snowcats, the crew would ferry the base supplies inland to Base Matienzo.

This was indeed good news. Perhaps we could tie up alongside the ice shelf too, knowing a supply ship annually called at Larsen Nunatak.

We slowly made our way through the Prince Gustav Channel, heading south toward the unknown. Our plan was to spend the night drifting in the southern part of the Prince Gustav Channel, close to Cape Longing (called C. Deseo on the map because Argentina claimed that sector of Antarctica; hence, their charts were in Spanish). Then, the following morning, we'd go straight to the Larsen Ice Shelf some forty-eight nautical miles farther southwest, fingers crossed.

I was looking forward to trying to reach that unreachable part of Antarctica, given that I had made several attempts over the years but always had to turn around due to severe ice conditions and safety reasons.

Now many people and various organs assisted me in my attempt to reach the Larsen Ice Shelf by sending me up-to-date information regarding that part of the world.

If we were able to reach the Larsen Ice Shelf as the world's first cruise ship, then history would be written. Emails poured in from everywhere, giving us support regarding our daring expedition cruise into a mysterious area. I felt it was the best opportunity we had to become a famous Antarctic expedition cruise ship if we succeeded.

The above image shows a satellite picture of the ice conditions on February 10, 2000. One incoming message said,

Quote:

As regards ice-shelf walkabouts then it is always best to remember that ice shelf edges are fickle. They can be 40 m high and stable or 2 m high and unstable. You might be confronted with a vertical ice face or a gentle low embayment.

They change without notice as icebergs calve. Provided a secure mooring is achieved the walkabout—at least locally—should present minimal problems. The ice is thick, and crevicing when present is manifested by wide, deep but visible rifts or chasms. It is along these that ice shelves flex with tidal oscillations. I would advise very careful considerations to any thoughts about heading much further south than Seal Nunataks bearing in mind the Weddell Sea multi-year pack ice clockwise gyre!

Unquote:

It was February 10, 2000, and I just had received a fairly fresh satellite picture from NOAA (National Oceanic Atmospheric Administration) of the ice situation from the Prince Gustav Channel to the Seal Nunataks, which was the beginning of the Larsen A Ice Shelf. All the bridge officers, including our expedition leader, assembled on the bridge, carefully studying the ice situation while reading the newly received message sent to us by a lady named Sarah Appleby. After a while, we agreed that the following morning, after the wake-up call, we would set the course south. We planned the trip based on the Q-Fax satellite photo and other images received from the BAS (British Antarctic Survey). We made approximate plans about what we could do if we reached the ice shelf.

It was now evening, and we desperately searched for a safe, ice-free place to spend the night adrift in a navigational box in the sea chart size 0.5 by 0.5 nautical miles. We could see Cape Longing in the distance on our starboard side, and we finally agreed to stay in a fairly ice-free place where we could stay adrift. All the passengers were excited and expectant about the next day, when we would continue to navigate south into the unknown and treacherous areas. We arrived at the navigational box and stopped one main engine to save fuel.

I knew well that all the passengers would the next day push the *Explorer* forward with their good spirits, crowding the bridge with red parkas, since they all wanted to be part of an unusual expedition day in the remote Antarctic wilderness, where no other expedition cruise ship had ever been before.

It was indeed a treacherous area since the ice was moving clockwise, and I was always somehow thinking about how to avoid the destiny of Sir Ernest Shackleton's *Endurance*, which was crushed in the ice of the Weddell Sea on October 27, 1915. I did not want the *Explorer* to be beset in the Weddell Sea ice, because if I made a mistake, we all would end up sitting on the ice, as the Shackleton party had, and would be on the first page of every newspaper on the planet with bold letters. What a nightmare.

I wrote in the captain's night-order watch book, "We stay in the box as marked in the chart until daylight. Start the second engine if needed. Please call Captain at 0600 hours or otherwise when needed. Have a good watch." Then I went to bed.

I could not sleep that night; my mind was full of thoughts—and potential nightmares. As a captain of the ship, that was my worst night I ever had had. Finally, I fell asleep.

The following morning was magical; the sky was clear, and the sun was just above the horizon and phenomenal. As I entered the bridge at 0630, a few expectant passengers were already there. A brief look at the radar confirmed that we were at the south end of the box, and we started the second main engine and resumed our trip south. It was clear to us that we were going to face an extraordinary challenge when looking at the ice ahead of us. Bear in mind that it was only some forty nautical miles to the Seal Nunataks, unless we had to crisscross our way there. We rapidly encountered bergy bits and then again huge icebergs mixed with growlers and all kind of ice as we slowly and carefully glided in between the ice in sometimes open ice free water. As we slowly made our way south, I felt our conquest could bring us a new record.

Despite my Antarctic experience—I already had made more than 115 ice voyages to that frozen continent—I didn't feel confident in what I was doing, and I felt like a pioneer on that attempt to reach the Seal Nunataks. I had come a long way from the time I'd started at sea as a young teenager in 1963. Now I was a hunter for fame and sought to bring our passengers to the Larsen Ice Shelf and back to Ushuaia. It was a hostile world down there, and for every nautical mile we made, I felt happy. Cape Longing slowly disappeared behind us, and we had no landmarks on the radar. We were farther south in that area than any cruise ship in the world had been. We had a course for Lindenberg Island, and we faced now pack ice 7/10, which soon became a lot more.

The ice became denser, and we had some twenty-five nautical miles left to go. It was still sunny, but the icebergs became more frequent. With the icebergs came bergy bits, growlers, and pack ice, which made us frequently alter the course a bit farther east and then directly more to the south because we found ourselves often in dead ends. We sailed on GPS positions to at least have a small idea about our location, as the chart was not accurate enough to trust our position. The GPS was correct, but the chart was not. We wrote in the chart the depth on the echo sounder, as per the rules (the echo sounder said there was no bottom). Finally, we headed directly east and then southeast, when we again encountered increasingly heavy pack ice.

The passengers stood on the top bridge and the bridge wings with their binoculars, looking for wildlife, and fortunately, the Weddell Sea is home to Weddell seals. We could see the relatively humble animals, which were famous for their deep dives, on ice attached to the continent. The bird life was not bad, and we could see Antarctic skuas, the raptors of the south, and petrels.

I, as usual, kept an eye on what was going on behind my back. I always tried to have an escape route from any situation. It was now two o'clock in the afternoon, and we had been sailing slowly for seven hours. I encouraged all the passengers to lift their binoculars in an attempt to see the ice shelf, so they did.

I finally had to give up when the weather Q-Fax produced a more workable image that showed that the pack ice went on for as far as we could make out with the sporadic cloud cover.

We were slowly battling the ice, when one of the passengers said, "This is really going to make the boys back at the golf club jealous."

The ice was on the move, and I could see in the binoculars that the previously ice-free areas behind us were closing in. This was not totally unexpected since it had happened to ships in Antarctica many times, but it was a significant setback for me because I wanted the Grand Old Lady to make another historic first. I knew well that ice was beyond anyone's control and hoped I wouldn't be stuck with the *Explorer* in moving pack ice. From a distance, the scene might have looked almost serene, but with the trained eye of an ice master, I knew well that if ice was closing in, it caused the hull to be under pressure and to shriek and creak. The pressure on the hull could be tremendous, and the ice screeched up the sides of the ship, which could be nerve-racking and unbearable, and crew and passengers were completely powerless. The *Explorer* was a thirty-one-year-old lady; hence, she had to be treated with silk gloves.

My head was full of thoughts, and I didn't want to have any of those experiences. I felt deflated when I had to turn around for safety reasons because the pack ice was on the move and had blocked the way ahead of us and behind our stern. The ice there gyres a lot, and it was potentially dangerous. It was a drama, and I was not to be frustrated because I couldn't make it that year either. I had to cheer myself up, and I knew I would try again as soon as the ice conditions became acceptable, which I doubted they would in that forgotten part of the world.

I was reluctant to announce to the passengers that we had to give up. I had no clue what they would think when we finally made the decision to announce over the PA system that we had to return to the Prince Gustav Channel. I guess for safety reasons, they were happy. However, we urgently had to find a safe way out from the ice that was closing in on us rapidly. The night slowly approached, and it was imminent that we find some open water with radar contact from land to figure out if we were drifting with the current. I understood the passengers were in good spirits, which was important to know. I slowly put my finger on the PA button, pressed it down, and announced that the *Explorer* had to return to the Prince Gustav Channel ASAP.

I presumed there would be no questions asked, as we'd tried our best to reach the Larsen Ice Shelf. Fortunately, the passengers understood that we had to regard safety first in that unpredictable area. That was my world, so to speak, and in my inner self, it kept my blood boiling.

The *Explorer* slowly headed back northeast, fighting the pack ice. We searched for sudden openings in the ice to find a safe way out, but they were hard to find. The ice conditions had changed rapidly for the worse, and once in a while, the ship lay completely still in the ice as we tried to push the ice and create new cracks with our 3,300-horsepower engines.

Luckily, the main engine-cooling water system was made to be trapped in the ice because she could take the cooling water from one of the ballast tanks to make sure the engines were running and not clogged by ice from the sea chests.

However, the ice was without question closing, so we urgently needed to find open water. The weather was cloudy, and but there was not too much wind yet.

I had been on the bridge for most of the day, and I felt tired. I was driving the *Explorer* myself because at least I knew the ship's hull could withstand my actions as we kept pushing the ice, trying to drive through it and running into every little crack we made, grinding and scraping the ice and the hull in out attempt to break through it.

I frequently thought about how the *Explorer* was a thirty-one-year-old ship. Though her hull was ice-strengthened, she was an old ice-working vessel and, hence, not in the best condition. Every hard contact with the ice could easily crack our frames or, even worse, open up the hull. It was unbelievable; the ice conditions had changed a lot, though we now returned more or less in the same path we had come from. Despite the wind and the cold, the scenery was spectacular. "It seems unreal, as though we are in a movie," said a passenger.

It was the Antarctic summer, and the weather could be unpredictable. As I said, though we were battling the ice, the scenery surrounding us was breathtaking; hence, I decided I would go for a walk on the boat deck to load my batteries and enjoy the beautiful scenery on my own for a while because I felt we were still far from reaching open water and safety, and I had to be on the bridge until we could park the ship in an ice-free spot miles away.

I knew that before we could finally relax for the night in a long-awaited place in an open spot of water, many hours remained for us to battle the ice in that part of the Weddell Sea. Farther south, some three hundred nautical miles from our location, Sir Ernest Shackleton's *Endurance* was trapped in the pack ice. The ice had gripped the ship tighter, pinching the sides of the vessel and causing the ship to roll over onto the side, and finally, it had sunk on November 21, 1915.

The new Q-Fax images received were as good a description as one could have had of the situation. The ice was closing ahead of us in our attempt to reach open water close to Cape Longing. The ice was also on the move in the Prince Gustav Channel, which certainly didn't make things better. That could mean pack ice strings that were hard to penetrate. We were in a dangerous part of the world, where one mistake could be fatal. The images revealed a clear change in the ice situation ahead of us for the worse.

When a ship is surrounded in a seemingly endless, icy white landscape as far as the eye can see in Antarctica, trying desperately to find the way out can be frustrating. When you suddenly see a thin black area in the distance, it is for sure open sea water.

The passengers on the bridge suddenly shouted, "I see open water! I see open water at the horizon!"

Since our speed was close to zero in the ice, those words were sweet music in our ears and gave us hope that we could reach safety before Antarctica embedded us in its darkness. In the distance, we all could see in our binoculars something dark at the horizon. Were the passengers, right? Did they possibly see open water?

Though the ship had a reinforced hull, I was continuously thinking about the *Explorer's* old frames in the forward part of the vessel. She was a worn-out Grand Old Lady; hence, she had to be treated with silk gloves when her hull rubbed the ice. Could she withstand this rough Weddell Sea ice, which was clearly on the move?

It was now five o'clock, and for the time being, we found ourselves in a narrow lane of water, and we ran along nicely for some hundred meters. Then a bang again shook the entire ship straight through. Passengers had to hold their glasses in the lounge as the boat shook back and forth in the ice.

We didn't want to have fog, which was only present when warm air met cold sea ice or air. The combination of fog and sea ice was a no-no in Antarctica. However, since the weather conditions could swiftly change, we never knew what to expect. Our progress was slow, with just a nautical mile in three hours, but it was better than nothing.

We still had a long way to go—some three nautical miles—through heavy ice mixed with pack ice to reach safety. The conditions had changed a lot since we'd come. I again made an announcement over the PA system, giving an update to the passengers and crew about the situation and saying, "Mother Nature has not been too kind to us on our mission, but we can see open water ahead of us, which is a good thing."

Luckily, we had been spared from any blackouts due to ice clogging the seawater intakes; the cooling water system from the ballast tank did a good job. After several hours of transferring pack ice, we found a gap of open water between two ice ridges, which meant we could increase the speed by one knot for a short while. The slow progress made me frustrated, especially since the time and effort in our attempt to reach the Larsen Ice Shelf had ended in failure. However, the *Explorer* forced her way forward, struggling to regain the open sea, which was now clearly visible.

Cape Longing was sighted, which was the place where we had drawn the navigational box on the chart for the night to come. It had been a long and demanding day for all of us, and I was exhausted. At least we had been where no other cruise ship had ever been before, which was a patch on the wound. We were now out of the pack ice, and as I looked back at the treacherous, icy white landscape, I could see that the ship's hull had left an orange color on the ice, with some huge icebergs as monuments. I thought, *Thank God we are safe.*

After managing to break out of the ice, we were adrift not far from Cape Longing. It was dinnertime, and I hosted a table for six passengers. With the day's events, there was no lack of conversational topics for the next two hours as we raised our glasses in a toast for an adventurous day.

The following morning, we headed for the Prince Gustav Channel, where we encountered several pack-ice strings. It was a time-consuming navigation because we had to stop the ship in front of the pack ice and then push the ice with lots of engine power to be able to break through. The ice strings were multiyear ice, and some were one hundred meters wide. Once we had safely passed the worst pack in the channel, we sped up and sent a message to the expedition cruise ship *Caledonian Star*, which was in the Antarctic Sound. We told the expedition leader,

Unquote:

Thus, we headed for the Antarctic Sound and Drake Passage toward Ushuaia in Argentina.

Chapter 28

The Warship *Piloto Pardo* Then Became the Cruise Ship Antarctic Dream

I WANT TO INCLUDE A follow-up regarding the Chilean warship *Piloto Pardo*, which had participated once upon a time in the rescue operation of the *Lindblad Explorer* on Christmas Eve 1979. In 2004, I participated in the rebuilding and conversion of this famous Chilean warship into the *Antarctic Dream*, which was Chile's first privately owned expedition cruise ship.

A number of wealthy people in Chile agreed to pay the conversion of the *Pilot Pardo* into a new cruise ship.

07/02/2004

cruise ship and pay for the remodeling of the vessel with me as the appointed first master of the converted warship. Hence, I was subsequently hired by the CEO of a Chilean Antarctic shipping company. Its representatives flew to Anchorage, Alaska, to hire me promptly as a master of the new cruise ship, which still did not exist. This took place while we were repatriating our passengers in Anchorage. It was agreed that I would go some four months later to the Talcahuano Shipyard as a supervisor for the rebuilding and then become the master of the ship called the *Antarctic Dream*.

The vessel *Piloto Pardo* was built for the Chilean Navy by Haarlemsche Scheepsbouw Maatschappij (Haarlem Shipbuilding Company) in Haarlem, Netherlands. She was launched on June 11, 1958 and commissioned on April 7, 1959. She was constructed specifically for servicing the scientific bases established in the Chilean Antarctic Territory. The ship measured eighty-three meters in length and was 11.9 meters wide, with a gross tonnage of more than two thousand metric tons and a draft of 4.6 meters. She had a twenty-three-millimeter ice-strengthened hull in the water line for polar navigation. The ship was christened the *Piloto Pardo* after Luis Pardo, the captain of the cutter *Yelcho*, which rescued the twenty-one stranded men of Sir Ernest Shackleton's *Endurance* expedition from Elephant Island, Antarctica, in August 1916.

She was decommissioned in January 1997, sold the next year to Orlando Paoa of Easter Island, and renamed *Hoto Matua*. In 2003, she was sold to Antarctic Shipping SA, converted into an Antarctic cruise ship in Talcahuano Shipyard (ASMAR), and renamed the *Antarctic Dream*. The refurbishment allowed a capacity of eighty passengers, with forty double cabins, all with exterior views.

However, there was a tremendous lack of competence in Chile with regard to the conversion of a cruise ship and the know-how of retired navy submarine officers. I asked myself how Chile, as a proud country, could accept some old and retired submarine officers suddenly being in charge of the rebuilding, when none of them had a clue about cruise ships or how a well-oiled expedition cruise ship was supposed to be constructed and operated under difficult conditions in Antarctic waters. Due to my extensive Antarctic experience since 1973, I was appointed to be the first master of the Chilean cruise ship, introducing Chile to the expedition cruise world with the *Antarctic Dream*. It was not an easy task for me, as the Chilean Navy was without doubt in charge of everything, and they complicated everything including for me though I was to become the Captain.

Hence, I spent five months in Talcahuano Shipyard, watching a ship slowly change into something wrong in all aspects. I doubted the ship could please our forthcoming passengers. Undeniably, every mistake possible regarding the conversion was made; therefore, I found myself writing lots of letters of complaint—and attaching photos of all the wrongdoing—to the seven richest families in Chile, who'd donated money for the rebuilding, regarding the incorrect rebuilding under the ex-Chilean Navy submarine officers in charge. It was a joke that ex submarine officers was doing this. What a disaster it was!

The bridge's aft wall was packed with electrical junction boxes, leaving no space for officers in the chart room, when all the boxes could easily have been installed in a converter locker, as per normal policy.

During the rebuilding, I once in a while tried to get the attention of the vessel's class company, the authority to approve the ship's passenger ship safety certificate (PSSC) and load line certificate. However, it was pointless, as the class was the Chilean Navy (Armada de Chile), and the vessel was still considered to be built under the rules of a Chilean warship; hence, the normal international PSSC requirements for a cruise ship were overruled and obsolete according to Chile, as the vessel was converted under Chilean Navy rules, whatever those rules were. Consequently, the conversion of the *Piloto Pardo* to the *Antarctic Dream* was fucked up in every aspect. Nevertheless, credit must be given to the engineers on board for how they dealt with the engine room problems as they occurred when the ship was finally sailing.

Further frustrating, I had been hired as a supervisor of the conversion and as the intended master on board with the purpose of sharing all my Antarctic experience with the new-born Chilean company Antarctic Shipping for the success of their first inaugural voyages to Patagonia and Antarctica with me as a galleon figure on board. The intention was that the ship could be a good competitor among the other thirty-three cruise ships in Antarctica.

The owner of a Chilean television company paid me a visit to figure out how much truth there was in my letters of criticism. Indeed, there was a lot of truth in my complaints. Consequently, he sent his son, who was in his twenties with me on a cruise to Antarctica to find out how the vessel was operating. I never did figure out what his conclusion was after our round trip to Antarctica and our safe return to Ushuaia in Argentina. I'm guessing the reason was that he could not even spell the word *ship*; hence, he was unable to deliver an appropriate report to his father, and on top of that, he was most of the time seasick. The owner of the television company sent his lawyer to attend as well to see how the vessel was doing. The sea trial was made, and the faults were rectified as they occurred. I felt the pressure on my shoulders when we finally headed south from Talcahuano to cruise in the Chilean inland sea waters for a month and a half, visiting some interesting hidden places.

Besides, it was annoying to know that some of the most senior people in charge of the rebuilding in the shipyard confiscated money under the noses of the seven Chilean donors for their own winning. One of them even bought a ranch! Everybody probably knows the price of a ranch—at least I do. Therefore, when I continued to ask Antarctic Shipping for navigational equipment and other items to meet the Chilean bridge officers' needs and mine as well, my requests were denied, and the answer was "There is no money available." I thought, *What the fuck? There is no money available? The ship is due to start cruising!* The superintendent, an ex-submarine engineer, suddenly got an apartment in Ushuaia, to everybody's surprise. All of us raised our eyebrows when we learned about that.

Yes, the company faced problems in the beginning, and the delivery was much delayed. However, once we finally started to cruise in the month of September, the snow was still hanging heavily on the Patagonian hills when we arrived at Ushuaia in the beginning of September. The cruise ship season in Ushuaia normally starts at the end of November, but we arrived at a cold and snowy Ushuaia. It was quite an experience to see for the first time Ushuaia covered in snow.

The vessel operated fairly well, but since there was no more money available, the bow thruster was undersized and could operate for only ten minutes at a time before it tripped. That was a huge problem since in the expedition cruise business, a vessel is supposed to do a close-up anchorage prior to the nearest landing area for the convenience of the passengers. However, that was not the case, as I had to play safety first, and it was impossible to rely on the vessel's bow-thruster unit. Bridge officers who have worked in that harsh, unusual environment, battling the elements, know that the weather conditions down there change rapidly and without warning; hence, there is an unconditional need to be able to rely on the vessel's engine and bow thruster. Due to that uncertainty, I always anchored up with safe margins all around (i.e., the vessel always had a safe swinging radius in case worse came to worse), not to forget the vessel only had one fixed propeller.

I sailed on the *Antarctic Dream* for the entire Antarctic season, which normally ended in the beginning of March, but we continued to cross Drake Passage down to Antarctica as the only vessel in that environment, with some unpleasant storms roaring in from the southwest, until the beginning of April, when we returned to Talcahuano Shipyard. After I'd spent nine months on board in a row, nobody had asked me if I wanted a vacation. I didn't have any plans of going on vacation either, since my monthly paycheck made me stay.

Chapter 29

A Medical Rescue Operation with the Royal Navy in the South Atlantic Ocean, Scotia Sea

It was October 1999, and the *Explorer* made the cruise to the Lost Islands of the South Atlantic Ocean, from Tenerife in the Canary Islands to the Falkland Islands as it had been doing for the last ten years. It was a one-month cruise with a cruise itinerary: Tenerife, Cape Verde, Ascension Island, Santa Helena, Tristan da Cunha, Nightingale Island, Gough Island, South Georgia, and to Port Stanley in the Falkland Islands.

No doubt it was a challenging cruise since there were lots of sea days between the islands, and we faced once in a while horrific storms that severely delayed us. Also, we had to refuel alongside a tanker on Ascension Island in order to reach the Falklands.

Just knowing we were heading south for the Southern Hemisphere, toward latitudes of the roaring forties and the furious fifties, was a challenge in itself since we could anytime encounter the perfect storm, which we did.

When we finally arrived at the volcanic island of Tristan da Cunha on latitude 37°10′ S, we found ourselves, as usual, drifting on a safe distance outside the village of Edinburgh, which was home to just one three-hundred-person village at the foot of an active volcano.

Tristan da Cunha is part of the British Overseas Territories, which includes Saint Helena and near-equatorial Ascension Island, which is some 3,730 kilometers to the north of Tristan da Cunha.

Suddenly, the bridge got a VHF call from the British high commissioner, who said, "We have a local nurse here by the name of Sandra who is suffering from a severe kidney pain and probably three kidney stones. Would it be possible for you to take her to Port Stanley ASAP for urgent medical treatment?"

My immediate response was "Yes, we'll take her to Port Stanley." Thus, we prepared to take Sandra on board.

Sandra was transferred from shore on board, along with her sister Felicity, via a local high-seas power boat and then transferred to an *Explorer rubber Zodiac* for her safe and smooth embarkation. This was done with huge difficulty, as the swell was notoriously high. Finally, she was safely on board and taken to the hospital cabin, where she was kept under constant surveillance of the ship's surgeon.

When all our passengers at the end of the day had returned on board, we sailed south for South Georgia. I felt I instantly had to make a public announcement over the ship's PA system to explain to everybody on board, including the crew, that we had taken Sandra on board due to a life-threatening situation. I knew my passengers were concerned, since they all knew that if Sandra's condition worsened, we'd have to cut the cruise short. Hopefully that would not be the case.

We now entered the world's most hostile ocean, and as expected, a strong gale had arisen, but the following morning, luckily, all was a joy. In that part of the world, the lows come in fast, and they sometimes disappear fast. Now the South Atlantic Ocean gave us a huge, long swell that was fairly comfortable for all of us.

Coming to South Georgia—the Gateway to the Antarctic, as Sir Ernest Shackleton called it—the normal clearing procedures into South Georgia were done in Cumberland Bay, in Grytviken at King Edward Point, but since the *Explorer* was well known there, we got permission to sail directly to Cooper Bay at the southeast end of the island without doing clearance into South Georgia.

After we had dropped the anchor in Cooper Bay, the ship's doctor suddenly came to see me on the bridge, saying, "Captain, Sandra's condition has deteriorated a lot, and she is in severe pain. I have given her morphine, but she needs urgently to get to Port Stanley as soon as possible."

Listening to his serious words, I felt instantly this was not good, and I figured out that my deepest nightmare was now most likely a fact: I had to cut the cruise short. I had to prioritize Sandra's well-being and survival since we were the only ship for a long period of time to visit Tristan da Cunha. The cruise director from the United Kingdom urged me to ASAP inform the passengers about the newly upcoming situation since information was now of the utmost importance regarding the matter. The cruise had to be cut short by two days on that remarkable wildlife island, though it was the highlight of the entire cruise, and the guests had demanded to see something out of the ordinary. Due to the circumstances, I was deeply concerned about whether some of our passengers were upset and would try to sue us, since in the United States, it is a subculture to sue somebody. Normally, the Americans have two reasons for lawsuits:

1) People with no actual damages are looking for a payday.
2) People with actual damages are looking for compensation.

However, I could not find a reason why anyone would look for a lawsuit since we had made a humanitarian emergency medivac from an inaccessible remote island in the deep South Atlantic Ocean. However, in South Georgia, like a patch on the wound, the passengers were able to make the Shackleton walk from Fortuna Bay to Stromnes Whaling Station. The *Explorer* landed the bravest and fittest guests in Fortuna Bay with rubber Zodiacs for these passengers to commence the overhill walk to Stromness Whaling Station on the other side of the mountains and island. I myself did the walk once, and it was challenging. The picture below shows a caricature of me.

SIR ERNEST SKOGLETON

It was a five-hour walk more or less for us, but one moment in Shackleton's odyssey really makes one's hair stand on end with emotion. As his party stopped for breakfast on top of those hills, where I once upon a time had walked with the brave ones as well, Shackleton wrote that at 7:00 a.m. on the dot according to the ship's chronometer, which they had carried all the way from the wreck of the *Endurance*, they heard the unmistakable sound of the Stromness steam whistles summoning the whalers to work. "Never," wrote Shackleton, "had any of us heard sweeter music. It was the first sound created by outside human agency that had come to our ears since we left Stromness Bay in December 1914." It was then May 20, 1916. Then the three men shook hands and walked down to the whaling station.

With the goal in sight for us, it was a fairly easy walk down to Stromness Whaling Station, but for Shackleton's three men in May 1916, the ground was slippery with ice.

At some point, we would blow the ship's horn when the passengers were on top of the hill to give them an impression of how Shackleton and his three men felt as they reached the top of the hill, powerless and exhausted, and then heard the steam whistles.

When everybody was back on board, we took up the anchor and headed urgently toward the open sea and the Falkland Islands. That evening, I had to explain to the passengers thoroughly during our six o'clock recap in the lounge the medical situation of Sandra. Prior to that, I contacted the CEO of Explorer Shipping Corporation in Chicago about the situation, and he gave me the go-ahead.

To my relief, the passengers appreciated my decision to sail straight toward Port Stanley in the Falkland Islands. However, Sandra's condition deteriorated, and the ship's doctor and I were counting the hours until we could reach the Falklands. We had some 650 nautical miles ahead of us, and I felt my responsibility was to bring Sandra to Port Stanley ASAP. Furthermore, we faced a severe gale storm that delayed our sailing time to Port Stanley.

As we sailed and followed the northern coastline of South Georgia toward the west, I had to call up the Royal Navy in the Falklands over the medium-wave radio frequency and ask them for their assistance. I asked if they could meet us midway to South Georgia, though the weather was severe.

Sandra had a British passport, and as such, I felt the Royal Navy would be cooperative. To my relief, they responded to my request and were undeniably cooperative, and they began a huge naval operation from the Falklands, which surprised all of us. As Sandra was a British citizen, I assume the Royal Navy saw an opportunity to climb out from their mothballs in the Falklands after the end of the Falkland War in June 1982.

Apparently, they and we felt something unusual was going to take place. They agreed to send a number of warships equipped with helicopters to have a rendezvous with us somewhere midway in the stormy Scotia Sea, with the tanker *Gold Rover* to refuel the Sea King helicopter midway in the air as they traveled between the warships, so they could reach Port Stanley.

The Scotia Sea is located at the northern edge of the Southern Ocean, at its boundary with the South Atlantic Ocean to the north and east and Drake Passage to the west. It is named after the expedition ship *Scotia*.

Entering the rough Scotia Sea, we began to pitch heavily after we passed Elsehul to the port. Elsehul is the outermost western bay of South Georgia. We now faced the open sea with the wrath of the Scotia Sea. Some 650 nautical miles kept the Royal Navy's three warships and us apart as we steamed toward each other with a bad upcoming weather forecast for the Scotia Sea. It was indeed a peculiar navigational situation.

The ship's doctor monitored Sandra twenty-four hours a day while her sister Felicity sat faithfully at her side in the ship's hospital. Meanwhile, I had frequent radio contact with the frigate HMS *Sutherland*, the ship in command of the three Royal Navy ships steaming toward us.

We regularly checked each other's GPS position and the ETA (estimated time of arrival) at the potential rendezvous point in the Scotia Sea. The *Explorer* was doing fine in the rough sea conditions, riding the waves like a duck, but the situation was more problematic for the HMS *Sutherland*. She was a slim warship, and as such, she was trying to keep her speed up for obvious reasons. She had the waves and sea from behind on her starboard quarter, while the *Explorer* was now pitching in the high seas.

The captain of the HMS *Sutherlands* later told me that the ship dove like a submarine in the rough seas, and the slim hull of the frigate disappeared in the waves, which made them slow down. I felt that the Royal Navy felt a big responsibilty in the medivac operation that suddenly had occurred in that remote part of the Southern Hemisphere.

The *Explorer* continued to pitch the Scotia Sea while closing in on the Royal Navy's HMS *Sutherland*. Suddenly, out of nowhere, fog rolled in, so we rapidly slowed down to a safeguarding speed since there was still a risk we could face potential growlers, which could be dangerous to us if we hit one of them. Hence, we made now some seven knots, and I informed the frigate HMS *Sutherland* that there was an impending risk of growlers close to South Georgia. We could meet growlers some 150 nautical miles west of South Georgia. It was a peculiar feeling to know the Royal Navy was out cooperating with us so far south, and we both knew that at some stage, we would rendevouz in the bumby Scotia Sea to transfer Sandra and her sister to them.

The wind force had increased to thirty-three knots, and we could now see on the radar the HMS *Sutherland* on our port side, making her way toward us. On the radar screen, I could see the HMS *Sutherland* make a big loop, and she then approached us from our port quarter. The fog was dense, and I stood on the port bridge wing with the navigation officer, Vince from the Phillipines, trying to spot the white spray from the HMS *Sutherland* as she tried to catch up with us in the huge seas. We slowed down to approximately six knots of speed at the request of the frigate.

Suddenly, in the fog, out of nowhere, we saw the forward top light of the frigate reflect in the sea spray as the warship pitched in the heavy seas, as did we. The HMS *Sutherland* called us up on the VHF radio to tell us about their presence.

I stood on the port bridge wing in the howling wind, feeling the sea spray in my face, while watching the British frigate. It was now a little bit too close to us, in my opinion, apparently trying to show off; hence, I asked myself if their bridge command had things under control. I thought about the safe navigation between our ships while I watched the bow of the HMS *Sutherland* once in a while disappear into the rough Scotia Sea. Her forward top light disappeared in the sea spray.

Though I had a raincoat on, I still became soaking wet on the bridge wing and sought shelter under the forward bridge wing wind protectors as the *Explorer* from time to time dove down into the rough seas. I kept the VHF phone handset in my hand, waiting for information from the frigate, but the radio was silent. I guessed the frigate was trying to stabilize their position in the rough seas in relation to the *Explorer* before they were ready to comunicate with me.

After some twenty minutes of silence, we finally made contact, and the master of the HMS *Sutherland* told me they were in the process of sending a Lynx helicopter with a military doctor to examine Sandra. For some unknown reason, after that, I referred to him over the VHF as "the flying doctor," which the bridge command of the frigate adopted as well. Of course, under the extreme wind conditions, I was concerned whether the helicopter could take off, fly the two hundred meters to us, and hover above our aft swimming pool deck.

Though the frigate was pitching heavily, suddenly, an RAF Lynx helicopter was launched with a British military doctor aboard. The short flying distance from the frigate to the *Explorer*'s aft deck took just a minute or so.

The flying doctor had to make a medical assessment of Sandra's condition and decide whether she would be airlifted or not. If Sandra needed to be airlifted, a huge Royal Navy operation would start and involve a shore base team as well.

The Lynx helicopter was suddenly seen hovering above our portside pool deck as the flying doctor was slowly lowered with the designated ship heli-fire team on standby. The doctor turned out to be a young fellow, probably newly graduated as a doctor and in need of medical practice—at least those were my thoughts about him.

After he touched down, we brought him rapidly to Sandra. Entering the hospital, he rapidly asked Sandra questions, such as if the pain was aching or sharp.

Sandra said, "Yes, I have pain that is coming and going."

Her answer seemingly made the doctor confused. He then looked at me with begging eyes and asked, "Captain, what is your feeling and opinion about this?"

I said, "Doctor, if you ask me, my answer is that it is obvious she needs urgently to be treated in a hospital, so take her off right now. Her condition has rapidly deteriorated, and now you are in doubt about what to do! I have called upon the assistance of the Royal Navy in this matter, as you are not sure what to do. If you can't decide whether Sandra shall be airlifted or not, then I will decide for you."

The doctor said, "Captain, these are words I wanted to hear from you, so now we'll take her off." He then used the radio in his flight helmet to call up the HMS *Sutherland* and tell them to prepare for an instantaneous medivac operation. Then he left with the Lynx helicopter, waving goodbye.

It was amazing to watch and hear over the radio the activity that took place, and I thought, *oh boy, was the Royal Navy only waiting for my final decision about whether Sandra should be airlifted or not?* Yes, that was clearly the case, and I suddenly felt flattered and thought, *Wow, were my words all that was needed?* Apparently, yes.

The bridge command on the HMS *Sutherland* told me to make Sandra ready for a medivac operation, along with her sister and their luggage. I went to Sandra and said, "Sandra, you will now be airlifted with a helicopter to the HMS *Sutherland*, which is sailing close to us. The weather is stormy, but you are in good hands. I wish you good luck and all the best." Then I gave her a hug in the bed and went to the port bridge wing, where I stood in the howling wind, watching the huge Sea King helicopter arrive and hover above the pool deck with a sound that overthrew the storm.

Once the helicopter was in position over the aft deck, they lowered the Heli-crew paramedics, who were escorted to the ship hospital with their own stretcher. They rapidly strapped Sandra down and then rushed back to the pool deck with the ship crew, carrying the stretcher to the pool deck.

Sandra was winched into the helicopter with her sister hanging close to her in a harness in the extreme wind, swinging back and forth under the wind of the rotor blades of the helicopter, which then flew to the HMS *Gold Rover* some two hundred nautical miles away. Because the journey was so long, the helicopter had to refuel midway in the air above the tanker before continuing some two hundred nautical miles farther toward the Falkland Islands.

When the Sea King helicopter was on its way over the stormy Scotia Sea, the captain thanked me over the radio for good cooperation, saying, "I'll see you in Port Stanley." Then they sped into the dark, rough seas toward the Falklands.

I informed the captain on the HMS *Sutherland*, "Once we arrive at Stanley, I will invite all the captains from the Royal Navy ships involved, the flight crews, and the base commander on board for the captain's farewell cocktail party with consequent dinner as a gratitude party for all of us.

Later on, I was told there was a Hercules C-130 monitoring the entire operation from above.

I increased the speed of the *Explorer*, and as per the policy, I informed the passengers over the PA system that we would resume our voyage toward the Falklands in the bumpy Scotia Sea. However, our policy was that we always slowed down during the dinner hours for the convenience of the passengers and to allow them to enjoy their dinner. I was told over the radio that the Falklands' government had arranged for a TriStar plane, which was ready to fly Sandra to the United Kingdom upon her arrival in the Falklands.

After two days' troublesome, rough crossing in the Scotia Sea, we could finally see in the distance, in the late afternoon, Cape Pembroke on the radar, as well as its lighthouse and, farther away, the narrows leading into Port William.

Normally, we arrived at 0700 hours, but since we were heavily delayed and the Royal Navy captains and officers involved in the remarkable operation were invited to our special welcome reception, I knew I had to go alongside ASAP, no matter what the wind conditions were. However, the wind was southwesterly (i.e., blowing off the jetty), as usual when there was a low pressure in the area, which was always to our disadvantage when going alongside.

Before the jetty was the bottleneck of the narrow Navy Point, the passage leading into

Stanley Harbor, which we had to pass with 0.02 nautical miles on each side on a southerly course. That usually was not a problem with wind some twenty to thirty knots, but our weather forecast said there was approximately fifty knots of wind that late afternoon. Normally, under those extreme wind conditions, one would stay outside and ride out the storm until conditions were more favorable.

I was deeply concerned about our arrival at Stanley Harbor and the floating jetty, and it was the only and first time I was really worried about going alongside. Over the VHF radio, I suddenly heard the well-known voice of our Port Stanley agent say, "Captain, we know these are stormy conditions, but I have here pilots from the RAF Mount Pleasant and captains from the Royal Navy base of East Cove Military Port at Mare Harbor in East Falkland, who were involved in this operation, standing at this moment on the jetty, waiting for your arrival."

I was under a lot of pressure to go alongside with a responsibility to please everybody; hence, I swiftly asked him, "Do we have sufficient space to arrive safely in this strong wind?"

He replied, "Yes, Captain, you have sufficient space to go alongside between the Ro-Ro ramp and the ship ahead of you". Whatever his opinion was about having sufficient space I could never figure out.

With his words, the decision was made. I knew that if I managed to bring the *Explorer* alongside in the strong gale winds, that evening would probably become historic. Those were not normal berthing conditions; in those conditions, any other cruise ship would have refused to enter Stanley Harbor, preferring to stay outside while riding out the storm and waiting for the wind to drop.

To gain time, prior to the arrival, I dressed myself in my usual gala uniform and threw a long raincoat on, and I went to the bridge as we passed Cape Pembroke. The wind was now hurricane force and just too much, and I asked myself a thousand times if I was doing the right thing by continuing sailing toward Stanley Harbor in an attempt to go alongside. If I failed, I'd have to swing around under some incredibly difficult conditions and steam out again into the deep ocean to ride out the storm. Though the *Explorer* could turn on a coin, it would have been under great difficulties.

As I thought about all the things that potentially could go wrong, I felt it was not on my agenda to turn around since I had already altered the course to port and due south, now in the darkness, toward the narrow Navy Point, facing the wind. As such, there was no way of return.

The wind howled in the superstructure of the ship and the rig when we sailed through Navy Point and turned again ninety degrees to port in the confined Stanley Harbor toward the inner bay, heading for the beached three masts of the iron bark *Lady Elizabeth*, which was partially beached in Whale Bone Cove.

Furthermore, to complicate things even more, we had been assigned a berth position between a trawler and the ro-ro ramp, which made me upset due to the agent's lack of judging distance. He clearly could have told the captain on the trawler the day before to move his ship more toward the end of the jetty to facilitate our arrival under those stormy conditions, but apparently, there was a shortcoming for Sullivan Shipping in Stanley.

Looking at the confined berthing space in my binoculars, I was furious because it seemed impossible to go alongside; hence, I took a deep breath when I knew I had to bring the *Explorer* alongside. All the Royal Navy officers were standing on the jetty under a shelter, watching my actions. I told myself, *I can make this. I can make this.* The berthing, under extreme difficulties and hard gale-force conditions, seemed close to impossible.

As we turned hard to starboard and toward the jetty, the wind took hold of the entire ship's side as I approached the jetty at a forty-five-degree angle. When I was some one hundred meters from the jetty, I let go the starboard anchor with half a shackle in the water, keeping the anchor chain as a spring. When the chain was tight, I gave hard starboard rudder and forced the *Explorer's* stern up against the wind and the jetty so we could get the stern lines ashore and the bow thruster full power to port.

It was a touch-and-go arrival, but amazingly, to my surprise, the tricky anchor operation worked, and we came alongside with sheer luck. Some of my passengers watching on the boat deck in their raincoats, along with the Royal Navy officers on the jetty, clapped. I had made the seemingly impossible-to-perform arrival.

I waved to all of them from the bridge wing in my happiness, though I was soaking wet in my gala uniform. I knew I had probably just done the most incredible arrival to a jetty in my entire seaman's life as well as in the history of Port Stanley harbor.

The successful medical rescue operation, which was conducted at maximum range from the Falkland Islands under some extreme weather conditions, demonstrates the value and capability of the British naval and air forces coordinated from the joint headquarters at Mount Pleasant in working together with an expedition cruise ship in sudden need of urgent medical assistance.

The gangway finally went down on the floating jetty, and when it was safe to come on board, all the Royal Navy officers and pilots rushed on board. I hurried down to the gangway hall to greet them all. They were all soaking wet for obvious reasons, and once they entered the lobby, each one of them was greeted with a big hug and a "Hooray!" from the welcoming passengers. The hugs undeniably flowed to the right and left. It was a remarkable event, and it was emotional to meet all the officers in person as they shook off the rainwater in the lobby.

The lounge and entire ship had been prepared and was ready for the captain's farewell cocktail party for the passengers and our invited guests.

For me as master, it was the first time the captain's farewell party had become a welcome party, as it was for our specially invited Royal Navy guests.

Once they were all seated in the lounge, I spontaneously shouted with my arms lifted high, welcoming the Royal Navy participants and saying, "Wow, we all made it!"

All the Royal Navy officers and pilots simultaneously stood and shouted, "Yes, Captain, we all made it!"

When all the Royal Navy officers and pilots lined up in the lounge in front of the passengers, it was a marvelous moment and probably an unforgettable event in all of our future memories. What we had accomplished and experienced together was emotional. The entire operation had been unique.

The operation took place under extreme, dangerous weather conditions, and it was the first time since the Falklands War that the Royal Navy had sailed so far out toward South Georgia with full speed, having no clue about the ice conditions, with a constant fear they could potentially hit a growler. It was the first time an RAF helicopter had to refuel while hovering above a tanker in a severe storm in the Scotia Sea when the fuel gauge's meter went down. The Royal Navy had learned a lot about many things.

The base commander of East Cove Military Port grabbed the microphone and made a short gratitude speech, thanking everybody involved for good cooperation and giving a special thanks to me for taking Sandra on board. He also said it was an excellent opportunity for the Royal Navy to carry out a joint drill under those kinds of rough weather conditions. He then handed to me a framed photo of a Phantom FGR-2 jet fighter from the 23 Squadron. All the pilots and officers involved had signed their names on the photo.

The helicopter pilot on the Sea King helicopter told me, "Captain, it was the first time for me I made a refueling operation midway in the air under stormy conditions, and believe me, I was looking constantly at the fuel meter to see if I could make it!"

The captain on the HMS *Sutherland* said, "Due to the high speed we kept, I was very concerned about hitting any growlers as we approached South Georgia."

Sandra was immediately flown on a TriStar plane to London for treatment.

The following year, when we again visited Tristan da Cunha, she came on board and gave me a big hug for what I had done for her.

Chapter 30

The Perfect Storm

As usual, after the completion of the European season, we made our way down to Tenerife in the Canary Islands and onward to the Southern Hemisphere and to Antarctica, starting with a cruise the Lost Islands of the South Atlantic Ocean, which was a one-month cruise.

On October 4, 2000, we sailed from Tenerife toward Ascension Island for refueling alongside the tanker *Maersk Gannet*, which was an operation of some five hours. During the bunker operation, the passengers were ashore for excursions. When the bunkering was completed, we dropped the anchor in Clarence Bay outside George Town Bay, waiting for our passengers to return. Once everybody was back on board, we sailed for Santa Helena, where we spent the entire day, and then we continued to Tristan da Cunha and Gough Island.

At Gough Island, the passengers did a Zodiac cruise in Elephant Bay, along the steep cliffs on the south side of the island. Landing is not possible, as Gough Island is a protected wildlife reserve and uninhabited except for the personnel—usually six people—of a weather station the South African National Antarctic Program has maintained with British permission on the island since 1956. It is one of the remotest places with a constant human presence. The island is situated in an area where low pressure frequently comes in from the west.

Since we were heading for the furious fifties with the lows suddenly coming in and had a four-day voyage ahead of us to South Georgia, I called up the meteorological weather station on the island and asked them for an update on the weather forecast. I had with me a handheld tape recorder because I wanted the passengers to take part in what was being said. The man, with his South African dialect, said, "Captain, give me a minute, and I will check." He then came back and said, "Captain, I cannot tell you what's going on, but it looks pretty bad in the southwest. There is something huge coming in, heading toward you. God bless you, and a have a safe voyage."

The navigational telex (NAVTEX) machine confirmed the incoming storm.

When all passengers were back on board, I gathered everybody in the lounge for an update on what we could expect weather-wise. I grabbed the microphone and played up the conversation with the weather station, and I said afterward, "Ladies and gentlemen, now you know as much as I know, and we all are in the same boat."

A seafarer hopes for fair wind and calm seas when he is sailing the high seas. However, sometimes hell can break loose with no time to react, and apparently, we had to secure the entire vessel inside and make it ready for whatever we might face.

As Gough Island slowly vanished behind us, we felt the wind was building up, and so was the swell, so I went down to make sure everything was secured. I instructed the staff captain to make sure that all doors on the outside decks were closed and that the steel plates on the forecastle had been fitted on the *Explorer*'s lounge windows to protect them. I told the passengers I recommended they all retire to their cabins and secure any lose items they had.

At approximately seven o'clock that night, I stood at the SB bridge wing, watching the swell and the waves build up. In the Southern Hemisphere, the low pressures move clockwise (i.e., if you point your right-hand fingers toward the wind, your thumb points toward the center of the low pressure; hence, you can easily follow how the low pressure is moving).

The *Explorer* was kind of sensitive to sea and swell coming from behind, and that was precisely what happened. The height of the waves had already built up to some seven meters, and I thought, *oh boy, if the waves continue to build up, I'll at some stage have to turn the vessel around to face the waves before it is too late.* I was constantly watching the barometer, which was rapidly falling. The wind was sixty knots and increasing. I thought about what the meteorologist on Gough Island had told me: "There is something really nasty coming up in the southwest, and God bless you." For sure we needed lots of blessings, as we were now caught in the storm and had to face it. My consolation was that the *Explorer* was like a duck, riding up and down in the high seas, but each wave rolling in from behind lifted the stern up, causing the bow to dip dangerously down into the sea.

I was now permanently on the bridge, watching the weather grow worse. The ship began to roll more heavily. The *Explorer* had no stabilizers, but she had extended bilge keels to minimize the rolling. When I saw the waves had become some ten meters in height, I made up my mind to turn the ship around as fast as possible, which turned out not to be that easy to do. I had to do it in a safe way and in the right moment to be able to get her around in the strong winds.

I had the control from the starboard bridge wing slow down the speed while I looked intently over my shoulder for a suitable moment between the huge waves. I suddenly saw a gap with space enough to get her around, and I gave hard starboard rudder and full ahead on the engine. The *Explorer* responded immediately and turned to starboard toward the powerful winds. I gave a sigh of relief when we faced the sea and the waves with an angle of five to ten degrees on the starboard bow.

We were all by ourselves in the middle of nowhere as the waves slammed into the ship, causing the ship to pitch heavily. We kept enough engine power, some two knots, which meant the ship was able to keep the bow up against the waves, keeping the waves from hitting the hull from the side. As per the rules, the ship had to keep its bow—the front end—pointing into the waves to plow through them safely, since a massive wave could strike the ship's side, roll the vessel over, and sink it. The wind and waves will try to turn the vessel and pushing against them requires forward momentum.

The water was black under the sunless gray sky, and by then, the bridge was crowded with passengers in red parkas.

The waves had increased in height to some thirty meters. The ship's air draft was twenty-two meters, and the waves came from nearly straight ahead. It was like looking up at mountains and towering walls of water. I knew all were asking themselves what would happen when a wave hit us.

We were stunned as we looked upward at the gigantic walls of water rolling in toward us as the bow prepared itself to face and battle the massive waves, which heaved the ship's bow upward until it came to a complete standstill. Then she pointed the bow downward, causing me to tell everybody on the bridge, "Hang on, everybody! Here we go!" And down we went, straight down like an elevator, with the abdominal parts of the body flying up into the throat. The thirty-meter waves raised the spinning propeller into the air, and strong vibrations hit the entire hull as she slammed down into the valley with a giant crash, sometimes with the ocean rolling in over the forecastle as the bow was totally submerged.

I said a silent prayer—*Rise. Come up. Please come up*—while the ocean tried to keep the bow submerged. It was as if the ship were thinking, *Can I, or can I not?* She was struggling and shaking with the enormous weight of tons and tons of water on the bow. She slowly raised the bow over the surface, and the water rushed back into the ocean over the sides like Niagara Falls as she went up again like an elevator. Everybody was silent and surely had the same thoughts I had.

But they all said simultaneously, "What a good show, Captain!" Well, it was indeed a bloody good show but dangerous. I knew none of them understood the seriousness of our fight with the elements.

I called several times down to the engine control room to make sure everything was okay down below, and each time, they said, "Captain, the engines are okay." My concern was that dirt or something else could possibly clog the fuel supply from the fuel tanks to the main engines. What a nightmare it would have been to lose engine power. The ship—and we—would never have survived. I understood how ridiculous it was to think about those things, as nothing could have been done anyway; the ship would have been doomed.

Each time she faced the enormous mountains of water, for some scary seconds, my eyes focused on the huge incoming waves as I gave constant orders to the helmsman to keep the bow from falling off course. I continuously had to adjust the speed, increasing or decreasing it, by using the variable pitch propeller. The *Explorer* was beaten in the rough seas, but though she was severely struggling, she was sturdy, she was strong, and she did what she was supposed to do.

I had been through some of the roughest seas on the planet in the past and plentiful storms—and occasionally both at the same time—but that was a storm I couldn't believe existed. The shrieking winds were trying to smash us to pieces as the incoming mountains of waves pounded us.

The night came, and darkness embedded us in uncertainty about what was to come, which made the situation even worse. The bridge was dark apart from the lights from the instruments. I kept the engine throttle always in my left hand while looking into the lights of the powerful spotlights ahead of us in an attempt to see which direction the gigantic waves came from and, consequently, be ready to take appropriate actions to keep the bow pointing toward the waves with a slight angle.

One mistake from the helmsman would have caused the ship to go down; hence, we had an additional helmsman who made sure no mistakes were made. So, it went for the entire night.

The sea spray was so intense and strong that the window wipers could hardly do their job, and they frequently slowed down, which took the visibility away. The bridge window frames squeaked and creaked from the wind pressure and sometimes from huge waves that smashed the armored glass windows. I could only hope they stayed intact. I knew about cruise ships, such as the German MV *Bremen*, whose bridge windows had smashed in the Drake Passage, and the entire bridge had flooded with water. That was something we did not need.

It was after midnight, and I figured out we were drifting backward in the storm, but at least we kept the bow up against the gigantic thirty-meter waves. They were not waves but mountains. I could hardly believe what I saw and experienced. Each time the ship came to a standstill on top of a wave, the bow then went down into the deep valleys between the crests, and the wind was obscured, so there was an unnatural stillness, a creepy silence that only enhanced the danger of the towering slope of water threatening us. As she went up again, the angle of the bridge tilted back. I had never seen water as menacing and cruel. The round clear view screen with the Bosch motor in front of the engine control handle was still rotating. Though it slowed down once in a while, it gave us an acceptable view while the waves smashed on the bridge windows.

A trip to the Southern Ocean is on many travelers' bucket lists, but it comes with its own set of challenges, and I don't mean choosing which parka to pack. Those are some of the roughest waters in the world. If you are seasick, that can mean big trouble, so I asked one of the deckhands to take a look down below. He came back after a while and said that nobody was up; everything was quiet. God, what a consolation to hear that. I felt kind of proud that so far everything was good. All of us on the bridge were stunned at what we saw. It was indeed a good show, as one man had said.

It was a never-ending nightmare, and the storm seemed to last forever. I had been on the bridge for some twenty hours, and once in a while, I was relieved by the staff captain, who took over control.

In the light of the searchlights, we saw that the water came aboard green and clear over the forecastle as the *Explorer* dropped into the deep valley ahead of her. Again, her bronze propeller broke clear of the surface, and then the slamming vibration instantly went through the ship, controlled by the pitch propeller, until she again entered the slope of the next wave. Each time, it seemed she could not rise in time to meet the next cliff of water that bore down on her.

It became dawn, and we then could see clearly what was going on. The sun slowly rose above the horizon on our starboard bow. We had made it safely through the night on God's providence.

Still, the wind force showed no sign of diminishing, and the wave height was frightening. All of us were in silence, watching the show that took place in front of our eyes. I noted that the direction of the wind and waves had slightly changed toward the north and northeast (i.e., the center of the low was moving toward the northeast).

The galley was unable to serve the passengers their breakfast, as the ship was heavily pitching in the high seas, and it would have been risky to work in the galley; hence, at 0800 hours, I made a public announcement to give an update on the situation and the weather forecast. I said, "I am sorry to say you have to stay where you are until the conditions improve. We are still trapped in this storm, and I do not know when things will improve, and the seas will calm down. Hopefully it will look better around noon."

The morning went by, and we continued to be pushed backward, still maintaining the course. Shortly after noon, we finally saw the barometer slowly rise. What a consolation it was to see that.

We all felt tired, and I continued to spend most of the time on the bridge, watchful and worried that things could go wrong. The staff captain relieved me and turned back to the task of controlling the pitch propeller. The deck crew made a check to see how much damage there was in the interior, but luckily, things was pretty much under control, as everything was well secured. Once in a while, we saw some enormous freak waves come from nowhere that made us all speechless and concerned. However, the *Explorer* was riding like a duck, and she faced them all one by one. Though she went down like a sub and stayed there, she struggled and came up again to our relief, showing the furious ocean "You can't beat me!"

Somehow, we managed to boil tea for some people, though the entire bridge tilted forward and backward frequently. The radio station had been closed since the storm started, as the radio operator was seasick. The water was leaking into the bridge from the wooden bridge door, so we had to put rags between the door and the frame.

Looking at the weather NAVTEX, we saw an improvement, and around three o'clock in the afternoon, the wind finally started to drop, and the waves calmed down a bit. It was a blessing to see that, and I knew we had made it through the roughest storm I had ever seen in my life. It was indubitably the perfect storm—scary and incredibly dangerous.

When the waves became approximately less than ten meters, I made a public announcement for everybody, telling them that at the end of my announcement, I would turn the ship around and resume the course toward South Georgia. Thus, it was done, and after a thirty-hour nightmare, we resumed the course to the south toward the furious fifties and sixties.

The passengers rushed up onto the bridge in happiness, and they all gave a big "Hooray!" They were proud they had survived probably the roughest storm ever out there, with thirty-meter waves. I again made a public announcement prior to the late evening dinner, telling them all, "Ladies and gentlemen, we were tossed by a huge, violent storm—in fact, the perfect storm—and all of us should be proud that we made it without any injuries. We are all heroes, and these thirty hours in the devil's eye have been a true-life experience none of us will ever forget. Enjoy your evening!"

Chapter 31

How Skog Passage Became a Reality

IT WAS FEBRUARY 15, 1998, and I was standing on the port bridge wing on the *Explorer* in the Antarctic Sound, at the western side of Joinville Island, close to Kinnes Cove and the Madder Cliffs, looking at the narrow passage ahead of me, which suddenly got my attention. It was apparently a small passage, and it was, to my surprise, an unnamed body of water. My first thought was *This passage must be navigable.*

We had arrived at our last Antarctic stop from the wild Weddell Sea. My passengers were ashore, and I could see most of them standing high up on the Madder Cliffs in their red parkas, looking down on the *Explorer*, which had been put adrift just to the south of the Madder Cliffs. There was plenty of water where we were drifting, since I had been there numerous times before.

Suddenly, an idea popped up in my head: I wondered if it was possible to go through the narrow passage ahead of me and still be afloat and pick up the passengers on the other side of the unnamed body of water. I was well acquainted with the water depth to the north of the passage; I knew, however, the water depth in that narrow was hopelessly unreliable and inaccurate. Nobody knew what was below the surface, and consequently, no one had gone through that unnamed body of water before.

There was, however, a fairly reliable rule in Antarctica: where the cliffsides descended steeply down into the sea, most of the time there was plenty of water close to the cliffs under the surface.

The *Explorer*'s draft was a safe five meters, or fifteen feet; hence, I suddenly felt I wanted to do something out of the ordinary. Therefore, I said a prayer to overcome my doubts while my eyes focused on the narrow passage ahead of me, which I now slowly approached.

My mind was set on how to slowly traverse the unnamed body of water. Perhaps I realized it was now or never if I wanted to make a serious attempt to safely navigate through the narrow from the south. I considered the arguments for and against, and I tried to scan the surface with my binoculars and assess the dangers below.

To my advantage, I knew there was plenty of water some 0.2 cables to the north of that narrow; however, I knew that any mistake I made could be the end of the *Explorer*'s story once and for all.

It took me some time to figure out in my mind if I actually had the guts to enter that unknown body of water, and I knew I was losing precious time as long as I was in doubt about what to do. The clock was ticking since the *Explorer* had to be shortly in the right position for the safe embarkation of the passengers to the north of the narrow.

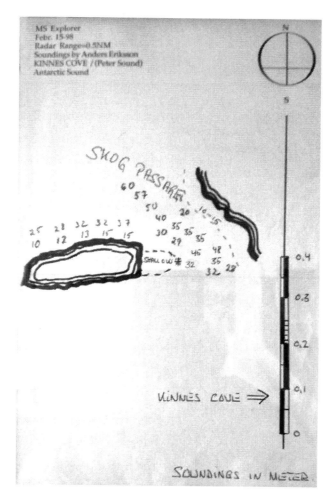

I suddenly ended up in deep doubt about what to do. I rapidly called up the Swedish Staff Captain Anders on the walkie-talkie, who was on duty, and asked him if he could take an echo-sounding Zodiac—a rubber boat fully equipped with echo-sounding equipment on the transom—and crisscross the sound ahead of us while giving me the depth figures over the radio. He agreed to do so, and when he was ready and warmly dressed, he took off. I, as usual, made the bridge's Decca radar ready for plotting, which we did when we undertook sounding and survey tasks in uncharted waters.

Over the VHF radio, I directed Anders on how to approach the areas of interest, and after an hour of crisscrossing the passage, he told me, "Peter, there is a huge underwater rock just to port of the middle part and clearly visible."

Apparently, that was the only obstacle in the narrow, and it appeared to be, as predicted, sufficient of water close to the steep cliffs. I had now the complete picture of the entire passage, and I told Anders to return to the *Explorer*.

Once he was back on board, I slowly approached the unnamed body of water, keeping my eyes focused on any possible additional rocks under the surface apart from the one we already knew existed. The water was clear, which was a big help, and there was no current. When the ship approached the spotted underwater rock, I could clearly see the rock when looking down from the port bridge wing, and I was aware that the speed was the key factor. It was a nasty rock but was clearly visible under the clear surface and the only obstacle in the passage. Slowly, we slipped through and entered the northern part of the narrow safely and afloat.

I couldn't believe what I just had done, and when the passengers returned, they all asked how it was possible for me to do this. The cruise director said, "Peter, why don't you claim this channel in your name as Skog Passage?"

The following day, I filled in the application form and sent it to the National Science Foundation in the USA. Four years later, on April 27, 2002, when I was in Iquitos, Peru, on the Amazon River, where I lived for fifteen years, I went to an internet café; opened my email; and, to my big surprise, read that Skog Passage was a reality. Everyone involved in the Antarctic expedition cruising world congratulated me. After four years of passing through the paper mill in the USA, New Zealand, and Great Britain, my request was approved. I had become immortal in Antarctica.

Epilogue

When I started at sea in 1963, it was a completely different era. Lost in my young teenage life about what to do, I went to sea since it was the only option I had to discover the world. In my teenage room, a world map hung over my head, and every night when I went to bed, I asked myself how it was possible for me to see this huge world. Every morning when I woke up, the first thing I saw was the map of the world on the wall above my bed.

Therefore, my destiny was set in my mind: I'd become a sailor because it was the only possibility I had to make my dream come true to see the world. I knew it would be a tough life in many ways but instructive. I would learn seamanship and the harsh sailor's life on the seven oceans—sometimes the hard way and from scratch in every aspect.

I was never involved in fights on board any ships as a deckhand because I knew that one wrong word from my side could end up in a bloody fight with disastrous consequences. I sailed with big, muscular boys from all over the world; hence, I knew the fine art of pulling out before disaster struck. As a young, innocent sixteen-year-old deck boy in the early 1960s, I worked on various cargo ships worldwide, with eight to eighteen cargo derricks. The world suddenly came in reach of my dreams, which made me feel confident.

After I graduated from the nautical college in Malmö, Sweden, in 1972, I became a third officer on board the cargo ship MS *Hakone*, sailing for the Swedish East Asia Company between Europe and the Far East. After some five months on board and my first circumnavigation of the globe, I suddenly got a call from the Broström Company in Gothenburg, who asked if I wanted to sign on to a passenger cruise ship, the *Lindblad Explorer*. I said, "No, I will not do that." However, I was told I had seven days to consider the offer. Nine days later, I called them back and accepted the offer. I didn't know that from that day on, my life would change forever, and I would experience the most incredible and marvelous things in this world.

It is impossible to describe adequately the adventures we had and what I experienced with my shipmates amid all the events that took place in the early 1970s during my expedition cruising life. I was fortunate to be a member of the *Lindblad Explorer* team in the early '70s, when we opened up the entire world to expedition cruising, including Antarctica. We paved the way for all the future cruise ships of all sizes coming behind us.

Indubitably, the captain deserves all the credit. He became my master in Antarctica and worldwide as we explored all the remote corners of the world.

On board the *Lindblad Explorer,* I learned close coastal navigation and the fine art of true navigation by using common sense and my eyes. I learned to trust my feelings and my senses, and my heart became my best friend. I learned not to even think about doing something if I was in doubt.

I developed a love-hate relationship with Antarctica. It was a nightmare most of the time due to the harsh climate, strong winds, and ice, with surprises and worries that affected all of us and sometimes led to serious events. Each time we left that remote continent, I told myself, *I hope I never come back to this godforsaken place,* but every time I returned to Antarctica, I was happy and full of joy because Antarctica became magic for me and was like a magnet.

As a master on board that Grand Old Lady, during the captain's welcome cocktail party, I told my passengers, "You can't go to the moon, but you can come to Antarctica, which is an outer-space experience. Antarctica is indeed as close as we can come to an outer-space experience."

Antarctica is like music; it will affect your mind, and the little voices will tell you to return. Yes, Antarctica affected me and my mind, and I ended up making a total of 125 ice voyages to that hidden continent at the bottom of the world, until 2008, when my expedition cruising life ended.

The *Lindblad Explorer* was a ship in the wilderness without a home port, and she had the whole world for an arena. She was the pioneer ship in Antarctica, and she opened up all the remote areas of the world for expedition cruising. As not only the *Lindblad Explorer* but also the *Explorer,* she wrote shipping history and continued to make firsts. This little red ship has a place in shipping history that far exceeds her size.

In 1997, we circumnavigated James Clark Ross Island in Antarctica as the first cruise ship ever to do so.

I always kept a diary and wrote down all the things of interest, which became an invaluable help when I started to write about my adventures in this book. I could have kept writing about many more incredible events, but then the book would have been gigantic, and therefore, I had to stop somewhere. My unsuccessful dive adventure in the Galápagos cave has persecuted me for the rest of my life with nightmares.

On board the *Lindblad Explorer* as well as the *Explorer,* I lived in a dream world in which all my dreams came true. My work as a deck officer made me happy every day because every day was a different challenge, and it kept my blood boiling. At the end of our bridge watches, we went down to our cabins and dressed ourselves in our best uniforms: white in the tropics—similar to the US Navy type, with a high collar—and black in the cold areas. Then we went down to the bar, where soft music slowly filled our hearts and made us emotional while we talked with the famous VIP passengers and listened to their life stories. Late-night dancing followed. Therefore, I never had any longing to fly home.

In August 1977, my then fiancée, who later became my wife, participated in a cruise from Japan to Bali, Indonesia, called the Western Pacific Cruising Expedition, which called on every Japanese island south of the Japanese mainland, including Iwo Jima, which was only populated by thirty Americans and sixty Japanese at the time. There we saw the copper reproduction of the American flag, which is a permanent war memorial. We visited Pagan Island, Saipan, and Tinian, where the events of the Pacific Second World War took place in the Marianas.

On that cruise, she became pregnant, and nine months later, in April 1978, I was blessed with a son, who was named Pontus. When Pontus became eleven years of age, he joined me on many of my cruises worldwide during his school vacations.

I am greatly obliged to many of my shipmates who sent me their private notes and material to enhance my stories. This helped me enormously in my attempt to describe the events as accurately as possible as they occurred.

The passengers in those years were the high society of the entire world. They were persons who could afford to cruise with us. Though all these VIPs were our passengers, we lived close together on a daily basis, and we got to know each other well, for better or worse.

The most praiseworthy aspect was that we visited places in Antarctica and all over the world with passengers who were well briefed and thoughtful. We put them ashore, augmented their lives, reembarked them, and pulled out from the landing sites. Nobody would even have known that the *Lindblad Explorer* had passed that way. She was designed to do just what that little red ship in the wilderness did so well, and she became my home for fifteen years. She made me feel that I was qualified in a field known by only a few people in those years.

In the 1970s, we did not have a GPS on board. Navigation in open waters was based on astronomical navigation from select stars and the sun and dead reckoning, along with radar observation from land and tidewater calculations done by the harmonic constants. Doing astronomical calculations by hand was time consuming, but ultimately, per the duty bridge officers' astronomical calculations, the discrepancy was no more than 0.5 to 0.8 nautical miles. Additionally, the ship's paper echo sounder was, in the 1970s, the most important equipment on the navigation bridge, and we always had to take into account the estimated current and the drift.

It was an honor to work daily with the world's most famous lecturers on board, such as Dr. Lyall Watson; Sir Peter Scott, son of Robert Falcon Scott; Edmund Hillary; Keith Shackleton; Roger Tory Peterson; Peter Puleston; Francisco Erize; Ron and Valerie Taylor from Australia; Bengt Danielsson and Thor Heyerdahl, both from the Kon-Tiki raft expedition in 1947; Sergio Aragonés, the head cartoonist from *Mad* magazine; Lorne Blair; Tom Ritche; Robert Hernandez; and more. They were all galleon figures on board and log keepers for the voyages.

On April 16, 2002, the US Board on Geographic Names approved the Antarctic geographic name Skog Passage, following the recommendation of the Advisory Committee on Antarctic Names (ACAN). As Skog Passage became a reality, I knew I had contributed a lot to the safe navigation of many bays and inlets in the Antarctic Peninsula.

I enjoyed every day of my life on board the little red ship until 2003, when she was sold to GAP (Great Adventure People) in Toronto, Canada. She made my dreams come true, and with her, I was finally able to see the world and fulfill my boyhood dreams. I was able to visit the places that I once upon a time had fantasized about as a young teenager when looking at the world map hanging on the wall above my bed.

Unfortunately, the *Explorer* sank on November 23, 2007, in the Bransfield Strait in Antarctica. After twenty hours of struggling to stay alive, she lost and went down to her eternal rest. When I learned she had gone down and lay to rest forever at the bottom of the Bransfield Strait, at a depth of some 2,400 meters, I had tears in my eyes, and my head was full of thoughts and memories from the ship that had changed my life forever.

On August 26, 2006, I became a member of the renowned Explorers Club in New York.

Conversion Table: Nautical Miles to Meters

Nautical Miles	Meters
0.1	185.2
0.2	370.4
0.3	555.6
0.4	740.8
0.5	926.0
0.6	1,111.0
0.7	1,296.0
0.8	1,481.0
0.9	1,666.0
1.0	1,852.0
2.0	3,704.0
3.0	5,556.0
4.0	7,408.0
5.0	9,260.0
6.0	11,112.0
7.0	12,964.0
8.0	14,816.0
9.0	16,668.0
10.0	18,520.0
11.0	20,372.0
12.0	22,224.0
13.0	24,076.0
14.0	25,928.0
15.0	27,780.0
16.0	29,632.0
17.0	31,484.0

18.0	33,336.0
19.0	35,188.0
20.0	37,040.0
21.0	38,892.0
22.0	40,744.0
23.0	42,596.0
24.0	44.448.0
25.0	46,300.0

Resources

Abercrombie and Kent
https://www.abercrombiekent.com/

able-bodied seaman
https://en.wikipedia.org/wiki/Able_seaman

Adamstown in the Pitcairn Islands
https://en.wikipedia.org/wiki/Adamstown,_Pitcairn_Islands

Admiralty Bay, Antarctica
https://en.wikipedia.org/wiki/Admiralty_Bay_(South_Shetland_Islands)

albatross
https://en.wikipedia.org/wiki/Albatross

Amerigo Vespucci
https://en.wikipedia.org/wiki/Amerigo_Vespucci

Antarctica
https://en.wikipedia.org/wiki/Antarctica

Antarctic Convergence
https://en.wikipedia.org/wiki/Antarctic_Convergence

Antarctic Dream cruise ship, *Piloto Pardo*
https://en.wikipedia.org/wiki/MV_Antarctic_Dream

Antarctic Shipping, *Antarctic Dream*
http://www.nedcruise.info/antarctic_dream.htm

Antarctic Shipping
https://www.adventuretravelnews.com/antarctic-shipping

Antarctic skuas
https://en.wikipedia.org/wiki/South_polar_skua

Antarctic Sound
https://en.wikipedia.org/wiki/Antarctic_Sound

Apia in Western Samoa
https://en.wikipedia.org/wiki/Apia

Arafura Sea
https://en.wikipedia.org/wiki/Arafura_Sea

Arctowski, Polish base in Antarctica
https://en.wikipedia.org/wiki/Henryk_Arctowski_Polish_Antarctic_Station

Ascension Island
https://en.wikipedia.org/wiki/Ascension_Island

Asmat and Agats, West Irian
https://en.wikipedia.org/wiki/Agats

Bahia Paraiso
http://www.antarcticmarc.com/bahia.html

Balboa, Panama
https://en.wikipedia.org/wiki/Balboa,_Panama

Bali
https://en.wikipedia.org/wiki/Bali

Baltra Island in the Galápagos
https://en.wikipedia.org/wiki/Baltra_Island

BAS (British Antarctic Survey)
https://en.wikipedia.org/wiki/British_Antarctic_Survey

Base Matienzo in Antarctica
https://translate.google.se/translate?hl=en&sl=es&u=https://es.wikipedia.org/wiki/Base_Matienzo&prev=search

Batangas Shipyard, Keppel, Philippines
http://www.keppelom.com/en/content.aspx?sid=3169

Bay of Biscay
https://en.Bay of Biscay - Wikipedia

Beagle Channel
https://en.wikipedia.org/wiki/Beagle_Channel

Bering Strait
https://en.wikipedia.org/wiki/Bering_Strait

Beaufort scale
https://en.wikipedia.org/wiki/Beaufort_scale

Bengt Danielsson
https://en.wikipedia.org/wiki/Bengt_Danielsson

Bismarck Strait, Antarctica
https://en.wikipedia.org/wiki/Bismarck_Strait

Black Sea
https://en.wikipedia.org/wiki/Black_Sea

Bo Svenson
https://en.wikipedia.org/wiki/Bo_Svenson

boatswain
https://en.wikipedia.org/wiki/Boatswain

Bosporus
https://en.wikipedia.org/wiki/Bosporus

Bounty Bay in the Pitcairn Islands
https://en.wikipedia.org/wiki/Bounty_Bay

Boyd Strait, Antarctica
https://en.wikipedia.org/wiki/Boyd_Strait

Bransfield Strait
https://en.wikipedia.org/wiki/Bransfield_Strait

Bulltofta Airport
https://en.wikipedia.org/wiki/Malm%C3%B6_Bulltofta_Airport

Callao, Peru
https://en.wikipedia.org/wiki/Callao

Cabo San Pío in Argentina
https://en.wikipedia.org/wiki/Cape_San_P%C3%ADo

Cape Finisterre
https://en.wikipedia.org/wiki/Cape_Finisterre

Cape Horn
https://en.wikipedia.org/wiki/Cape_Horn

Cape Longing in Antarctica
https://en.wikipedia.org/wiki/Cape_Longing

Cape Pembroke
https://en.wikipedia.org/wiki/Cape_Pembroke

Cape Verde Islands
https://en.wikipedia.org/wiki/Cape_Verde

Captain James Cook
https://en.wikipedia.org/wiki/James_Cook

Captain Peter Skog
http://www.captainpeterskog.com/

Captain William Bligh
https://en.wikipedia.org/wiki/William_Bligh

Carcass Island
https://en.wikipedia.org/wiki/Carcass_Island

Carl Anton Larsen
https://en.wikipedia.org/wiki/Carl_Anton_Larsen

Carlos Menem
https://en.wikipedia.org/wiki/Carlos_Menem

Caroline Islands
Caroline Islands - Wikipedia

Cecil and Kitty Bertrand
https://www.falklandsbiographies.org/biographies/40

chief mate
Chief mate - Wikipedia

Christensen Nunatak in Antarctica
https://en.wikipedia.org/wiki/Christensen_Nunatak

Christopher Columbus
https://en.wikipedia.org/wiki/Christopher_Columbus

coatimundi bear
https://en.wikipedia.org/wiki/Coati

Compañía Argentina de Pesca https://en.wikipedia.org/wiki/Compa%C3%B1%C3%ADa_Argentina_de_Pesca

Cooper Bay in South Georgia
https://en.wikipedia.org/wiki/Cooper_Island

Crystal Sound
https://en.wikipedia.org/wiki/Crystal_Sound

Cumberland Bay, South Georgia
https://en.wikipedia.org/wiki/Cumberland_Bay

Darwin Station, Galápagos
https://www.galapagosislands.com/santa-cruz/charles-darwin-station.html

David Rockefeller
https://en.wikipedia.org/wiki/David_Rockefeller

deck boy
https://www.merriam-webster.com/dictionary/deck%20boy

Deception Island, Antarctica
https://en.wikipedia.org/wiki/Deception_Island

Des and Jen Bartlett
https://biblio.co.uk/9780812818253
https://en.wikipedia.org/wiki/Des_Bartlett

Devil's Crown, Galápagos Islands
https://www.galapagosislands.com/floreana/devils-crown.html

DNV (Det Norske Veritas)
https://en.wikipedia.org/wiki/DNV_GL

Donald M. Kendall
https://en.wikipedia.org/wiki/Donald_M._Kendall

Drake Passage
https://en.wikipedia.org/wiki/Drake_Passage

Dr. Lyall Watson
https://en.wikipedia.org/wiki/Lyall_Watson

Edinburgh, Tristan da Cunha
https://en.wikipedia.org/wiki/Edinburgh_of_the_Seven_Seas

Edmund Hillary
https://en.wikipedia.org/wiki/Edmund_Hillary

Ellesmere Island
https://en.wikipedia.org/wiki/Ellesmere_Island

Endurance, ship in Antarctica
https://en.wikipedia.org/wiki/Endurance_(1912_ship)

Ernest Shackleton
https://en.wikipedia.org/wiki/Ernest_Shackleton

Falklands War
https://en.wikipedia.org/wiki/Falklands_War

Fangataufa Atoll
https://en.wikipedia.org/wiki/Fangataufa

Falalis Island in Federated States of Micronesia, map
https://mapcarta.com/16510088

Fletcher Christian
https://en.wikipedia.org/wiki/Fletcher_Christian

Florida Water
https://en.wikipedia.org/wiki/Florida_Water

Francisco Erize
https://es.wikipedia.org/wiki/Francisco_Erize

Frank Wild
https://en.wikipedia.org/wiki/Frank_Wild

Franz Josef Land, Russia
https://en.wikipedia.org/wiki/Franz_Josef_Land

frigate bird, Galápagos Islands
https://en.wikipedia.org/wiki/Magnificent_frigatebird

Galápagos Islands. (The Enchanted Islands)
https://en.wikipedia.org/wiki/Gal%C3%A1pagos_Islands

Gaucho, South America
https://en.wikipedia.org/wiki/Gaucho

Gäveskär
https://commons.wikimedia.org/wiki/Category:G%C3%A4vesk%C3%A4r

Genovesa Island (Tower Island)
https://en.wikipedia.org/wiki/Genovesa_Island

Georgetown, Ascension Island
https://en.wikipedia.org/wiki/Georgetown,_Ascension_Island

Gerlache Strait
https://en.wikipedia.org/wiki/Gerlache_Strait

Gibraltar
https://en.wikipedia.org/wiki/Gibraltar

Gin Cove in Antarctica
https://en.wikipedia.org/wiki/Gin_Cove

Giovanni Agnelli
https://en.wikipedia.org/wiki/Gianni_Agnelli

Godthul, South Georgia
https://en.wikipedia.org/wiki/Godthul

Gothenburg, Sweden
https://en.wikipedia.org/wiki/Gothenburg

Gough Island, South Atlantic
https://en.wikipedia.org/wiki/Gough_Island

Grandidier Channel
https://en.wikipedia.org/wiki/Grandidier_Channel

Great Barrier Reef
https://en.wikipedia.org/wiki/Great_Barrier_Reef

Grytviken
https://en.wikipedia.org/wiki/Grytviken

Guadalcanal
https://en.wikipedia.org/wiki/Guadalcanal

Hannah Point, Antarctica
https://en.wikipedia.org/wiki/Hannah_Point

harmonic constants, tidewater
https://en.wikipedia.org/wiki/Tide

Helsinki
https://en.wikipedia.org/wiki/Helsinki

Henry Kissinger
https://en.wikipedia.org/wiki/Henry_Kissinger

Herbert Sound, Antarctica
https://en.wikipedia.org/wiki/Herbert_Sound

Hercules C-130
https://en.wikipedia.org/wiki/Lockheed_C-130_Hercules

Hope Bay, Antarctica
https://en.wikipedia.org/wiki/Hope_Bay

Husvik, South Georgia
https://en.wikipedia.org/wiki/Husvik

IAATO
https://iaato.org/what-is-iaato

iceberg
https://en.wikipedia.org/wiki/Iceberg

ice class 1A
https://en.wikipedia.org/wiki/Ice_class

Ifalik Island in the Caroline Islands
https://en.wikipedia.org/wiki/Ifalik

Illiria, cruise ship
https://www.ship-rex.com/illiria-cruise-ship---photograph-3455-p.asp

intertropical convergence zone
https://en.wikipedia.org/wiki/Intertropical_Convergence_Zone

Isla Picton, Isla Lennox, and Isla Nueva in Chile
https://en.wikipedia.org/wiki/Picton,_Lennox_and_Nueva

Iquitos, Peru
https://en.wikipedia.org/wiki/Iquitos

Jack Elofsson
http://www.arcticflyfishing.com/about.htm

Jacques Cousteau
https://en.wikipedia.org/wiki/Jacques_Cousteau

James Cook
https://en.wikipedia.org/wiki/James_Cook

James Ross Island in Antarctica
https://en.wikipedia.org/wiki/James_Ross_Island

James Wolfensohn
https://en.wikipedia.org/wiki/James_Wolfensohn

Johan Gunnar Andersson
https://en.wikipedia.org/wiki/Johan_Gunnar_Andersson

Kaohsiung, Taiwan
https://en.wikipedia.org/wiki/Kaohsiung

Kathleen Bruce
https://en.wikipedia.org/wiki/Kathleen_Bruce

Keith Shackleton
https://en.wikipedia.org/wiki/Keith_Shackleton

killer whale (orca)
https://en.wikipedia.org/wiki/Killer_whale

Kinnes Cove, Antarctica
https://data.aad.gov.au/aadc/gaz/display_name.cfm?gaz_id=109630

king crabs
https://en.wikipedia.org/wiki/King_crab

King Edward Point
https://en.wikipedia.org/wiki/King_Edward_Point

King George Island
https://en.wikipedia.org/wiki/King_George_Island

Kockum Shipyard in Malmö
https://en.wikipedia.org/wiki/Kockums_Naval_Solutions

Kodiak Island, Alaska
https://en.wikipedia.org/wiki/Kodiak_Island

Kon-Tiki
https://en.wikipedia.org/wiki/Kon-Tiki_expedition

Lady Elizabeth, iron barque
https://en.wikipedia.org/wiki/Lady_Elizabeth_(1879)

Lamotrek Island in the Caroline Islands.
https://en.wikipedia.org/wiki/Lamotrek

Lars-Eric Lindblad
https://en.wikipedia.org/wiki/Lars-Eric_Lindblad

Larsen Ice Shelf in Antarctica
https://en.wikipedia.org/wiki/Larsen_Ice_Shelf

Larsen Nunatak in Antarctica
https://en.wikipedia.org/wiki/Larsen_Nunatak

Las Palmas
https://en.wikipedia.org/wiki/Las_Palmas

Lavoisier Island
https://en.wikipedia.org/wiki/Lavoisier_Island

Lawrence Blair
https://en.wikipedia.org/wiki/Lawrence_Blair

Leith Harbor, South Georgia
https://en.wikipedia.org/wiki/Leith_Harbour

Lemaire Channel
https://en.wikipedia.org/wiki/Lemaire_Channel

Lindblad Explorer
https://en.wikipedia.org/wiki/MV_Explorer_(1969)

Lindenberg Island, Antarctica
https://en.wikipedia.org/wiki/Lindenberg_Island

Livingston Island, Antarctica
https://en.wikipedia.org/wiki/Livingston_Island

Lockheed bribery scandal
https://en.wikipedia.org/wiki/Lockheed_bribery_scandals

Lockheed Corporation Aviation
https://en.wikipedia.org/wiki/Lockheed_Corporation

Lorne Blair
http://www.sophia-anastasia.com/people/Lorne_Blair.php

Luis Marden
https://en.wikipedia.org/wiki/Luis_Marden

Luis Pardo
https://en.wikipedia.org/wiki/Luis_Pardo

Lynx helicopter
https://sv.wikipedia.org/wiki/Westland_Lynx

Madder Cliffs in Antarctica
https://en.wikipedia.org/wiki/Madder_Cliffs

magnetic north pole
https://en.wikipedia.org/wiki/North_Magnetic_Pole

Malmö
https://en.wikipedia.org/wiki/Malm%C3%B6

Marañón River, Peru
https://en.wikipedia.org/wiki/Mara%C3%B1%C3%B3n_River

Mare Harbor in the Falkland Islands
https://en.wikipedia.org/wiki/Mare_Harbour

Maxwell Bay, Antarctica, Fildes Peninsula
https://en.wikipedia.org/wiki/Maxwell_Bay_(Antarctica)

Michael Rockefeller
https://en.wikipedia.org/wiki/Michael_Rockefeller

Micronesia
https://en.wikipedia.org/wiki/Federated_States_of_Micronesia

Milt Machlin
https://en.wikipedia.org/wiki/Milt_Machlin

Moruroa Atoll
https://en.wikipedia.org/wiki/Moruroa

Mount Flora, Hope Bay, Antarctica
https://en.wikipedia.org/wiki/Mount_Flora

Mount Pleasant in the Falkland Islands
https://en.wikipedia.org/wiki/RAF_Mount_Pleasant

Nathaniel Palmer
https://en.wikipedia.org/wiki/Nathaniel_Palmer

National Science Foundation (USA)
https://en.wikipedia.org/wiki/National_Science_Foundation

Nelson Rockefeller
https://en.wikipedia.org/wiki/Nelson_Rockefeller

Neptune's Bellows, Deception Island, Antarctica
https://en.wikipedia.org/wiki/Neptune%27s_Bellows

Neumayer Channel
https://en.wikipedia.org/wiki/Neumayer_Channel

NOAA
https://en.wikipedia.org/wiki/National_Oceanic_and_Atmospheric_Administration

Nylands Brigade
https://sv.wikipedia.org/wiki/Nylands_brigad

Ocean Harbour, South Georgia
https://en.wikipedia.org/wiki/Ocean_Harbour

Odessa
https://en.wikipedia.org/wiki/Odessa

Okinawa
https://en.wikipedia.org/wiki/Okinawa_Island

Olivia Hussey
https://sv.wikipedia.org/wiki/Olivia_Hussey

Operation Highjump
https://en.wikipedia.org/wiki/Operation_Highjump

ordinary seaman
https://en.wikipedia.org/wiki/Ordinary_seaman

Otto Nordenskjöld
https://en.wikipedia.org/wiki/Otto_Nordenskj%C3%B6ld

PA system
https://en.wikipedia.org/wiki/Public_address_system

Palmer Station, Antarctica
ttps://en.wikipedia.org/wiki/Palmer_Station

Panama Canal
https://en.wikipedia.org/wiki/Panama_Canal

Papeete, Tahiti
https://en.wikipedia.org/wiki/Papeete

Papua, Indonesia
https://en.wikipedia.org/wiki/Papua_(province)

Paradise Bay
https://en.wikipedia.org/wiki/Paradise_Harbor

Paso Mackinlay
https://es.wikipedia.org/wiki/Paso_Mackinlay

Pendulum Cove, Deception Island
https://en.wikipedia.org/wiki/Pendulum_Cove

Petermann Island
https://en.wikipedia.org/wiki/Petermann_Island

Piloto Pardo
https://en.wikipedia.org/wiki/Luis_Pardo

Pitcairn Islands
https://en.wikipedia.org/wiki/Pitcairn_Islands

Pohnpei, Micronesia
https://en.wikipedia.org/wiki/Pohnpei

Point Barrow, Alaska
https://en.wikipedia.org/wiki/Point_Barrow

Port Lockroy
https://en.wikipedia.org/wiki/Port_Lockroy

Port Pattison Bay, Falkland Islands
https://www.alamy.com/port-pattison-bay-on-carcass-island-in-the-falklands-image6383528.html

Port Stanley, Falkland Islands
https://en.wikipedia.org/wiki/Stanley,_Falkland_Islands

Prince Bernhard of the Netherlands
https://en.wikipedia.org/wiki/Prince_Bernhard_of_Lippe-Biesterfeld

Prince Gustav Channel in Antarctica
https://en.wikipedia.org/wiki/Prince_Gustav_Channel

Prince Olav Harbour
https://en.wikipedia.org/wiki/Prince_Olav_Harbour

Provideniya, Siberia
https://en.wikipedia.org/wiki/Provideniya

PSSC (passenger ship safety certificate)
https://www.transportstyrelsen.se/en/Shipping/Vessels/Vessel-Categories/Passenger-Ships

Puerto Cortés
https://en.wikipedia.org/wiki/Puerto_Cort%C3%A9s

Puerto Williams in Chile
https://en.wikipedia.org/wiki/Puerto_Williams

Punta Arenas
https://en.wikipedia.org/wiki/Punta_Arenas

Punta Cormorant, Galápagos Islands
https://www.visitgalapagos.travel/visitor-sites/punta-cormorant-galapagos-islands.html

Queen Juliana of Holland
https://en.wikipedia.org/wiki/Juliana_of_the_Netherlands

Raroia Atoll
https://en.wikipedia.org/wiki/Raroia

Rarotonga
https://en.wikipedia.org/wiki/Rarotonga

Raúl Alfonsín
https://en.wikipedia.org/wiki/Ra%C3%BAl_Alfons%C3%ADn

Rene Wassing
https://www.papuaerfgoed.org/en/the_disappearance_of_michael_rockefeller

Rio Gallegos, Argentina
https://en.wikipedia.org/wiki/R%C3%ADo_Gallegos,_Santa_Cruz

Robertson Island in Antarctica
https://en.wikipedia.org/wiki/Robertson_Island

Robert Hernandez
https://www.expeditions.com/why-us/expedition-team/staff-bio/robert-hernandez/

Roger Tory Peterson
https://en.wikipedia.org/wiki/Roger_Tory_Peterson

Ron and Valerie Taylor
https://en.wikipedia.org/wiki/Ron_and_Valerie_Taylor

Rum Cove in Antarctica
https://en.wikipedia.org/wiki/Rum_Cove

San Bernardino Strait
https://en.wikipedia.org/wiki/San_Bernardino_Strait

San Cristóbal Island, Galápagos
https://en.wikipedia.org/wiki/San_Crist%C3%B3bal_Island

Santa Cruz Island, Galápagos
https://en.wikipedia.org/wiki/Santa_Cruz_Island_(Gal%C3%A1pagos)

Santa Helena Island
https://en.wikipedia.org/wiki/Saint_Helena

Sea King helicopter
https://en.wikipedia.org/wiki/Westland_Sea_King

Seal Nunataks in Antarctica
https://en.wikipedia.org/wiki/Seal_Nunataks

Sergio Aragonés
https://en.wikipedia.org/wiki/Sergio_Aragon%C3%A9s

Sir Clements Markham
https://en.wikipedia.org/wiki/Clements_Markham

Sir Joseph Banks
https://en.wikipedia.org/wiki/Joseph_Banks

Sir Peter Scott
https://en.wikipedia.org/wiki/Peter_Scott

Skagen
Shttps://en.wikipedia.org/wiki/Skagen

Smith Island, South Shetlands
https://en.wikipedia.org/wiki/Smith_Island_(South_Shetland_Islands)

Snow Island, Antarctica
https://en.wikipedia.org/wiki/Snow_Island_(South_Shetland_Islands)

Sorol Island in the Caroline Islands
https://en.wikipedia.org/wiki/Sorol

South Georgia
https://en.wikipedia.org/wiki/South_Georgia_Island

South Shetland Islands
https://en.wikipedia.org/wiki/South_Shetland_Islands

Soviet Union
https://en.wikipedia.org/wiki/Soviet_Union

Spanish Sahara
https://en.wikipedia.org/wiki/Spanish_Sahara

Spitsbergen, Arctic
https://en.wikipedia.org/wiki/Spitsbergen

Stromness Bay, South Georgia
https://en.wikipedia.org/wiki/Stromness,_South_Georgia

Talcahuano Shipyard in Chile
https://www.trusteddocks.com/shipyards/5175-asmar-talcahuano-shipyard

Tenzing Norgay
https://en.wikipedia.org/wiki/Tenzing_Norgay

Thor Heyerdahl
https://en.wikipedia.org/wiki/Thor_Heyerdahl

Tierra del Fuego
https://en.wikipedia.org/wiki/Tierra_del_Fuego

Tonga
https://en.wikipedia.org/wiki/Tonga

Tongatapu
https://en.wikipedia.org/wiki/Tongatapu

Tristan da Cunha
https://en.wikipedia.org/wiki/Tristan_da_Cunha

Trobriand Islands
https://en.wikipedia.org/wiki/Trobriand_Islands

Truk Island, Chuuk Lagoon
https://en.wikipedia.org/wiki/Chuuk_Lagoon

Tuamotu Islands
https://en.wikipedia.org/wiki/Tuamotus

Ucayali River, Peru
https://en.wikipedia.org/wiki/Ucayali_River

Ulithi Atoll and Mogmog
https://en.wikipedia.org/wiki/Ulithi

United States Board on Geographic Names
https://en.wikipedia.org/wiki/United_States_Board_on_Geographic_Names

Ushuaia, Argentina
https://en.wikipedia.org/wiki/Ushuaia

USS *Sennet*, submarine
https://en.wikipedia.org/wiki/USS_Sennet_(SS-408)

Uwus in Agats, West Irian
https://en.wikipedia.org/wiki/Agats

VDR (video data recorder)
https://en.wikipedia.org/wiki/Voyage_data_recorder

Virus, movie
https://en.wikipedia.org/wiki/Virus_(1980_film)

V-Ships
https://vgrouplimited.com/technical-management/

Wallenius Lines
https://www.walleniuslines.com/

Weddell Sea in Antarctica
https://en.wikipedia.org/wiki/Weddell_Sea

West Point Island, Falklands
https://en.wikipedia.org/wiki/West_Point_Island

Western New Guinea
https://en.wikipedia.org/wiki/Western_New_Guinea

Wiencke Island, Antarctica
https://en.wikipedia.org/wiki/Wiencke_Island

Woleai Island
https://en.wikipedia.org/wiki/Woleai

Yangtze River
https://en.wikipedia.org/wiki/Yangtze

Yap Islands, South Pacific
https://en.wikipedia.org/wiki/Yap

Yokohama fender
http://www.yokohama-fenders.gr/yokohama-fenders/

Zodiac
https://en.wikipedia.org/wiki/Inflatable_boat

About the Author

Captain Skog has been a professional seaman since 1963 and has sailed innumerable times to the remotest corners of the globe. Born in Finland, he lived in Sweden for most of his life, yet he is truly an international man and is fluent in English, Spanish, German, and, of course, Swedish. A graduate of the nautical academy in Malmö, Sweden, he first went to sea as a deck boy while still a young teenager. In 1974, he discovered the thrill of expedition cruising when he began working on the *Lindblad Explorer*, the ship that invented expedition cruising. He worked first as a second officer and later as chief officer.

While sailing on the *Explorer*, Captain Skog became well acquainted with the polar regions and ice navigation. His first Antarctic experience dates back to 1974, when he sailed during the austral summer expeditions to the Antarctic Peninsula. Over the following five years, those extraordinary voyages, which were full of surprises from a navigational point of view, became an overwhelming favorite. To date, he has more than one hundred Antarctic ice voyages to his credit and is widely recognized as one of the most skillful ice pilots in the business.

His Arctic experience started in 1974, when he sailed to Baffin Bay, cruising the Canadian Arctic, Pond Inlet, Lancaster Sound, and Resolute Island. The voyage continued close to the magnetic north pole and the upper part of Greenland's west coast, south of Thule Base. He has also sailed the southern and eastern coasts of Greenland as far north as the ice permitted, turning back near latitude 74 degrees. He has taken several voyages to the Svalbard Archipelago, circumnavigating quite a few times the west island of Spitsbergen and sailing through Hinlopen Strait to the solid Arctic ice at latitude 81 degrees north.

Each summer in the 1970s, between his Antarctic voyages, Captain Skog returned to the Arctic. In the summers of 1998, 1999, 2000, and 2001, he visited the Norwegian Arctic. In the middle of the 1970s, as a chief officer, Captain Skog became part of a team introducing new corners of the world to intrepid travelers in Micronesia, Indonesia, and the entire South Pacific.

In 1991, aboard the *Frontier Spirit* (now the *Bremen*), the captain sailed to Point Barrow, Alaska, to begin a transit through the fabled Northwest Passage. Unfortunately, impenetrable pack ice prevented the transit, and the ship turned back at Hershel Island. Despite having cruised to the Arctic, the British Isles, Europe, the South Pacific, the inshore waters of Alaska, and throughout the remote islands of the South Atlantic Ocean, as well as the length of the Amazon River to Iquitos, Peru, Captain Skog feels most at home in the ice of the Antarctic Peninsula.

In 2003–2004, Captain Skog sailed on board the MS *Andrea* as an ice master to the Antarctic Peninsula, and the same year, he contributed to the success of the MS *World*'s first Antarctic voyage. In the summer of 2004, Captain Skog sailed on board the *Spirit of Oceanus* (formerly the *Renaissance 5*) as master again in Alaska and the Bering Sea area, which this time included the Russian Far East. In the summer of 2005, Captain Skog sailed on Australia's first expedition cruise ship, the *Orion*, to the Kimberley coast and East Timor as the first cruise ship in decades in those waters. Shortly after that, he sailed on the *Corinthian II* in the Mediterranean Sea and during the Antarctic season in 2005–2006. In 1997, as master of Abercrombie and Kent's *Explorer*, he became the first person to pilot a cruise ship through an unnamed passage in Antarctica. On April 16, 2002, the US Board of Geographic Names named the passage in his honor. The award was given in recognition of his experience in the Antarctic and his contribution to soundings of poorly charted areas to ensure the safety of landings and enhance British admiralty charts.

In 2006–2007, Captain Skog was the master of Chile's first expedition cruise ship, the *Antarctic Dream* (formerly the *Piloto Pardo*), cruising in Antarctica, Patagonia, and the Chilean coast for nine months. In November 2006, Captain Skog became a member of the Explorers Club in New York. Captain Skog has become a symbol of mankind's compelling desire to know, feel, and understand what lies beyond the next horizon. He exhibits an intellectual passion for expedition cruising that permits the human mind to go from Arctic to Antarctic waters and all points between.

Made in the USA
San Bernardino,
CA